Wolf Schmid
Figurally Colored Narration

Narratologia

Contributions to Narrative Theory

Edited by
Fotis Jannidis, Matías Martínez, John Pier,
Wolf Schmid (executive editor)

Volume 81

Wolf Schmid

Figurally Colored Narration

Case Studies from English, German, and Russian Literature

DE GRUYTER

ISBN 978-3-11-135798-0
e-ISBN (PDF) 978-3-11-076310-2
e-ISBN (EPUB) 978-3-11-076316-4
ISSN 1612-8427

Library of Congress Control Number: 2021952272

Bibliographic information published by the Deutsche Nationalbibliothek
The Deutsche Nationalbibliothek lists this publication in the Deutsche Nationalbibliografie;
detailed bibliographic data are available on the Internet at http://dnb.dnb.de.

In memory of Johannes Holthusen,
my academic teacher

Preface

The present book deals with a hitherto neglected device in narrative texts: the intrusion of figural evaluations and designations into the narrator's discourse. *Figural* means: belonging to the discourse of a character.

The book studies figurally colored narration (FCN) using three literatures: anglophone, German, and Russian. I searched for FCN in short narrative genres in particular, since the device is by nature more often represented there.

Figural coloring of the narration is most easily recognized in works narrated by a non-diegetic narrator, i.e., a third-person narrator who does not participate in the story being told, the diegesis. This is because FCN presupposes a clear axiological and linguistic difference between narrator and character, which is only present (in the guise of the difference between narrating and narrated self) in a few diegetically narrated works.

Notwithstanding the necessary prioritization of short narrative forms and non-diegetic narrators, I have also included individual novels that exhibit the phenomenon, and in one case a novel with a diegetic narrator, Dostoevskij's *The Adolescent*, is examined in detail.

The texts have not been selected from the point of view of literary history, but exclusively in terms of the presence of FCN. The examination of the texts likewise does not pursue questions of literary history, but is carried out exclusively from a typological point of view. Interpretations of the texts under consideration should not, therefore, be anticipated. The examples concern manifestations of FCN and their possible functions.

The level of detail in which the texts are addressed is somewhat varied. This follows from their differing relevance to the phenomenon under investigation.

Dostoevskij plays a special role among the authors discussed. This is due to the fact that the tension between narrator and character in this author's works, both non-diegetically and diegetically narrated, manifests itself in a typically Dostoevskijan multi-voicedness. Dostoevskij was an author who was particularly aware of the problem of representing consciousness, as occasional remarks by his narrators attest. In no other author can one find so many and such varied manifestations of FCN as in Dostoevskij.

*

The English versions of the quotations are drawn from recognized published translations where available. If a published translation is not sufficiently adequate, or is unsuitable for demonstrating the point at stake, I have revised the

https://doi.org/10.1515/9783110763102-001

translation. Such cases are marked "tr. rev." In some cases, it was not possible to find an appropriate – or indeed any – published translation. It is important in our context that perspectival nuances are reflected in translation. Not a few translations are at fault for correcting the original after finding it to be stylistically deficient. The search for a suitable translation is particularly delicate with English as the target language, since in comparison with German there are relatively few translations of Russian works into English. Some authors are almost exclusively read in one canonical translation, e.g., Thomas Mann in Lowe-Porter's version. Translations of primary texts that are my own, rather than drawn from published sources, are marked by asterisks.

For the sake of uniformity and bibliographical research, the Russian personal names and work titles are rendered in the international transliteration system, i.e., not Chekhov, but Čexov. The translated quotations also use (or have been silently modified to use) this system.

*

I sincerely thank my Hamburg colleague in English Literature, Prof. Peter Hühn, who critically read the entire manuscript and provided numerous suggestions for revision.

Since I am not a native speaker of English, I had to rely on a knowledgeable and critical proofreader. Such a corrector appeared in the shape of Dr. Alastair Matthews, to whom I extend my sincere thanks.

My thanks also go to the two anonymous reviewers who gave me valuable advice on corrections.

Contents

1 Introduction: Narrator and Figure

1.1 Figurally Colored Narration: Initial Definition

The present book deals with *figurally colored narration* (FCN),[1] a narrative phenomenon that is widespread in modern literature but has received little attention
in narratological research.[2] It is about a device that, in terms of narrative perspective, is situated between the authentic text of the narrator and that pattern of
mind representation that in an international context is referred to as *free indirect
discourse* (FID; *erlebte Rede, style indirect libre, nesobstvenno-prjamaja reč* [the
latter meaning, in verbatim translation, "improperly direct speech"]).[3]

The procedure under consideration is to be found in segments of the narration that meet the following conditions:

- The narrative text is figuralized to varying degrees of density and clarity, i.e.,
  it takes up particular features and fragments of a character's text (mainly
  evaluations and designations).
- The figural element is not explicitly marked, i.e., there are no quotation
  marks, *verba dicendi, putandi*, or their equivalents.
- In contrast to FID, figurally colored narration does not give the impression of an immediate representation of the character's current acts of
  consciousness.

In view of the latter stipulation, one cannot simply call FCN a device of mind representation. The consciousness of the character is represented only insofar as it
is contained in the figural features and fragments brought into the narrative discourse. And these features and fragments do not refer to the current consciousness activity of the character, but rather to his or her general mindset, to constant, typical attitudes.

---

1 The English term coined by me (Schmid 2010, 166) is not common in the anglophone field. In
German, I prefer the term *uneigentliches Erzählen* (Schmid 2014, 195–197). In Russian, the term
nesobstvenno-avtorskoe povestvovanie ("improperly authorial narration") has become established (see below, chapter 2).
2 Stanzel (1979, 225; 1984, 174) states that a comprehensive investigation of this "interesting
phenomenon in the modern novel," which he himself calls *reflectorization of the teller-character*
(see below, section 2.8), is still pending.
3 The Russian linguist Elena Padučeva (2011) uses "quasi-direct speech" as the equivalent of
FID. On my concept of FID and its development in German and Russian literature, cf. Schmid
2023.

https://doi.org/10.1515/9783110763102-002

1.2 An Example: Anton Čexov, "Rothschild's Violin"

Let us begin by looking at an example of the device. It is taken from Anton Čexov's tale "Rothschild's Violin" (Skripka Rotšil'da, 1894) and forms its opening. The use of figurally colored narration is a technique typical of this author's late novellas. The narrative text of the tale begins with the following words:

> Городок был *маленький, хуже деревни,* и жили в нём почти одни только старики, которые *умирали так редко,* что даже *досадно.* В больницу же и в тюремный замок гробов требовалось *очень мало.* Одним словом, *дела были скверные.* (Čexov, *PSS*, VIII, 297; italics mine – W. Sch.)

> The town was small, *more wretched* still than a village, and it was filled almost entirely with old folk, who *died so seldom* that it was a *crying shame.* And in the hospital and the prison the demand for coffins was *low.* In a word, *business was bad.* (Čexov, *S*, 281; italics mine – W. Sch.)

The narrative opening presents the external and internal situation of a figure who is not yet named. The selection of the elements (a small town, "old folk," "hospital," "prison," "coffins") and their evaluation (the town is "small, more wretched still than a village"; the old folk die so rarely that it is "a crying shame"; "the demand for coffins" is "low"; "business" is "bad") follows the spatial and ideological (axiological) perspective of this not-yet-named figure, who – as far as we can tell – is dissatisfied with his or her life situation. Although the aforementioned elements are chosen from the life horizon of this subject and are presented with his or her evaluations, the author of these three sentences is not a figure, but the narrator. The choice of unfavorable life circumstances follows the horizon of the still-unknown character but does not originate from a concurrent act of thinking or speaking in the diegesis. The content of the three statements is not to be understood as the reflections of a figure who, in an interior monologue, realizes his or her life situation. Instead, all the signs of an inner process are missing, such as the expressive linguistic function (in the sense of Bühler 1918/20; 1934) or syntactic traits that point to a summing-up soliloquy. In this respect, we are not dealing with free indirect discourse, even though the passage in question is often referred to as such (Levitan 1976, 42). Free indirect discourse is always a more or less narratorially reworked reproduction of the speech, thought, or evaluative acts of a narrated figure or a collective. Such an act is not present here, is not mentioned later, and cannot be assumed on the basis of what follows. We have here the narration of the narrator, who adapts his text to the horizon of a figure in individual thematic and axiological features, i.e., in selection and evaluation – a mode of presentation that we describe as *figurally colored narration.*

The subject from whose horizon the narrator has selected and evaluated the features of the narrative's opening is mentioned in the continuation of the introductory paragraph:

> Если бы Яков Иванов был гробовщиком в губернском городе, то, наверное, он имел бы собственный дом и звали бы его Яковом Матвеичем; здесь же в *городишке* звали его просто Яковом, уличное прозвище у него было почему-то — Бронза, а жил он бедно, как простой мужик, в небольшой избе, где была одна только комната, и в этой комнате помещались он, Марфа, печь, двухспальная кровать, гробы, верстак и всё хозяйство. (*PSS*, VIII, 297)

> Had Jakov Ivanov been a coffinmaker in the provincial capital, he would no doubt have had his own house, and people would have addressed him respectfully as Jakov Matveič. Here in this little backwater, though, he was simply Jakov, and for some reason he had also been nicknamed "Bronze". He lived humbly enough, like an ordinary peasant, in a small old hut that had only one room, which housed Jakov, Marfa, the stove, a double bed, the coffins, a workbench, and all their belongings. (Čexov, *S*, 281–282)

The coffinmaker Jakov Ivanov is not actually introduced, but in the conditional sentence ("Had Jakov Ivanov been a coffinmaker in the provincial capital ...") he is assumed to be known. The conditional sentence in the irrealis mood contains essential negative information: Ivanov has no house of his own, and he is not addressed by his first name and patronymic, which in Russia is a form of address for persons of respect. The second part of the long Russian sentence that describes the coffinmaker's living conditions contrasts the provincial capital with the sober reality of the "little backwater," which in turn contains two pieces of information: firstly, "here" Ivanov is addressed by his first name only, and his nickname is "Bronze" for some reason,[4] and secondly, "here" the coffinmaker lives as poor as a peasant. His meagre living conditions are illuminated by the enumeration of the things that are housed in the only room of the small old hut. Among the objects mentioned is Marfa, who, we can assume, is the coffinmaker's wife, whose illness marks the beginning of the story. The fact that Marfa is only mentioned as part of a series of objects ("stove," "double bed," "coffins," "workbench") indicates that the sober enumeration made by the narrator follows the coffinmaker's horizon of values and way of thinking. The subordinate mention of

---

4 This nickname functions in two equivalence relations: 1. it is associated with the poor, turbulent Bronze Age (Russian: *bronzovyj vek*), with which the Golden Age contrasts in the name of Roth-Schild, Jakov's antagonist; 2. bronze, as a designation of metal, contrasts with the wood of the mostly hollow bodies that Jakov handles: the coffins, the violin, the willow with the large cavity, and so on. On these oppositions, which cannot be discussed in detail here, see Schmid 2018b.

Marfa, who is included in the list of objects, also indicates the low importance Ivanov attaches to his wife. When Jakov presents his terminally ill wife to the feldsher as his *prédmet* ("object"), he uses a term that in the nineteenth century referred to someone to whom one is attached with affection.[5] Nevertheless, the unintentional, unconscious, but actual meaning "object" is present in Jakov's use of the term.

The entire first paragraph of the narrative denotes the initial situation of the story. The selection of the objects and the negatively evaluated facts connected with them, as well as the combination of heterogeneous moments into a situation that expresses a quality of mood, thus follows the spatial and ideological standpoint of the hero, the coffinmaker Jakov Ivanov, who ekes out a living from people's deaths. The temporal point of view from which it becomes possible to describe the situation in this manner is also that of the coffinmaker. The narrative begins on the threshold between backstory and actual story, in the phase immediately before the occurrence of those events (Marfa's death, Jakov's illness) that will trigger the main mental event, Jakov's inner transformation.

A situation is always constituted only in the consciousness of a latent story-forming subject who experiences reality and reduces its complexity to a few moments. Who is this subject here? At first it seems as if it is Jakov's consciousness that has joined the town, the old people, and the bad business situation together to form a situation. But in his consciousness there is no such situation, at least not a current one. We therefore do not have a case of classic FID that reflects current consciousness here, but rather the narration of a narrator who, in the selection and evaluation of the thematized objects, orients himself around the standpoint of the character. Although the chosen elements are factors that determine the coffinmaker's state of mind, and their specification is linked to the hero's horizon, it is the narrator who has chosen them from the many that make up the coffinmaker's horizon and linked them together to form a situation. Thus, this is the form we have called *figurally colored narration*.

At this point it becomes clear that the reader's identification of FCN is an attribution based on interpretation. A different view of the character could in principle lead to the identification of a different form of presentation from FCN (although this is not very likely in the case of "Rothschild's Violin").

---

5 Cf. *Slovar' russkogo jazyka v 4-x tomax*. Moscow: Russkij jazyk, 1983, s. v. "predmet 5."

1.3 Demarcation from Related Devices

In the Čexov example, the figural element was relatively easy to identify due to the evaluations that differed greatly from the doxa, that which is generally considered true and correct. The axiological coloring does not always give such clear indications of a figural point of view. A problem arises when the narrative text itself is already strongly subjectively colored. Then it can be difficult to decide whether evaluations and other parameters of subjectivity come from the narrator or the figure. We find such a case of narrative oscillating between authentic narratoriality and veiled figurality in Thomas Mann's novella *Death in Venice* (Der Tod in Venedig, 1912):

> Der Autor der klaren und mächtigen Prosa-Epopöe vom Leben Friedrichs von Preußen; der geduldige Künstler, der in langem Fleiß den figurenreichen, so vielerlei Menschenschicksal im Schatten einer Idee versammelnden Romanteppich, „Maja" mit Namen, wob; der Schöpfer jener starken Erzählung, die „Ein Elender" überschrieben ist und einer ganzen dankbaren Jugend die Möglichkeit sittlicher Entschlossenheit jenseits der tiefsten Erkenntnis zeigte; der Verfasser endlich (und damit sind die Werke seiner Reifezeit kurz bezeichnet) der leidenschaftlichen Abhandlung über „Geist und Kunst", deren ordnende Kraft und antithetische Beredsamkeit ernste Beurteiler vermochte, sie unmittelbar neben Schillers Raisonnement über naive und sentimentalische Dichtung zu stellen: Gustav Aschenbach also war zu L., einer Kreisstadt der Provinz Schlesien, als Sohn eines höheren Justizbeamten geboren. (Mann, VIII, 450)

> The author of the lucid and massive prose epic about the life of Frederic of Prussia; the patient artist who with long toil had woven the great tapestry of the novel called "Maya," so rich in characters, gathering so many human destinies together under the shadow of one idea; the creator of that powerful tale entitled "A Study in Abjection," which earned the gratitude of a whole younger generation by pointing to the possibility of moral resolution even for those who have plumbed the depths of knowledge; the author (lastly but not least in this summary enumeration of his maturer works) of that passionate treatise "Intellect and Art" which in its ordering energy and antithetical eloquence has led serious critics to place it immediately alongside Schiller's disquisition "On Naïve and Reflective Literature": in a word, Gustav Aschenbach, was born in L –, an important city in the province of Silesia, as the son of a highly-placed legal official. (Mann, *Death in Venice*, 202)

This is how the second chapter of the novella begins. Its hero no longer needs to be introduced. He is known to us from the walk through the Munich English Garden described in the first chapter. Now he is presented to us in his self-image, as a powerful "creator" of literary narratives, as a "patient artist," as a preceptor of youth, and as the author of "passionate treatises." In the selection of themes and in its syntactic structure, the presentation is clearly narratorial, but traces of the self-conception of the described person are evident in the choice of words and in the evaluations. And at the same time, the shadow of narratorial irony falls over these figural traces. "The author of the lucid and massive prose epic," "the patient artist who with long toil had woven the great tapestry of the novel," "the creator of that powerful tale," "the gratitude of a whole younger generation," "the possibility of moral resolution" – these pathetic qualities cannot be read without an ironic intonation. Here we have a case of *text interference* (see below, section 3.1), the overlapping of the character's text (CT) and the quoting narrator's text (NT). In text interference, CT and NT, with their respective intentions of meaning, are simultaneously present. The phrases and evaluations of the writer Gustav von Aschenbach, who is intoxicated by his own greatness and significance, are overlaid by the voice of the (non-diegetic) narrator, who presents himself throughout as sober and critical.[6] Thus, the entire presentation becomes double-voiced.[7] Nevertheless, this presentation, with its interference between CT and NT, is difficult to distinguish from an authentically narratorial but thoroughly ironic performance. Irony is a two-level figure in which the meaning of a first user is axiologically counterdetermined by the intention of the quoting user. But irony need not be accompanied by text interference. In our case, the narrator could be speaking ironically without reference to the character's text, which is not present and is not quoted subsequently either. Here we have a case in which FCN cannot be clearly distinguished from an authentic narratorial text.

On the other hand, there are problems of demarcating FCN from FID. Let us consider the end of Aleksandr Solženicyn's camp narrative *A Day in the Life of Ivan Denisovič* (Odin den' Ivana Denisoviča, 1962), whose hero was sentenced to ten years in a Soviet forced labor camp because he had allowed himself to be captured by the Germans as a prisoner during World War II. In this thematically and formally innovative work, FCN, which had been avoided as a bourgeois-formalist method in Russian literature of the 1940s and 1950s, prevailed with all its might, and thus the novella gave important impulses to the further development of complex perspective in the Russian prose of the 1960s and 1970s–1980s (Holthusen 1968, 241–245; Schmid 1979; Koževnikova 1994, 245).

There are sections in this novel that are undeniably FCN. One of them deals with the problem of the footwear with which the camp inmates are provided:

Никак не годилось с утра мочить валенки. А и переобуться не во что, хоть и в барак побеги. Разных порядков с обувью нагляделся Шухов за восемь лет сидки: бывало, и вовсе без валенок зиму перехаживали, бывало, и ботинок тех не видали, только

---

6 On the distinction between *diegetic* and *non-diegetic* narrators, which corresponds to the opposition of "homodiegetic" and "heterodiegetic" narrators in Genette (1972, 252), an opposition problematic in terms both of system and of word formation, cf. Schmid (2010, 68–74).
7 On the category of "double-voicedness," cf. Baxtin ([1929] 2000, 86; tr. 1981, 185–186).

лапти да ЧТЗ (из резины обутка, след автомобильный). Теперь вроде с обувью под-
наладилось. (Solženicyn, *MSS*, III, 10)

No sense in getting your boots wet in the morning. Even if Šuxov had dashed back to his
hut he wouldn't have found another pair to change into. During eight years' imprisonment
he had known various systems for allocating footwear: there'd been times when he'd gone
through the winter without valenki at all, or leather boots either, and had had to make shift
with bast sandals or a sort of galoshes made of scraps of motor tyres – "Četezes" they called
them, after the Čeljabinsk tractor works. Now the footwear situation seemed better ... (Solženicyn, *OD*, 14)

This paragraph is clearly not presented in FID. Neither a current interior monologue nor the recollections of the protagonist are presented; rather, it is the narrator's voice one hears, which, in the narratorial overview of the story of shoe
allocation in the prison camp, approaches as closely as possible the evaluative
and linguistic horizons of the protagonist and uses special expressions from
camp language. The main factor suggesting that we are dealing with the narrator's point of view here is that the abbreviation ČTZ is explained, in the original
Russian version in the language of the hero's environment ("rubber shoe, trail
automobile"), in the translation even with the resolution of the letters ČTZ = *Čel-
jabinskij traktornyj zavod* ("Čeljabinsk tractor works").

Although FCN and FID exhibit differing structures, it is not always possible
to separate them from each other in Solženicyn's text. Distinguishing one from
the other is made difficult above all in places where figural elements that correspond to the current situation of the protagonist become more frequent. As a result, the final sentences of the novel can be considered either the reproduction of
a current process in the character's consciousness, summing up the day's events
as he falls asleep, i.e., as FID, or as the words of the narrator who, independently
of the current situation in the character's consciousness, weighs up the day's
"successes," i.e., as FCN:

Засыпал Шухов вполне удоволенный. На дню у него выдалось сегодня много удач: в
карцер не посадили, на Соцгородок бригаду не выгнали, в обед он закосил кашу,
бригадир хорошо закрыл процентовку, стену Шухов клал весело, с ножевкой на
шмоне не попался, подработал вечером у Цесаря и табачку купил. И не заболел, пе-
ремогся.
Прошел день, ничем не омраченный, почти счастливый. (Solženicyn, *MSS*, III, 111)

Šuxov went to sleep fully content. He'd had many strokes of luck that day: they hadn't put
him in the cells; they hadn't sent the team to the settlement; he'd pinched a bowl of kasha
at dinner; the team-leader had fixed the rates well; he'd built a wall and enjoyed doing it;
he'd smuggled that bit of hacksaw-blade through; he'd earned something from Cezar in the
evening; he'd bought that tobacco. And he hadn't fallen ill. He'd got over it.
A day without a dark cloud. Almost a happy day. (Solženicyn, *OD*, 142–143)

Particularly when a backstory is being told, the problem of demarcation arises. The reader will ask himself whether the backstory involves memories that come to the character, such that the past is shaped in FID, or whether the narrator, without the involvement of the character at this point, is summarizing the backstory in FCN.

A passage on the cusp between the two possibilities can be found in Katherine Mansfield's story "The Fly" (1922). In conversation with his boss, old Woodifield mentions the grave of the former's son, who is buried in Belgium in a cemetery for fallen soldiers. The mention of the boy's grave is a terrible shock to the boss:

> The boy had been in the office learning the ropes for a year before the war. Every morning they had started off together, they had come back by the same train. And what congratulations he had received as the boy's father! No wonder; he had taken to it marvellously. As to his popularity with the staff, every man jack of them down to old Macey couldn't make enough of the boy. (Mansfield, *Stories*, 347)

FCN and FID can be distinguished here in various ways. The most acceptable is probably to treat the first part of the quotation (italics) as FCN and the second (no italics) as FID. FCN is hard to identify in narratives that are strongly figural in perspective. The figural coloring of the narration is not easily noticed in these cases because there is a lack of contrast with the narratorial context.

A novel told mostly from the changing heroes' perspective is Hermann Broch's *The Sleepwalkers* (Die Schlafwandler, 1932).[8] The second part of the trilogy is centered on the bookkeeper August Esch:

> Esch hatte das Offert für die Mannheimer vorbereitet; er brauchte bloß das Zeugnis beizulegen. Eigentlich war er froh, dass die Dinge so gekommen waren. Es war nicht gut, immer an einem Platz zu sitzen. Man musste hinaus, je weiter desto besser. Und man musste sich umtun; so hatte er es auch stets gehalten.
>
> Nachmittags ging er zu Sternberg & Co., Weingroßhandlung und Kellereien, sein Zeugnis holen. Nentwig ließ ihn an der Holzbarriere warten, saß *dick und rundlich* an seinem Schreibtisch und rechnete. (Broch, *Schlafwandler*, 187; my italics – W. Sch.)

> Esch had drawn up his application for the Mannheim post; he now needed only the reference to enclose with it. Actually he was glad that things had turned out as they had. It wasn't good for a man to vegetate all the time in one place. He felt he must get out of Cologne, and the farther the better. A fellow must keep his eyes open; as a matter of fact he had always done that.

---

8 On the representation of consciousness in this novel, cf. Cohn 1966, 31–48; 1978, 52–55.

> In the afternoon he went to the office of Sternberg & Company, wholesale wine merchants, to get his reference. Nentwig kept him waiting at the counter, and sat at his desk, *fat and slouching*, totting up columns. (Broch, *Sleepwalkers*, part 2, ch. 1; italics mine – W. Sch.)

"Fat and slouching" – these words are structurally ambivalent. Formally, they can be attributed to the narrator, but in the context, which is rich in FID, they are more likely to be attributed to the hero as his evaluation of the perceived person. This oscillating attribution is characteristic of works in which figural perspective dominates.

To be clear once again: what is constitutive for FCN is figural selection, evaluation, and naming without actually transmitting the current content of a figure's consciousness. The identification of FCN depends on whether axiological and stylistic features that deviate from objective, sober statements are attributed to the narrator (FCN) or to a figure (no FCN), and this is a subjective act of interpretation.

1.4 The Naturalness of FCN

Essentially, FCN is not a particularly sophisticated technique, just a very natural means of everyday storytelling. Whenever a person reports about another person's experiences or adventures, he or she will involuntarily adopt to a certain extent the point of view of that person in both the literal and figurative sense of the term. The narrator will take over the person's field of vision, visualize the objects that appear in front of the person, and make himself and the listener aware of them, i.e., he will adapt the choice of objects to be narrated to the perspective of the person about whom he is reporting. Depending on his ideological and axiological proximity to the person, the narrator can also adopt the person's evaluations, either in an authentic empathetic act or, in an ironic deception, just for the sake of appearances. Various intermediate stages between empathy and satirical unmasking are possible.

The narrator may also be tempted to adapt his choice of words to the character. This in turn can happen with different attitudes, from empathic solidarity to merciless mockery.

It is not possible to report on another person without taking on his or her spatial, temporal, axiological, linguistic, and perceptual point of view to some extent.[9] Thus, FCN is nothing other than the literary modeling of this everyday convergence between a teller and the person he is telling about.

There are of course differences between literary FCN and the everyday adoption by a reporter of the perceptual, evaluative, and linguistic horizon of the person he is telling about. In everyday life, the given context and situation, but above all the intonation of the teller, will signal that he or she is taking on the position of another person and, moreover, what evaluative accents he or she is rendering and overlaying it with.[10] In literary composition, the figurality is usually covert. It must first be identified, and then the narrator's own evaluation must be reconstructed. In this respect, FID is easier to identify than FCN. In FID, deictics, language function, and – in certain languages – tense and mood signal the presence of the character's text in the narrative text. In FCN such grammatical signs are usually missing, and the reader is completely dependent on the symptoms of selection, evaluation, lexis, and syntax.

In standard literary narrative it is quite common for the narrator to select the objects as they fall within the field of the character's perception. Let us look at an example from Thomas Mann's novel *The Magic Mountain* (Der Zauberberg, 1924). The novel's hero, Hans Castorp, is on his way by train to Davos, to the mountain sanatorium, where he is going to visit his cousin:

> [...] der Zug wand sich gebogen auf schmalem Pass; man sah die vorderen Wagen, sah die Maschine, die in ihrer Mühe braune, grüne und schwarze Rauchmassen ausstieß, die verflatterten. Wasser rauschten in der Tiefe zur Rechten; links strebten dunkle Fichten zwischen Felsblöcken gegen einen steingrauen Himmel empor. Stockfinstere Tunnel kamen, und wenn es wieder Tag wurde, taten weitläufige Abgründe mit Ortschaften in der Tiefe sich auf. Sie schlossen sich, neue Engpässe folgten, mit Schneeresten in ihren Schründen und Spalten. Es gab Aufenthalte an armseligen Bahnhofshäuschen, Kopfstationen, die der Zug in entgegengesetzter Richtung verließ, was verwirrend wirkte, da man nicht mehr wusste, wie man fuhr, und sich der Himmelsgegenden nicht länger entsann. Großartige Fernblicke in die heilig-phantasmagorisch sich türmende Gipfelwelt des Hochgebirges, in das man hinan- und hineinstrebte, eröffneten sich und gingen dem ehrfürchtigen Auge durch Pfadbiegungen wieder verloren. (Mann, III, 13)

> The train wound in curves along the narrow pass; [one] could see the front carriages and the laboring engine vomiting great masses of brown, black, and greenish smoke, that floated away. Water roared in the abysses on the right; on the left, among rocks, dark fir-trees aspired toward a stone-grey sky. The train passed through pitch-black tunnels, and

---

9 On the five parameters of point of view, cf. Schmid 2010, 100–105.
10 In section 3.5 we will discuss a famous case of FCN in an extra-artistic and extra-fictional oral context, in which the identification of the figural part failed because of the lack of signaling intonation.

when daylight came again it showed wide chasms, with villages nestled in their depths. Then the pass closed in again; they wound along narrow defiles, with traces of snow in chinks and crannies. There were halts at wretched little shanties of stations; also at more important ones, which the train left in the opposite direction, making one lose the points of the compass. A magnificent succession of vistas opened before the awed eye, of the solemn, phantasmagorical world of towering peaks, into which their route wove and wormed itself: vistas that appeared and disappeared with each new winding of the path. (Mann, *Magic Mountain*, 5)[11]

The narrator selects the objects and their characteristics as they appear to the traveling hero. In this respect, the description of the journey is figurally perspectivized. But the evaluation of the views presented can hardly be called figural. The Hamburg merchant's son Hans Castorp is introduced in the first sentence of the novel as an "unassuming young man" (*Magic Mountain*, 3; "Ein einfacher junger Mensch," Mann, III, 11). And even if his eye is "awed," what it sees will hardly have been perceived in Castorp's simple consciousness as a "solemn, phantasmagorical world of towering peaks." In this respect the description is more narratorial than figural.[12]

When in literary narrative a current activity of consciousness of the character is presented, and the selected objects reveal the character's view and evaluation, we speak of *free indirect perception* (Palmer 2004).[13] If the selection and evaluation are accompanied by interior speech and figural reflection, we speak of *free indirect discourse*. Neither of these two modes is present in this case. FCN is not present here either, as that would require a figural coloring of the evaluations. We must exclude FCN because of the elaborate expression of admiration for the sublime views of nature. Neither the admiration nor its expression fits the mental profile of the "unassuming young man" as presented at the beginning of the novel. What we have here is rather an approach – quite common in everyday narration – in which the narrator moves to the spatial point of view of the figure and

---

11 The English translation emphasizes the figural element in that it renders the German "*man sah die vorderen Wagen*" with "*he* [literally: one] could see the front carriages" (italics mine – W. Sch.).

12 It could even be called authorial, since the description of the majestic mountain world is obviously a reflection of the impressions the author received in 1912 during his visit to his wife, who was taking a cure in Davos. However, such biographical speculation clearly exceeds the limits of what is permissible in Literary Studies.

13 Willi Bühler (1937, 131, 153) calls this device – analogously to *erlebte Rede* – *erlebte Wahrnehmung*, Bernhard Fehr (1938) *substitionary perception*, Laurel Brinton (1980) *represented perception*.

selects the objects according to how they are perceived by the figure, thereby expressing his own narratorial evaluation.

The naturalness of FCN can also be seen in the fact that clearly narratorial narration not infrequently becomes increasingly figuralized as the narrator moves closer to the character. A passage from the second chapter of the third part of Hermann Broch's novel *The Sleepwalkers* can serve as an example. The third part of the trilogy is dedicated to the merchant Wilhelm Huguenau, who is drafted into military service in 1917 and deserts from the front in Belgium:

> Umgeben von der klaren Luft, die den Frühling vorbereitet, zieht der Deserteur waffenlos durch die belgische Landschaft. Eile würde ihm nicht frommen, bedächtige Vorsicht frommt ihm besser, und Waffen würden ihn nicht schützen; er geht sozusagen als nackter Mensch durch die Gewalten hindurch. Sein unbefangenes Gesicht ist ihm besserer Schutz als Waffen oder eilige Flucht oder falsche Ausweispapiere.
>
> Belgische Bauern sind misstrauische Kerle. Vier Jahre Krieg haben ihren Charakter nicht veredelt. Ihr Korn, ihre Kartoffeln, ihre Pferde und Kühe haben dran glauben müssen. Und wenn ein Deserteur sich zu ihnen flüchten will, so sehen sie ihn doppelt misstrauisch an, ob es nicht der Mann ist, der einmal mit dem Gewehrkolben ans Hoftor getrommelt hat. Und wenn so einer auch ein erträgliches Französisch spricht und sich als Elsässer ausgibt, es hilft ihm in neun von zehn Fällen nicht viel. Wehe dem, der bloß als Flüchtling und trauriger Hilfeheischender durch das Dorf wanderte. Wer aber, wie Huguenau, ein treffendes Scherzwort rasch auf der Lippe hat, wer mit strahlend freundlichem Gesicht ins Gehöft tritt, der kann leicht ein Lager auf dem Heuboden erhalten, der mag des Abends mit der Familie in der dunklen Stube sitzen und von den Gewalttaten der Preußen erzählen und wie sie es im Elsass getrieben haben, er wird Beifall finden, er erhält auch sein Teil von den spärlichen versteckten Vorräten, und wenn er Glück hat, besucht eine Magd den Fremdling im Heu. (Broch, *Schlafwandler*, 388–389)

Bathed in the limpid air that heralds the spring, the deserter made his way unarmed through the Belgian landscape. Haste would have served him little, prudent caution served him better, and weapons would not have protected him at all; it was, one might say, as a naked man that he slipped through the armed forces. His untroubled face was a better protection than weapons or hurried flight or forged papers.

For the Belgians were suspicious fellows. Four years of war had not improved their disposition. Their corn, their potatoes, their horses and cows had all had to suffer. And when a deserter came to them looking for sanctuary they examined him with twofold suspicion, lest he might be one of the men who had beaten on their doors with a rifle-butt. And even if the fugitive spoke passable French and gave himself out as an Alsatian, in nine cases out of ten that would have availed him little. Woe to the man who strayed into a village merely as a fugitive timidly imploring help! But a man who came like Huguenau with a ready jest on his lips, with a beaming and friendly face, found it easy enough to have beer smuggled to him in the barn, or even to sit with the family of an evening in the kitchen and tell tales of the Prussians' brutality and violence in Alsace; such a stranger was welcomed and got his share of the hoarded provisions; with luck he might even be visited in his bed of hay by one of the maids. (Broch, *Sleepwalkers*, part 3, ch. 2)

With the beginning of the second paragraph, the perspective changes. Whereas in the first paragraph the deserter's fate was still presented narratorially, in the second paragraph the figural perspective increasingly, barely noticeably and not at all marked, comes to the fore, admittedly not without the perspective occasionally slipping back into the narratorial mode.

What we can conclude from the above discussion is the following: telling about someone else's experiences means adopting his or her point of view, at least in the parameters of space and time, often also in perception and evaluation, sometimes even in language. This is the reason for the widespread use of hybrid text-interference modes in literature since the beginning of the nineteenth century.

1.5 FCN in the Torah and in Homer

Figurally colored narration is by no means a modern device. Its naturalness alone prevents that. We already find it in the Torah and in Homer.

In chapter 24 of Bereshit/Genesis, Abraham sends his oldest servant to his homeland to find a wife for his son Isaac. The servant successfully courts the beautiful Rebekah, who has generously supplied him and his camels with water at the well, thus giving, without knowing it, the sign requested by Isaac from heaven. Rebekah's brother Laban accepts the courtship, and Rebekah sets out with her maidservants to the land of Canaan.

Genesis 24:61 states:

> And Rebekah rose, with her young women, and they mounted the camels and went after the *man*, and the *servant* took Rebekah and went off.

Menakhem Perry (2007, 281) sees a "bifurcation into two perspectives" in the appellations (italicized here): on the one hand the perspective of the members of the family, who know that the wooer is a *servant*, and on the other hand the perspective of Rebekah, who is going "after the *man*." Perry calls this device of coloring the narrator's voice with a hue that originates in a narrated character's text *combined discourse*.[14]

In the twenty-fourth canto of Homer's *Iliad*, Priam, led by Hermes, goes to Achilles to ask him to hand over Hector's body:

---

14 One of the anonymous assessors of this book notes that *combined discourse* is the Tel Aviv School's equivalent of FID.

χερσὶν Ἀχιλλῆος λάβε γούνατα καὶ κύσε χεῖρας
δεινὰς ἀνδροφόνους, αἵ οἱ πολέας κτάνον υἷας. (24.478–479)

He [Priam] took the knees of Achilles and kissed his hands,
the terrible ones, man-killing, that had killed many of his children.[15]

That the passages I have italicized are not simply a standing epithet of the narrator, but reflect Priam's view of Achilles, is evident from the context. In line 22.423, Priam had said about Achilles: "he killed my children in their bloom" (γάρ μοι παῖδας ἀπέκτανε τηλεθάοντας), and in lines 24.505–506, Priam's view of Achilles and his own course of action toward the murderer of his children is made explicit:

ἐγὼ δ᾽ ἐλεεινότερός περ,
ἔτλην δ᾽, οἷ᾽ πώ τις ἐπιχθόνιος βροτὸς ἄλλος,
ἀνδρὸς παιδοφόνοιο ποτὶ στόμα χεῖρ᾽ ὀρέγεσθαι.

I deserve even greater pity,
because I endure what no man on earth has ever endured,
that I kiss the hands of the man who killed my children.

The figural expression profiles the pain of the old man pleading for his son's corpse. The FCN provides insight into the brokenness of the father, who accuses and kisses his son's murderer at the same time.

In the *Odyssey* we find a spot of FCN when Odysseus reveals himself to his son Telemachos:

[...] ἐγὼ τοιόσδε, παθὼν κακά, πολλὰ δ᾽ ἀληθείς,
ἤλυθον εἰκοστῷ ἔτεϊ ἐς πατρίδα γαῖαν.
αὐτάρ τοι τόδε ἔργον Ἀθηναίης ἀγελείης,
[...]
ὣς ἄρα φωνήσας κατ᾽ ἄρ᾽ ἕζετο, Τηλέμαχος δὲ
ἀμφιχυθεὶς πατέρ᾽ ἐσθλὸν ὀδύρετο δάκρυα λείβων.
ἀμφοτέροισι δὲ τοῖσιν ὑφ᾽ ἵμερος ὦρτο γόοιο
(16.205–207, 213–215)

[...] I, just as you see me, after sufferings and many wanderings,
have come in the twentieth year to my native land.
But this, you must know, is the work of Athene.
[...]
So saying, he sat down, and Telemachos,
flinging his arms about *his good father*, wept and shed tears,
and in the hearts of both arose a longing for lamentation.
(Tr. Murray/Dimock 1995, 133–135; italics mine – W. Sch.)

---

15 I owe the reference to the quotation and its context to Irene de Jong (1987, 119–120; 2014, 52).

In this scene of anagnorisis, which is crucial for the whole story, the narrator refers to Odysseus in a way that corresponds to the son's evaluation. Simon Grund (forthcoming), referring to this passage, states that "the evaluative attribute ἐσθλὸν ('good, brave') can be taken as an instance of *embedded focalization* [for this term see below, section 2.10], in the case of which evaluative judgements and the perspective of a textual character are conveyed in the narrator's speech."

In her book on the presentation of the story in the *Iliad*, Irene de Jong (1987) collects a number of examples of what she calls *figural narration* or – after Mieke Bal (1981) – *embedded focalization*. Her aim is to show that Homer does use figural narration, which has been denied by many scholars. However, it should be underlined here that Bal's concept of embedded focalization and de Jong's concept of figural narration do not correspond exactly to my concept of FCN. Both terms are broader, including what I call the indirect representation of perception, thought, and emotion (see below, sections 2.1 and 2.10).

2 Figurally Colored Narration: Terms and Definitions

2.1 Terminological Clarification

In the following, the most important terms, descriptions, and definitions of FCN in German, Russian, and English research will be presented. In order to provide a terminological basis for distinguishing between the patterns of mind representation to which FCN belongs, I will first present the patterns of the explicit representation of consciousness that are fundamental to narrative literature in my conceptualization.[1]

The concentration on the representation of consciousness results from the fact that in most cases, FCN includes those features of the character's text that are connected with the mindset of the figure. Thus, FCN can also include designations and evaluations that are simply part of a figure's mindset, without being articulated in external or internal speech at the moment in question.[2] The following overview is limited to patterns of the representation of consciousness for this reason.

2.1.1 Patterns of the Explicit Representation of Consciousness

The explicit representation of consciousness can be divided into *marked* and *covert* patterns. The representation of consciousness is marked when graphic means (quotation marks, italics, blocking, and the like) or so-called *inquit* formulas ("he thought...," "she felt...") indicate the figural origin of the corresponding segments of the narrative discourse. The representation of consciousness is, of course, also marked in the case of the narratorial consciousness report ("Such

---

1 I am concerned here only with the patterns of the *explicit* representation of consciousness. For the *implicit* representation of consciousness, which is based on indexical and symbolic signs such as the character's speaking and behavior, cf. Schmid (2017, 59–62); cf. there (23–56) for a detailed description of the patterns of explicit mind representation and an earlier version of the following scheme.

2 On my distinction between manifest, phenotypic character *discourse* and latent, genotypic character *text*, which corresponds to the entire subject sphere of the figure and contains the character's disposition to a certain perceptual, ideological-axiological, and linguistic perspective, cf. Schmid 2010, 120–121. The term *character's text* is here taken to mean the genotypic complex of all the exterior and interior speech, thoughts, and perceptions of a given figure.

https://doi.org/10.1515/9783110763102-003

thoughts went through her mind"). Covert representation pertains when the figural text is not easily recognizable as such but is formally presented as narrative discourse. This applies in particular to FID.

Table 1: The Six Patterns of the Explicit Representation of Consciousness

A.	Marked representation of consciousness
1.	Direct interior discourse:
	extended form: direct interior monologue,
	stream of consciousness in the first person;
	reduced form: quoted figural designation.
2.	Indirect and autonomous indirect representation of perception, thought, and emotion.
3.	Consciousness report.
B.	**Covert representation of consciousness**
4.	Free indirect discourse (FID);
	free indirect monologue;
	stream of consciousness in the third person.
5.	Free indirect perception.
6.	Figurally colored narration (FCN).

These six patterns will now be compared with the types commonly used in English-language scholarship.

2.1.2 Brian McHale's Scale of Speech Reproduction

Brian McHale's typology of forms of speech representation (1978, 258–259) comprises seven types on a sliding scale from diegesis to mimesis (both in the Platonic sense: from narratorial summary to direct imitation):

1. Diegetic summary: "involving only the bare report that a speech event has occurred, without any specification of what was said or how it was said"
2. Summary, less "purely" diegetic: "represents, not merely gives notice of, a speech event in that it names the topics of conversation"

3. Indirect content paraphrase: "without regard to the style or form of the sup-posed 'original' utterance"
4. Indirect discourse, mimetic to some degree: "gives the illusion of 'preserv-ing' or 'reproducing' aspects of the style of an utterance"
5. Free indirect discourse: "may be mimetic to almost any degree short of 'pure' mimesis"
6. Direct discourse: "the most purely mimetic type of report"
7. Free direct discourse: "direct discourse shorn of its conventional ortho-graphic cues"

Our pattern 1 corresponds to types 6 and 7 in McHale; the extended form (direct interior monologue and stream of consciousness in the first person) and reduced form (quoted figural designation that often appears erratically in the narrative text) are not treated as separate types in McHale's scale.

Our pattern 2 (indirect representation) corresponds to McHale's types 3 and 4, which differ in the stronger narratorial or figural coloring of the reproduced speech. McHale's types 3 and 4 are not represented separately in our typology. Our differentiation between indirect and autonomous indirect representation has no correspondence in McHale. Autonomous indirect representation occurs when the expressivity and syntax of figural indirect discourse go beyond the syntactic restrictions of the pattern, or when the indirect representation adopts the consti-tutive characteristics of direct discourse (graphic markings, use of the first and second person; for examples from Dostoevskij and Virginia Woolf, see Schmid [2017, 36–37]).

Our pattern 3 (consciousness report) corresponds to McHale's types 2 and 3.[3] FID, free indirect interior monologue, and stream of consciousness (in the third person), listed under 4 in my table, correspond to McHale's type 5. My pattern 5 (free indirect perception) does not figure as a separate type in McHale, and nor does McHale's typology of 1978 provide for figurally colored narration (my pat-tern 6);[4] only in McHale (2014, 819) is this pattern noted, under its different names.

---

3 Types 2–3, which come close to pure diegesis (in the Platonic sense: the narrator's report), are summarized by Leech and Short (1981) and by Semino and Short (2004) under the designation NRSA, "narrative report of speech acts." Toolan (2006, 709–710) extends the pattern to include the representation of consciousness: "narrative report of thought acts."
4 Even in Michael Toolan's (2006) overview of the forms for rendering speech and conscious-ness, figurally colored narration is not considered.

2.1.3 Dorrit Cohn's Triad of Modes for Rendering Consciousness

In *Transparent Minds*, the first monograph on consciousness in narrative literature, Dorrit Cohn (1978, 14) proposes a triad of modes. In contrast to McHale's
scale, which orders the forms in which the *speech* of the characters is presented,
Cohn is concerned with the forms that render *consciousness*. For "consciousness
in third-person context" Cohn distinguishes the following three modes:[5]

1. *Psycho-narration*: "the narrator's discourse about a character's conscious-
    ness" (Cohn 1978, 14; this pattern corresponds to the consciousness report in
    our terminology. However, Cohn also subsumes the indirect representation
    of thoughts under this form. Her sample sentences for this are *He knew he
    was late* and *He wondered if he was late.*)
2. *Quoted monologue*: "a character's mental discourse" (in our terminology: in-
    terior monologue in direct discourse)
3. *Narrated monologue*: "a character's mental discourse in the guise of the nar-
    rator's discourse" (in our terminology: interior monologue in FID)

2.1.4 Alan Palmer's Triad of Rendering Mind

Alan Palmer (2004) has proposed a differently named, but in substance largely
identical triad:

1. Direct thought (*She thought, "Where am I?"*)
2. Free indirect thought (*She stopped. Where the hell was she?*)
3. Thought report (*She wondered where she was*)

Palmer, who already in 2002 strongly opposed the speech-category approach,
cannot hide the fact that his types 1 and 2 correspond to the patterns of direct and
free indirect discourse. Significantly, he originally wanted to avoid the "swamp"
of free indirect discourse in his book completely (2004, 56).

---

5 In the tradition of Käte Hamburger (1957; 1968), Cohn treats the representation of consciousness in the first and third person separately, and for further differentiation she draws on the
evaluative relationship between narrator and figure for the three techniques: a representation of
consciousness presented by a distanced or even ironic narrator is "dissonant"; the representation is "consonant" if the narrator, as Cohn not unproblematically formulates, "remains effaced
and [...] readily fuses with the consciousness he narrates" (1978, 26).

2.2 Leo Spitzer: "Contagion"

We now move on to considering theories in which the concept of FCN is defined, or even mentioned, even if under a different name.

The earliest known description of FCN is by Leo Spitzer. Spitzer's remarks on "language mixing" (1923a) are often cited for their discovery of the phenomenon of "contagion of the narrator's language by the characters' language" or "contamination of the narrator's language by the language of the fictional characters" (Stanzel 1979, 48, 247; tr. 1984, 26, 192). Spitzer's essay deals with a special feature of prose style in Alfred Kerr's criticism, which Spitzer calls *Sprachmischung* ("mixing of languages") and – in the 1928 version – *Sprachmengung* ("blending of languages"). In the narrative excerpts examined, phonetic, grammatical, and syntactic peculiarities of the characters' language, often dialectal peculiarities, are "mixed" or "blended" with the narrator's language. This results in "a strange and inextricable mixture, an as-if form, a kind of 'contagion' of the author's language by the characters' language" ("ein sonderbares und unentwirrbares Gemisch, eine Als-ob-Form, eine Art 'Ansteckung' der Autorensprache durch die Figurensprache"; Spitzer 1923a, 98).[6] The term *language* simplifies the complex device involved. In addition to lexical and syntactic aspects, the device naturally also affects the evaluation that the linguistic phenomena connote.

With the concept of contagion, which he introduces cautiously and with metaphorical reservation and uses only once more, with distancing quotation marks (1923a, 99), Spitzer nonetheless pinned down a mode of representing the language of narrated figures or collectives that is important for narrative works from early realism on. Narratology has adopted Spitzer's term *Ansteckung* in various languages (*contagion*, Russian *zaraženie*).[7] "Contagion" is a method of covertly representing a character's language and evaluative positions, and is to be sharply distinguished from a similar method of marked representation, which is referred to in my scheme as *quoted figural designation*. Spitzer (1928, 330) described this latter procedure as the "imitation of individual words in the narrative report"

---

6 Spitzer (1923b) describes a similar process on a larger scale in Charles-Louis Philippe's novel *Bubu de Montparnasse*. Individual explanatory sentences of the narrative text in the gnomic present tense, which seem to be spoken by an objective narrator, turn out to be "pseudo-objective motivation," i.e., they actually present the subjective reasoning with which the characters motivate their actions.

7 In her overview article on FID in medieval and modern French literature, Sophie Marnette (forthcoming) observes how there is a "trend toward a *parler vrai* ('true speech')" that "pervades the narration itself so that the vocabulary used in the reported discourses is often found in the very discourse of the narrator, a technique often described as 'contamination' by scholars."

("Nachahmung einzelner Worte im Berichttext") and demonstrated it using an example from a German translation of *The Brothers Karamazov*: "Starr blickte er [Dmitrij Karamazov] dem 'Milchbart' in die Augen" ("He [Dmitrij Karamazov] looked the 'milksop' straight in the eye"; Dostoevskij, *BK*, 911). Spitzer comments: "One sees, as it were, a beam of subjectivity, the tone of Mitja's voice, break out from the factual report" (Spitzer 1928, 330). While the quoted figural designation is marked by quotation marks, the "contagion" device lacks any indication of the figural origin of the corresponding segments of the narrative text.

In her typology of the three basic techniques for rendering consciousness, Dorrit Cohn refers to Spitzer's *Ansteckung*, which she calls "stylistic contagion," with respect to a passage from Joyce's *Portrait of the Artist as a Young Man*.[8] As her designation suggests, she understands this to be merely a stylistic phenomenon:

> Applied to the techniques for rendering consciousness, the phrase "stylistic contagion" can serve to designate places where psycho-narration verges on the narrated monologue, marking a kind of midpoint between the two techniques where a reporting syntax is maintained, but where the idiom is strongly affected (or infected) with the mental idiom of the mind it renders. (Cohn 1978, 33)

From the examples that Spitzer cites from Kerr's prose, it is clear that "stylistic contagion" always conveys an evaluation of the character in question. The contagion thus becomes a place of axiological interference between the primary speaker (figure) and the secondary speaker (narrator), and thus a process of – in the Baxtinian sense – double-voicedness.

2.3 Mixail Baxtin: "Anticipated and Disseminated Reported Speech"

Inspired by Spitzer, Mixail Baxtin also speaks of "contagion" (*zaraženie*) in the book that was published under the name of Valentin Vološinov with the misleading title *Marxism and the Philosophy of Language* (1929).[9] This book is mainly

---

8 In her dissertation on Hermann Broch's novel *The Sleepwalkers*, Dorrit Cohn (1966, 36) also uses Spitzer's term "stylistic contagion" to describe a style "in which the author's voice takes on the coloring of the character's, his images and habits of thought."

9 On Baxtin's authorship and his distance from Marxism, see Bočarov (1993) and my summary (Schmid 2020, 25, note 26). The books of Vološinov (1927; 1929) and Pavel Medvedev (1928), which can be attributed to the factual authorship of Baxtin, were published by Vitalij Maxlin in

concerned with the relationship between the "authorial context" and "reported speech," i.e., characters' discourse. [10] Among the manifold phenomena of "speech interference" (*rečevaja interferencija*), the most important of which is FID (in Vološinov's terms: *nesobstvennaja prjamaja reč'*, "quasi-direct discourse" [1929, 149; tr.: 1973, 137]), Vološinov (1929, 146) lists a "modification of direct speech" which he calls "anticipated and disseminated reported speech" (*predvosxiščёnnaja i rassejannaja čužaja reč'*):

> The presetting of the reported speech and the anticipation of its theme in the narrative, its judgements, and accents may so subjectivize and color the author's context in the tints of his hero that that context will begin to sound like "reported speech," though a kind of reported speech with its authorial intonations still intact. To conduct the narrative exclusively within the purview of the hero himself, not only with its dimensions of time and space but also in its system of values and intonations, creates an extremely original kind of apperceptive background for reported utterances. It gives us the right to speak of a special modification: *anticipated and disseminated reported speech* concealed in the authorial context and, as it were, breaking into real, direct utterances by the hero. (Vološinov 1973, 135)

This "anticipated and disseminated reported speech" is equivalent to our FCN. As an example of the method, which is widely used in the prose of Andrej Belyj and his successors, but whose classic cases must – as Vološinov points out – be sought in Dostoevskij's works, a paragraph from the beginning of Dostoevskij's tale "A Nasty Anecdote" (Skvernyj anekdot, 1862) is cited:

> [...] однажды зимой, в ясный и морозный вечер, впрочем, часу уже в двенадцатом, три *чрезвычайно-почтенные* мужа сидели в комфортной и даже роскошно убранной комнате в одном *прекрасном* двухэтажном доме на Петербургской стороне и занимались *солидным* и *превосходным* разговором на *весьма любопытную* тему. Эти три мужа были все трое в генеральских чинах. Сидели они вокруг маленького столика, каждый в *прекрасном* мягком кресле, и между разговором тихо и *комфортно* потягивали шампанское. (Dostoevskij, *PSS*, V, 5; italics are Vološinov's)

> Once in winter, on a cold and frosty evening – very late evening, rather, it being already the twelfth hour – three *extremely distinguished* gentlemen were sitting in a *comfortable*, even sumptuously appointed, room inside a *handsome* two-story house on Petersburg Island and were occupied in *weighty* and *superlative* talk on an *extremely remarkable* topic. All three

---

a three-volume edition under the title *Baxtin under the Mask* (Baxtin pod maskoj) with the Moscow publishing house Labyrinth in 1993. Further on, the book *Marxism and the Philosophy of Language* will be cited under the name of Vološinov.

10 The translators of the book render the Russian expression *čužaja reč'* – which in the English translations of Baxtin's writings is usually translated with "someone else's speech" or "another person's speech" – not quite correctly as "reported speech," a term which in other contexts is used as a translation of "FID."

gentlemen were officials of the rank of general. They were seated around a small table, each in a *handsome* upholstered chair, and during pauses in the conversation they *comfortably* sipped champagne. (Vološinov 1973, 135; italics are Vološinov's)[11]

Baxtin (alias Vološinov) remarks that this passage cannot be accepted as a serious description by an author or a narrator. The "colorless, banal, insipid" epithets, consistently used in their banality and monotony, which are set in italics in his quotation, make the passage appear extremely "wretched and banal" in style. In reality, the qualifying adjectives correspond to the evaluations of the generals portrayed and are given ironic and mocking accents in the context of the narrative.[12]

In the book *Discourse in the Novel* (Slovo v romane), which Baxtin wrote in 1934–1935 (but which, for political reasons, could not be printed in part until 1972 and in full until 1975; tr. Baxtin 1981), FCN is treated as a manifestation of the phenomenon of "heteroglossia" (*raznorečie*; cf. Tjupa 2014), which Baxtin believed was constitutive for the novel. Baxtin finds many instances of heteroglossia in the English comic novel, and he quotes examples of the device from Dickens's novel *Little Dorrit*.

The conference was held at four or five o'clock in the afternoon, when all the region of Harley Street, Cavendish Square, was resonant of carriage-wheels and double knocks. It had reached this point when Mr Merdle came home *from his daily occupation of causing the British name to be more and more respected in all parts of the civilized globe capable of appreciation of wholewide commercial enterprise and gigantic combinations of skill and capital.* For, though nobody knew with the least precision what Mr Merdle's business was, except that it was to coin money, these were the terms in which everybody defined it on all ceremonious occasions, and which it was the last new polite reading of the parable of the camel and the needle's eye to accept without inquiry. (Dickens, *Dorrit*, book 1, ch. 33; italics are Baxtin's 2012, 55–56)

In the italicized text, Baxtin ([1934–35] 2012, 55–56; tr. 1981, 304) sees "someone else's speech" (*čužaja reč'*) introduced into the narrative discourse. This introduction occurs "in a concealed form" (*v skrytoj forme*), that is, without the formal markers that usually signal the speech of another. Baxtin calls the intruding speech of someone else the "hidden, diffused speech of another" (*skrytaja forma rassejannoj čužoj reči*). For him, the examples he quotes in this book illustrate the "double-accented, double-styled hybrid construction" (*dvuakcentnaja i dvustil'-*

---

11 The translation here is that of Vološinov's translators.
12 For the "double-voicedness" of this passage and Baxtin/Vološinov's idea of the agonal structure of "speech interference," see below, chapter 3.

naja gibridnaja konstrukcija) in which "two utterances, two languages" intermingle (cf. below, section 3.3).

When someone else's words introduced into the narrative discourse contain justifications or explanations, Baxtin speaks of "pseudo-objective motivation." He thereby takes up the term *pseudoobjektive Motivierung*, coined by Leo Spitzer (1923b) to denote explanations and justifications that the narrator seems to put forward in his own name but that in fact come from one of the characters' texts.

As an example of "pseudo-objective motivation," Baxtin quotes the following sentence from Dickens's *Little Dorrit*:

> But Mr Tite Barnacle was a buttoned-up man, and consequently a weighty one (*Dorrit*, book 2, ch. 12)

2.4 Natal'ja Koževnikova: "Improperly Authorial Narration"

In Russian Literary Studies, the device of figurally colored narration has been referred to as "improperly authorial narration" (*nesobstvenno-avtorskoe povestvovanie*) since the fundamental works of Natal'ja Koževnikova (1971; 1976; 1994). In her first description, Koževnikova models the device – somewhat tortuously – as an "extension" of elements of skaz or FID "to those constructive elements of the work that are traditionally associated with the author's discourse" (1971, 104). Although it is often not possible to clearly demarcate "improperly authorial narration" from FID, especially since the former often initiates or includes the latter, it is important to distinguish between the two devices (1971, 104–105). FID serves to reproduce the characters' speech or thought, whereas "improperly authorial narration" is a mode of description or narration (1971, 105) by the narrator. Therefore, the term chosen by Koževnikova, *nesobstvenno-avtorskoe povestvovanie* ("improperly authorial narration"), is not entirely appropriate. In FCN the narration is basically narratorial, but tinged by the characters' evaluations and expressions.[13]

---

13 Another important Russian work on the figuralization of narrative, Sokolova (1968), subsumes all the very different phenomena of the "unification of the subject levels of the author and the hero" under her category of "quasi-authorial discourse" (*nesobstvenno-avtorskaja reč'*). The broad definition equates "quasi-authorial discourse" with the more general phenomenon of interference between narrator's text and character's text (see below). This not only eliminates the difference between indirect discourse and FID, but also the difference between FCN and FID. There is a detailed and critical review of Sokolova's concept in Schmid (1973, 55–56, 68–69).

The following conclusions can be drawn for "improperly authorial narration" from Koževnikova's careful observations on the stylistic types of Russian prose of the 1920s:

1. "Improperly authorial narration" is mainly created by the stylistic means of figural lexis. The syntax corresponds to the book-language structure of the "author" (always meaning, of course, the narrator): "Fragments of the text reflect the hero's use of words in the form of individual fragments, masked quotations, but the words of the character, his or her evaluations, are not separated from the author's discourse" (1971, 105).

2. In Russian prose of the 1920s there are two stylistic types of "improperly authorial narration." In works "with a tendency to mimetic reproduction of figural expressions" (*s ustanovkoj na charakternost'*), the skaz type dominates; in works "with a tendency to literary stylization" (*s ustanovkoj na literaturnost'*), a type that is close to FID and has a quotation-like character dominates (1971, 106).

3. Two different narrative principles are realized in "improperly authorial narration": "representation by means of someone else's style and presentation with a socially determined perspective" (1971, 109).

4. "Improperly authorial narration" can also reflect the language use of an entire milieu (1971, 112).

5. The milieu-specific designation of a phenomenon implies the perspective of the corresponding milieu and characterizes the position of the narrator (1971, 112). This also applies to epochs that are represented by specific designations in historical novels (1971, 113).

6. Orientation on the characters' point of view can take place without using the stylistic devices of the characters' discourse. This is a "non-coincidence of the subject and stylistic structure of narration" (*nesovpadenie sub"ektnoj i stilističeskoj struktur povestvovanija*; 1971, 118).

Koževnikova (1971) uses examples from Russian literature of the 1920s to discuss in detail various perspectival and stylistic nuances of the figuralization of narration. Her observations, however, suffer from an overly simplistic concept of "point of view" (*točka zrenija*) that excludes axiological and stylistic facets.[14]

---

14 Although she cites Boris Uspenskij (1970) several times, where "phraseology" appears alongside "evaluation," "spatio-temporal characteristics," and "psychology" as a "tier" (*plan*) of "point of view," Koževnikova reduces this complex phenomenon to that partial parameter that is called *perceptual point of view* in Schmid (2010, 104–105). In noting the "non-coincidence of the subject and style structure of narration," Koževnikova follows Uspenskij's observation

Koževnikova presents a somewhat different concept in her monograph *Types of Narration in Russian Literature of the 19th and 20th Centuries* (1994), in which she gives "improperly authorial narration" its own chapter. One of the two types subsumed under this device is "quoting narration" (*citatnoe povestvovanie*): the words of a character in one of his or her speeches are quoted in the narrative text. The majority of the examples given of this explicitly mark the words from the character's discourse by means of quotation marks or italics, and are therefore examples of the type that I call *quoted figural designation* and assign to the marked representation of consciousness.[15] Where the marking is missing, the examples Koževnikova gives are nicknames or mythological names that the narrative text takes from one of the characters' texts. The very specific name form serves as a marker here.[16] In some of the examples of "quoting narration" that Koževnikova gives, the attribution to the character's text is made explicitly through phrases such as "according to his words," "as she expressed herself," and the like. All such procedures for marking someone else's words mean that FCN is no longer defined as a covert adoption of segments of the character's text. According to Koževnikova, the second type of "improperly authorial narration" is the "orientation" of entire text fragments "on the word-use of a portrayed milieu or figure," whereby these text fragments "are not directly connected with a situation of speech" (Koževnikova 1994, 228). For Koževnikova, this is the basis of "improperly authorial narration" as an independent narrative type.

Koževnikova presents this second, "extended" type in a series of examples illustrating different forms of origin. One of them is the adoption of open or covert quotations from the speech of a character. As an example, Koževnikova uses the description of the joint purchases of the hero Akakij Akakievič and the tailor Petrovič in Nikolaj Gogol's tale "The Overcoat" (Šinel', 1842):

---

that the points of view on the different tiers do not necessarily coincide. On Uspenskij's tiered model of point of view, see Schmid (1971; 2010, 95–99).

15 Koževnikova does not make the distinction I systematically draw between marked and covert representation of consciousness.

16 Boris Uspenskij (1970, 47–57; tr. 1973, 33–41) treats such cases of quoted figural designation under the heading "Influence of someone else's speech on the authorial speech" or "Influence of the character's speech on the authorial text." The idea of "influence" of the character's text on the narrative text, under which Uspenskij also subsumes FID, suggests a corresponding activity of the character, which as a rule is out of the question. The activity here is entirely on the part of the narrator, who repeats, imitates, parodies. Like Koževnikova later, Uspenskij draws most of his examples of the supposed "influence" of the character's text on the narrative text from the works of Lev Tolstoj, who – as Uspenskij (1970, 48; tr. 1973, 34) explains – considers it necessary to emphasize by using italics that a word taken over does not belong to him but was temporarily borrowed, so to speak, from a character.

В первый же день он отправился вместе с Петровичем в лавки. Купили сукна очень хорошего – и не мудрено, потому что об этом думали еще за полгода прежде и редкой месяц не заходили в лавки применяться к ценам; зато сам Петрович сказал, что лучше сукна и не бывает. На подкладку выбрали коленкору, но такого добротного и плотного, который по словам Петровича, был еще лучше шелку и даже на вид казистей и глянцевитей. Куницы не купили, потому что была точно дорога, а вместо ее выбрали кошку лучшую, какая только нашлась в лавке, кошку, которую издали можно было всегда принять за куницу. (Gogol', *PSS*, III, 155)

On the first possible day, he went shopping in company with Petrovič. They bought some very good cloth, and at a reasonable rate too, for they had been considering the matter for six months, and rarely let a month pass without their visiting the shops to inquire prices. Petrovič himself said that no better cloth could be had. For lining, they selected a cotton stuff, but so firm and thick that Petrovič declared it to be better than silk, and even prettier and more glossy. They did not buy the marten fur, because it was, in fact, dear, but in its stead, they picked out the very best of cat-skin which could be found in the shop, and which might, indeed, be taken for marten at a distance. (Gogol', *O*, 8)

In this quotation there are indeed traces of "improperly authorial narration," but the text passage is not very suitable as an example of our FCN, since it explicitly marks the figural parts twice: «сам Петрович сказал» ("Petrovič himself said") and «по словам Петровича» ("Petrovič declared"). In this second type of "improperly authorial narration," Koževnikova does not make a distinction between marked and covert forms. The difference does not play a role for her. For us, however, it is decisive, because according to our system, the adoption of text segments or features of the character's text, marked in one way or another, belongs to the pattern of quoted figural designation. The markedness gives this type of "improperly authorial narration" a special semantic and pragmatic character that sets it apart from FCN, which is always unmarked.

The concept on which this book is based also differs from Koževnikova's in a second essential point. In her examples, Koževnikova focuses mainly on the reproduction of the speech and narrative of the characters, i.e., on forms of external speech. Naturally, she is especially interested in authors who, on the one hand, cultivate a colorful character's text in which dialectisms and folk expressions are richly represented, and, on the other hand, stage skaz narrators who tell about their heroes in folk language. She finds rich examples of both structures in the work of Nikolai Leskov. The present book is not about the narrative repetition or imitation of specific expressions of the characters, but about the adoption of axiological and stylistic features of the genotypical character's text, the mental subject sphere of a figure or a collective.

2.5 Elena Padučeva: "Quotation"

In Elena Padučeva's monographs *Semantic Investigations* (1996, 354–361) and *The Linguistics of Narrative. The Case of Russian* (2011), which are authoritative for recent Russian textual philology, FCN is treated only briefly, with reference to Jakobson 1957 (*kvazicitirovanie*) and Wierzbicka 1970 (*citirovanie*), under the rubric of "quotation" (*citirovanie*). While Padučeva clearly separates FCN from FID (referring to Banfield 1982 and Koževnikova 1994), a more refined typology of the device is missing, and the fundamental distinction from quoted figural designation, i.e., the reduced variant of direct discourse marked by graphic signs such as quotation marks and italics, has not been drawn. For Dostoevskij, in whose narratives quoted figural designation occurs quite frequently, Padučeva only states succinctly that he "often arranges the quotation as direct discourse" (1996, 357). However, the missing explicit marking gives FCN a different semantic structure and pragmatic meaning than quoted figural designation. There is no indication in *Semantic Investigations* or in *The Linguistics of Narrative* that explicit marking fundamentally changes the narrative gesture and narrative semantics of figural designation as compared to the pattern called "quotation." Insofar as Padučeva does not differentiate between marked and covert modes of "quotation," her concept corresponds to that of Natal'ja Koževnikova, where this distinction is irrelevant.

Padučeva, like Koževnikova, clearly distinguishes "quotation" (i.e., FCN) from FID (in her terms: "quasi-direct speech" [QDS], *nesobstvennaja prjamaja reč'*, but also *svobodnyj kosvennyj diskurs*, which is the Russian translation of *free indirect discourse*):

> Quotation [i.e., FCN] and QDS [i.e., FID] are similar [...] in that in both cases the narrator cedes his right in part to the character. There is an important difference between these two phenomena, however. The QDS phenomenon consists of the narrator (SELF) handing over to the character (OTHER) the right to the speech act, i.e., he withdraws completely from the utterance in favor of the character. In quotation there is only a partial invasion by OTHER of the utterance made by SELF. This lack of distinction between QDS and quotation is, in the final analysis, the result of underestimating the role of speech act in the structure of the text. (Padučeva 2011, 240)

However, Padučeva's view that in FID (or QDS) the narrator "withdraws completely from the utterance in favor of the character" is an adoption of Banfield's highly problematic one-voice thesis. Furthermore, Padučeva affirms the dubious thesis of a basic difference in voicedness between FCN (double-voiced) and FID (single-voiced):

Quotation and QDS also differ functionally. In quotation there are two voices "singing together" [*dvuxgolosie*]: to the voice of SELF, which is the rightful owner of speech, is added
– wrongly from the point of view of the ideal grammatical model – the voice of OTHER.
Whereas QDS tends towards the monological interpretation, the voice of OTHER (i.e., a
character) can completely oust the voice of SELF (the narrator). (Paducheva 2011, 240)

It seems questionable whether there should be such considerable differences between quotation (FCN) and QDS (FID). In chapter 3 of this book we will present
arguments against this rigid, static, and overly simplistic opposition.

2.6 German Slavic Studies: "Improper Narration" and "Free Indirect Narration"

The German Slavist Johannes Holthusen (1968) coined the term *uneigentliches
Erzählen* ("improper narration") and documented the device in his studies of Russian literature of the 1960s with examples from the prose of Boris Pasternak, Vera
Panova, Vladimir Tendrjakov, and Aleksandr Solženicyn. Holthusen initially
also considered the term *free indirect narration*, but then decided on the term "improper narration," which indicated the proximity to the standard Russian term
for FID, namely *nesobstvenno-prjamaja reč'* (in verbatim translation: "improperly
direct speech").

The term *free indirect narration* would be misleading, as it suggests that what
is told falls within the current realm of experience of the narrated character. But
this is not the case with FCN, because it is narration by the narrator who adopts
or – better – seems to adopt some of the characters' not necessarily actual but at
least typical evaluations and designations.

However, the term *free indirect narration*, which Holthusen occasionally considered, is suitable for denoting another configuration that occurs quite frequently in narrative texts but is also clearly distinguishable from FCN, namely
the reproduction of the report or the narration of a figure by a figurally perspec-
tivizing narrator.[17]

Puškin's novella "The Station Supervisor" (Stancionnyj smotritel', 1831) contains such a structure: the sentimental traveler who figures as the primary

---

17 On the phenomenon of *free indirect narration* in this sense, cf. Herdin 1905, 85: "assumption
of the narrative role by the reporter" (*Übernahme der Erzählerrolle durch den Berichterstatter*);
Steinberg 1971, 17-27: "reported speech" (*berichtete Rede*, with examples from narratives in German, English, and French); Spitzer 1928, 329–330: "reported free indirect discourse" (*berichtete
erlebte Rede*).

narrator gives the station supervisor's account of the alleged abduction of his daughter by a passing hussar in a figural perspective, so that in the middle part of the abduction story the father's account is hardly distinguishable from the traveler's narrative. In reality both narrate, the father as the logically secondary and temporally primary narrator and the traveler as the logically primary and temporally secondary narrator, whereby the implicit evaluations of the father are empathetically and sympathetically adopted by the traveler, with small, hardly noticeable accents of distancing.

The reproduction of the story of the abandoned father by the sentimental travel writer oscillates between a sober report of the facts and the figural depiction of the inner world of the betrayed father. The figural segments contain FID and free indirect perception. At one point, however, at the culmination of the plot, the free indirect narration violates the perspective limits set for it. The father, who has gained access to his daughter's St. Petersburg apartment through a ruse, becomes a witness to the tender tête-à-tête of his "lost sheep" with the raging "wolf." At this point the sentimental traveler bursts out:

> Бедный смотритель! Никогда дочь его не казалась ему столь прекрасною; он по неволе ею любовался. (Puškin, *PSS*, VIII, 104)

> Poor supervisor! Never had his daughter appeared so beautiful to him; he could not help admiring her. (Puškin, *Prose*, 101; tr. rev.)

The two sentences can hardly reflect the father's report. Could the unhappy father have so openly explained to the traveler his most secret emotions on witnessing the tender reunion of his lost sheep with the wolf? Would he have been able to do so at all if he had been aware of his own emotions? Here the narration clearly goes beyond the horizon of the reporting father and violates the pattern of free indirect narration (cf. Schmid 2023).

In my book *The Text Structure in Dostoevskij's Stories* (1973, 1986, 60, 134-141), I covered a frequent phenomenon in Russian narrative art since Aleksandr Puškin's *Evgenij Onegin*, whereby "individual words or parts of sentences are interspersed in a narratorial report which in their thematic, evaluative, lexical, syntactic and/or language-functional characteristics betray that they do not actually belong to the narrative text, but rather come from the horizon of consciousness and the language repertoire of the portrayed characters."[18]

---

18 On this stylistic-semantic phenomenon produced by the method of incorporating figural features into the narrative text, which has been used in Russian narrative prose since Puškin, cf.

This is the procedure that I now call FCN. I distinguished between two types:

1. The *contagion* of the narrative report by the character's text.
2. The more or less evaluative *reproduction* of parts of typical parts of the character's speech.

Both types differ from quoted figural designation in that the parts of the character's text are not separated from the narrative text by special graphic symbols or equivalents.

My *Elemente der Narratologie* (Schmid 2005; 2008; 2014, 195–197) took up Holthusen's term "uneigentliches Erzählen" and demonstrated the procedure with examples from Dostoevskij, Čexov, and Solženicyn. In the English translation of the book, *Narratology* (2010, 166–168), I chose the term *figurally colored narration*.

2.7 Hugh Kenner, Susan Swartzlander, and Lucy Ferriss: "Uncle Charles Principle"

In the anglophone world, the term "Uncle Charles Principle," introduced by Hugh Kenner (1978, 15–38), has become established for the device of FCN.[19] It is named after a sentence from Joyce's *Portrait of the Artist as a Young Man*:

Uncle Charles repaired to the outhouse.

The seemingly narratorial expression "repaired" is here colored by the idiosyncratic use of words by the hero portrayed. Kenner writes:

If Charles spoke at all about his excursions to what he calls the outhouse, he would speak of "repairing" there.
Not that he does so speak, in our hearing. Rather, a speck of his characterizing vocabulary attends our sense of him. A word he need not even utter is there like a gnat in the air [...]. This is apparently something new in fiction, the normally neutral narrative vocabulary

---

the seminal analyses by Viktor Vinogradov (1939). According to Vinogradov, Gogol' modified the device with elements of skaz and Dostoevskij combined Gogol's social typification with Puškin's individualization of the narrative style in his polyphonic novel. Vinogradov does not, however, have a specific name for the method called FCN in this book.

19 Cf. McHale 2014, 819; Fludernik 1993, 325–326; Ferriss 2008. McHale (1978) does not consider this device in his scale of forms of speech reproduction (see above).

pervaded by a little cloud of idioms which a character might use if he were managing the narrative. (Kenner 1978, 17)

The "Uncle Charles Principle" says: "the narrative idiom need not be the narrator's" (Kenner 1978, 18).

Kenner finds another case of the "Uncle Charles Principle" in the first sentence of Joyce's story "The Dead":

> Lily, the caretaker's daughter, was literally run off her feet.

The use of the word "literally," when "figuratively" is meant, does not point to the narrator but corresponds to the language repertoire of the heroine. The word "literally" is "tinged with her idiom" (Kenner 1978, 16).

It is important that Kenner refers to the "Uncle Charles Principle" not only in terms of diction but also in terms of syntax. And so he gives a number of examples where Joycean syntax mirrors the priorities of a character. In Kenner's view, Joyce linked stylistic decisions to the tastes of the corresponding character. "The Uncle Charles Principle entails writing about someone much as that someone would choose to be written about" (Kenner 1978, 21).

Kenner finds further examples in *Ulysses*, but their assignment to the "Uncle Charles Principle" is questionable. In the description of a funeral, for example, Kenner hears the narrator break through Bloom's direct interior monologue:

> Holy water that was, I expect. Shaking sleep out of it. He must be fed up with that job, shaking that thing over all the corpses they trot up. What harm if he could see what he was shaking it over. Every mortal day a fresh batch: middleaged men, old women, children, women dead in childbirth, mean with beards, baldheaded business men, consumptive girls with little sparrow's breasts. All the year round he prayed the same thing over them all and shook water on top of them: sleep. On Dignam now. (Joyce, *Ul*, 106)

Kenner interprets this passage in a specific way:

> Here something has subtly happened. What commenced as Bloom's list of mortuary variousness has insensibly become the narrator's: "consumptive girls with little sparrows' breasts" seems too shapely in its cadence to have sprung from Bloom's mind. (Kenner 1978, 28)

Kenner postulates a change of perspective in the middle of Bloom's direct interior monologue. One might well ask: why couldn't Bloom himself think or speak of "consumptive girls with little sparrows' breasts"?

Kenner sees two designating instances at work in the narrative text: the narrator, who names the objects according to the linguistic and social norm, and

Bloom, the Jewish outsider, who is not familiar with the Christian ceremony. Joyce thus achieves an effect that we call *defamiliarization* after Viktor Šklovskij (Schmid 2005), a term that Kenner does not use.

> The priest took a stick with a knob at the end of it out of the boy's bucket and shook it over the coffin. (Joyce, *Ul*, 105–106)

The designation of the Catholic holy-water devices without mentioning the *nomen proprium*, which in this case is a "description without knowledge" (Kenner 1978, 30), is reminiscent of Lev Tolstoj's defamiliarization of the war banner as a stick with a shred of cloth attached to it.

Kenner's argument that the voice or idiom of the narrator resounds in the middle of Bloom's monologues does not correspond to the "Uncle Charles Principle," which is based on the fact that the voice and idiom of the character resonate in the narrative text. However, Kenner sticks to the "Uncle Charles Principle," which in *Ulysses*, as he notes, "despite appearances is not abandoned" (1978, 35).

In the "Eumaeus" episode, Kenner finds "Bloom written about as he would choose. The result is a contrived stylistic disaster" (1978, 35):

> Copious in its fecund awfulness, it is Joyce's return to the tonic of his method: the Uncle Charles Principle *in excelsis*, a stylistic homage in Bloom's style to Bloom, and in some ways the book's most profound tribute to its hero, Ulysses, first among Homer's word-men. (Kenner 1978, 38)

Kenner's point that the "Uncle Charles Principle" in Joyce not only affects lexis but can also encompass syntax is picked up by Susan Swartzlander ([1989] 1992) in a study of Ernest Hemingway's early narrative "Up in Michigan." She shows that for Hemingway, as for Joyce, the syntax and rhythm of characters' speech can also infect narrative discourse. "Like Joyce, Hemingway used a narrative voice that adopts not just the idiomatic phrases, but also the speech rhythms, syntax and attitudes representative of the characters in 'Up in Michigan'" (Swartzlander 1992, 34).

Kenner regards the "Uncle Charles Principle" as a uniquely Joycean device. Following in his footsteps, the American writer Lucy Ferriss (2008, 180–183) and her Trinity College students find the device in a number of American short stories, e.g., by Bernard Malamud, Shirley Jackson, Isaac Bashevis Singer, Flannery O'Connor, and Saul Bellow. The short story is particularly fertile ground for the UCP, as Ferriss observes: "So long as Uncle Charles is strongly present in the scene, even if he is not the 'focalizer,' the language of the narration belongs momentarily to him more than to Joyce or Joyce's narrator. [...] In the short story it is a strategy whose detection may be the very key that unlocks the narrative."

Ferriss, admittedly, seems to have a different understanding of UCP than what is meant by our FCN. In the texts she studied, FCN in our sense is rarely found. A figural coloring merely dominates passages in which the consciousness of the corresponding figure is presented, which thus correspond to FID. Our stipulation that FCN does not present current acts of consciousness of the character is not met.

When examining more recent authors, Ferriss comes to the conclusion: "Uncle Charles is hard to find." And her study of texts in the third person written by a dozen prominent writers since 1985 reveals: "The UCP has vanished." The device, whose climax Ferriss locates in Joyce, is, as she postulates, replaced by another device, which she calls APP after John Updike's early story "A&P." APP is characterized in Ferriss's description by a poetic stylization that is due not to the character but to what she calls the author (meaning the narrator). The poetic stylization includes, again in Ferriss's description, devices such as assonance, internal half-rhyme, and metric regularity. To illustrate the difference between the two devices, Ferriss (2008, 186) explains:

> The APP, we might say, differs from the UCP in this inversion:
> Narrative idiom need not be the narrator's. (UCP)
> Focalizing idiom need not be the focalizer's. (APP)

On the basis of these characterizations, we have to conclude that APP is the reversal of the principle of text interference. In the latter, the character's text penetrates the narrative discourse in this or that way. In APP, conversely, the narrative text penetrates the character's discourse. This can lead to the extreme called poetic or ornamental prose, in which a network of authorial-narratorial poetization can be found on the substrate of the narrative text, including the characters' discourse (Schmid 2014d). But in APP it cannot be the case that "the focalizer" has "borrowed whatever language he or she needs from the author's idiomatic field," as Ferriss (2008, 186) has it. Narratorialization is a late procedure in the ideal genesis of the work (Schmid 2010, 209–210), a device that is located above the heads of the characters and and of which the characters know nothing.[20]

---

20 It is interesting for questions of cultural and mental history that Ferriss parallels the replacement of UCP by APP with the replacement of theater by film: "In the latter half of the 20th century, film gradually overtook theater as our chief dramatic vehicle, and the APP overtook the UCP as the chief departure from the 'normal vocabulary' of the story. [...] It is [...] possible that the rise of both film and the APP derive, ironically, from a way of experiencing a world in which

2.8 Franz Stanzel: "Reflectorization of the Teller-Character"

In his *Theory of Narrative*, in which he summarized the typologies he had developed since the 1950s and polished them for the then-current scholarly discourse, Franz Stanzel (1979, tr. 1984) calls the procedure with which we are concerned *reflectorization of the teller-character* or *assimilation of a teller-character to a reflector-character* (1984, 168–169).[21] However, he notes that a comprehensive study of "this interesting phenomenon in the modern novel" has not yet been undertaken (1984, 172).

In order to clarify this "assimilation," Stanzel assumes catalogues of characteristics for narrator and reflector figures. These catalogues of concrete features will, of course, only be of limited importance for identifying the presence of the two instances in textual passages, since the crucial axiological and stylistic features cannot be firmly assigned to either of the two instances. Stanzel demonstrates how he imagines the postulated "assimilation" using a textual example from Katherine Mansfield's story "The Garden Party," which is shortened a little here:

> "But we can't possibly have a garden party with a man dead just outside the front gate."
> That really was extravagant, for the little cottages were in a lane to themselves at the very bottom of a steep rise that led up to the house. A broad road ran between. True, they were far too near. They were the greatest possible eyesore, and they had no right to be in that neighborhood at all. They were little mean dwellings painted a chocolate brown. [...] When the Sheridans were little they were forbidden to set foot there because of the revolting language and of what they might catch. But since they were grown up, Laura and Laurie on their prowls sometimes walked through. It was disgusting and sordid. They came out with a shudder. But still one must go everywhere; one must see everything. So through they went. (Mansfield, *Stories*, 204)

Stanzel argues that it is not a narrator who speaks in the passage, but rather an "anonymous reflector-character" revealing a bias that connects him with the Sheridans:

---

we increasingly find no fixed truths. In a world of fixed truth, authorial diction intrudes, God-like, on 'normally neutral' narrative, whereas characterological idiom provides a helpful inflection of the drama, a way of proposing that 'to repair' to the outhouse is one individual, acceptable modulation of simply going there. In a world of relative truths, by contrast, authorial diction is no more God-like than any other diction and so can be played with – just as film angle is played with; just as notions of identity, history, and the like are all 'fair game'" (Ferriss 2008, 190).

21 In the German original (1979, 220–238), Stanzel speaks of *Personalisierung* of the teller-character. A better English equivalent of *Personalisierung* would have been *figuralization*, as Fludernik (1996, 134) notes.

An authorial teller would have to break the illusion of this bias by virtue of the external perspective available to him. [...] Because the reflectorized teller has no existential basis in this story, he must be considered a transformation of the teller-character. Making an authorial narrator think and speak as if he were one of the characters of the story is called reflectorization. (Stanzel 1984, 172)

The example from "The Garden Party" to which Stanzel refers is a special case of FCN in which the figure whose axiological perspective is adopted is a collective, in this case the Sheridan family. Such a case, collective FCN, is also present in the example quoted above, the description of the "extremely distinguished gentlemen" with which Baxtin/Vološinov documents "anticipated and disseminated reported speech."[22]

Stanzel's description of the procedure in terms of "assimilation of a teller-character to a reflector-character" does not exactly correspond to the imperative of minimal categorical effort, and one could also critically ask whether readers will characterize the procedure in the example from "The Garden Party" with the term "assimilation." After all, the term implies a certain solidarity. In reproducing figural evaluations, the narrator of Mansfield's narrative seems to distance himself from the Sheridan family.

Moreover, it should be borne in mind that the "assimilation" procedure is not present in the entire narrative text in the example. Individual sentences, such as "True, they were far too near" or "It was disgusting and sordid," are closer to classic FID, which in the first case is bound to the Sheridans' collective and in the second case reflects the inner speech or point of view of Laura and Laurie from the time "when the Sheridans were little."[23] Of course, it is often difficult to decide between FCN and FID, especially since the two patterns often alternate in texts and the former often marks the transition from pure narrative text to the latter. But in this sample text, the two different patterns can be identified relatively clearly.

Stanzel presents the personal-philosophical diagnosis according to which the "reflectorization of the teller-character" can be explained on the one hand as "an expression of the suspension of the boundaries of consciousness between the individual characters," but on the other hand also as "the traces of an incomplete individualization of the characters by the author in the process of writing." This

---

22 For collective FCN, Stanzel (1984, 266, footnote 72) refers to an observation by Seymour Chatman (1975, 254), according to which a "communal or sympathetic mode" is expressed at the beginning of Virginia Woolf's novel *Mrs Dalloway*.

23 Fludernik (1996, 136), who perceives these words as ironical FID, as a "transcript" of the feelings of brother and sister, opts for this reading.

conclusion is to be understood in the sense that "a complete separation of the imaginative world of the author/teller from that of the fictional characters had not been achieved" (1984, 179). This explanation is too laborious in its implied assumptions to be convincing. Before postulating the "suspension of the boundaries of consciousness," one could note here the – apparent – adoption of figural (individual and collective) evaluations and designations by the narrator. What the narrator apparently accepts is actually meant to be rejected by the reader. The "assimilation" postulated by Stanzel here actually serves to portray the Sheridan family critically.

In an earlier essay, Stanzel (1975, 295) described an increasing convergence of narrative consciousness with character consciousness as the developmental law of James Joyce's prose. He states that the rapprochement between authorial and personal media in *Ulysses* finally goes so far that there is an "overflow of the consciousness content [*Überfließen des Bewusstseinsinhalts*] of the different characters toward the narrative medium." At this stage, what Stanzel observes could still be described with Spitzer's term "contagion." By further opening or abolishing the boundaries between the characters' and the narrator's consciousness, and by expanding the narrative consciousness to a supra-individual or collective consciousness, this development reaches a point where narration can only be understood in the image of a "literary primordial generation of consciousness content" ("literarische Urzeugung von Bewusstseinsinhalt"; Stanzel 1975, 295). According to Stanzel, the development of storytelling in Joyce's work thus reflects the history of narrative art in a retrograde manner.[24]

---

24 Not more than thirty pages later, in the chapter on the "typological circle," Stanzel ([1979] 1984) takes up the device again, this time under Spitzer's designation *Ansteckung der Erzählersprache durch die Figurensprache* (1979, 247–249; tr. "'contamination' of the narrator's language by the language of the fictional characters"; 1984, 192–193), with textual examples from Thomas Mann's *Buddenbrooks* and Jane Austen's *Mansfield Park*. Pseudo-empathetic contagion, of course, does not only concern languages, but also values and ideologies. For Jane Austen, Stanzel refers to Roy Pascal (1977, 56), from whom he also takes his quotation from *Mansfield Park*. Pascal, however, classifies the procedure as "free indirect speech" and has no separate category for what we call FCN. Pascal (1977, 55), for his part, refers to Graham Hough ([1970], 1978, 49–52), who observes the phenomenon of "colored narrative" for the passage from *Mansfield Park* cited by Pascal and Stanzel and determines the place of this device in Austen's work.

2.9 Monika Fludernik: "Reflectorization" and "Figuralization"

In her more recent book *Towards a "Natural" Narratology* (1996), Monika Fludernik takes up the concept of *reflectorization* from Stanzel's English version of the *Theory of Narrative*. Drawing on Stanzel's prime example from Mansfield's "Garden Party," she defines the procedure as "the narrator's taking on the personality (linguistic and ideological) of a character or [...] a group of characters whose views are presented as if 'through their minds'" (1996, 135). She declares an artificial narrator figure, which she calls a "reflectorized teller character," to be the origin of the irony transposed from the reflectorization in "The Garden Party":

> The reflectorized teller character in this schema is a construct, combining the *knowledge* of the narrator with the focalization and language of a character present on the scene, but is identical to neither the narrator nor a specific identifiable character. (Fludernik 1996, 135)

In the creation of this narrator figure, Fludernik obviously succumbs to Stanzel's problematic formula of "adaptation of a narrator figure to a reflector figure." Would it not be more appropriate to speak of the adoption of the figural perspective (in all its facets) by the one and only narrator, who does not directly express his (and the author's) distance from the characters' evaluations but lets them be deduced instead?

Another textual example, from George Eliot's *Romola*, shows how Fludernik models reflectorization: the viewpoint is that of the character, while the language, "both stylistically and formally," belongs to the narrator. The text passages from "The Garden Party" and *Romola* show the basic structure of reflectorization:

> The two passages from "The Garden Party" and *Romola* thus illustrate the phenomenon of reflectorization in its complex interrelating of an external viewpoint (the narrator's) and a specific character's or group of characters' point of view and language. Neither passage can be read as bona fide free indirect discourse, and that primarily on account of the descriptive and summarizing tenor of the texts. (Fludernik 1996, 137)

There is, Fludernik argues further, no realistic indication in the two texts cited that the reflectorization is a representation of a "specific thought act" of the characters. This is why there needs to be a source that knows the characters' mindsets and is responsible for condensing their viewpoint into a typicalized representation of it. This source must be located on a higher textual level, and this leads to the necessity of an implied author. Although I subscribe to the category of the implied or – as I prefer to call him – the abstract author (cf. Schmid 1973, 23–25; 2010, 36–51; 2014b), I see no need to bring it into play at this particular point. In the cases presented by Fludernik, why can the source of knowledge about the characters' mindsets and values not simply be the fictive narrator? Nothing in the latter's configuration contradicts this possibility.

Using two narratives, D. H. Lawrence's *England, My England* (1922) and Fay Weldon's "Weekend" (1978), Fludernik's case studies demonstrate the complex "interweaving" of the characters' perspectives on the one hand and their interference, as I would call it, with the narrator's view on the other. The decisive criterion for assigning text segments to one instance or the other is the evaluation expressed in each case. In Lawrence's narrative, the decision is made more difficult by the fact that the narrative text is formulated colloquially and the figural and narratorial parts do not differ stylistically, meaning that language is largely irrelevant as an indicator of the speaking and thinking instance in any given case. In Weldon's "Weekend," reflectorized narration serves to express an "indefinable omnipresence of discourses" (Fludernik, 1996, 143) to which the voice of the ironic narrator also belongs.

In the same book, Fludernik splits Stanzel's category of reflectorization into two concepts. In addition to her own concept of reflectorization, which we have discussed here and which she leaves with Stanzel's name, she also uses an alternative mode that she calls "figuralization." The complex differentiation between the two modes is rich in assumptions and is based on an idiosyncratic idea of the instances involved in the narrative. In the sense of Ann Banfield's model of the replacement of the narrator by an "empty deictic center," Fludernik postulates a figural perspective in the case of figuralization that cannot be related to any instance, neither to one of the characters of the narrated story nor to a narrator (who does not exist for her here):

> The major difference between reflectorization and figuralization [...] lies in the narratorial and (implicitly) dissonant tone of the former and the reflectoral and empathetic style of the latter. Both techniques employ free indirect discourse or expressive style to designate a specific viewpoint. In the case of figuralization that viewpoint cannot be aligned with a character on the story level, whereas in the case of reflectorization either there is a particular character available who is indeed the topic of the passage [...] or the viewpoint relates to a complex of attitudes [...] A final, third, crucial difference between figuralization and reflectorization therefore lies in the evocation of fictional personae. Figuralization renders perspectivizations of story matter that – within the reflectoral mode of narration – remain divorced from a specific focalizer; reflectorization, on the other hand, on account of the authorial mode of presentation, thematizes a clash between authorial language and a definite character's (or a group of characters') outlook and perspective. (Fludernik 1996, 151)

Even if we do not share the numerous assumptions behind this approach (not least the Banfield credo), we can understand the difference between the techniques by deriving the following oppositions from the definition above:

1. Reflectorization (in Fludernik's sense) presupposes a character or a group of characters present in the story whose way of thinking and speech is reproduced in the narrative text outside of direct or free indirect discourse. Figuralization cannot be attributed to a figure or a narrator.
2. Reflectorization is double-voiced and serves as an ironic distancing. It uses a typified language to reflect stereotypical opinions and attitudes. Figuralization is monophonic and serves the purposes of empathic immersion.
3. In reflectorization, the narratorial performance clashes with a figural evaluation position. In figuralization, the story is perspectivized in ways that have no relation to a focalizer (this problematic term is probably to be understood here as a term for the figure whose point of view the narrator adopts).[25]

2.10 Mieke Bal and Irene de Jong: "Embedded Focalization"

Figurally colored narration is a special case of what Mieke Bal (1977a) calls *focalisation transposeé*, Bal (1978; 1981; 1985) and Irene de Jong (1987, 2001) *embedded focalization*:

> [...] events are focalized by a character, who is not, however, the narrator of her own perceptions, thoughts, and emotions. These are presented to us by the primary narrator-focalizer. (de Jong 2001, 71)

> [It] is one of the special characteristics of narrative texts that a primary narrator-focalizer can *embed* the focalization of a character in his narrator-text, recounting what that character is seeing, feeling or thinking, without turning him into a secondary narrator-focalizer (who would voice his own focalization in a speech). (de Jong 2014, 50).

De Jong (2014, 50–51) distinguishes an *explicit* and an *implicit* form of embedding. The first is present when the figural part is marked by a verb of seeing, feeling, or

---

25 The term *focalizer*, or its French equivalent *focalisateur*, is a creation of Mieke Bal (1977a, 33; 1977b, 116) that Gérard Genette (1983, 48), the originator of the term *focalisation*, harshly rejected. In his view, only the narrator can "focalize." The English version of her narratology, in which Bal has abandoned the idea of a communication of focalization and the corresponding instances, covers only the *focalizer*, but he solely figures as "the point from which the elements are viewed" and no longer as an active agent (Bal 1985, 104).

thinking. However, such cases are explicitly excluded by our initial definition of FCN (see above, section 1.1).

The implicit embedding of focalization is dependent, according to de Jong (2014, 51), on "evaluative words, interactional particles, moods, or deictics that reveal a character's focalization." However, I would by no means recognize all the cases de Jong lists under "implicit embedding of focalization" as FCN. Many of these cases lack the features *evaluation* and *style*. Our FCN forms only a subset of the cases subsumed by Bal and de Jong under the broader concept of embedded focalization.

Let us conclude this chapter by reviewing the crucial features of FCN:
- FCN is narration by the narrator (whether in the third or first person) that adopts salient features of a character's or of a collective's text.
- These features mainly concern evaluation and designation. Syntax may also be involved.
- The figural part is not explicitly signaled in any way.
- FCN is to be sharply distinguished from FID. Unlike FID, which represents actual acts of consciousness of a character, FCN involves not current acts of consciousness of the character but typical segments of the character's text in which the character's way of thinking is expressed.

3 Figurally Colored Narration as Text Interference

3.1 The Structure of Text Interference

In chapter 1 we introduced the concept of *interference between the narrator's text and the character's text*, or, more concisely, *text interference*. In a first attempt, we defined this as the the overlapping of the character's text and the quoting narrator's text. One might ask why we speak of *texts* and not of *discourses*. In our use of the term, text is distinguished from *discourse* in that it contains the whole *subject sphere* of the entity in question, its perceptual, ideological, and linguistic point of view, in pure, uncontaminated form. This genotypic form in which the narrator's text and the character's text must be conceived is, of course, an abstraction of the phenotypic form in which the discourses that can be directly observed exist in the narrative text. In other words, the term *text* is here taken to mean the complex of all the exterior and interior speech, thoughts, and perceptions of an entity. Interference between the two texts is not limited to words or statements, but rather pertains to the entire complexes of the two entities' acts of perception and ascriptions of meaning, including their own ideologies and evaluative positions. That is why the concept of *text* used here encompasses, alongside linguistically manifested speech, exterior as well as interior, acts whose status remains that of thought, perception, or merely evaluation.

To clarify the terminology, the *narrative discourse* (the text of the narrative work as a product of the narrator) is divided into the *narrator's discourse* and the *characters' discourse*, whereby the characters' *discourse* functions as quotations within the arrangement of the narrator's discourse. Since the beginning of modern narrative in the eighteenth century, the narrator's discourse often does not produce a pure narratorial text but tends instead to intersperse it with features characteristic of the characters' texts. Similarly, a character's discourse may contain narratorial features. The narrator is responsible for both phenomena: the penetration of figural features into his own (the narrator's) discourse and the narratorial revision of the character's discourse. The unmixed, genotypic texts, i.e., the *narrator's text* (NT) and the *character's text* (CT), must be distinguished from the narrator's discourse and the character's discourse, which can also contain figural and narratorial features respectively (cf. Schmid 2010, 118–121).

Text interference is a hybrid phenomenon in which *mimesis* and *diegesis* (in the Platonic sense) are mixed, a structure that unites two functions: the reproduction of the characters' text (*mimesis*) and the actual narration (*diegesis*). Text interference appears in various forms, of which FID has most often been the subject of academic study. In these forms, the interference results from the way that,

https://doi.org/10.1515/9783110763102-004

in one and the same segment of the narrative text, certain features point to NT and others, in contrast, to CT. As a result of the distribution of features from both texts and the expressive function (in the sense of Bühler's 1918/20 *Kundgabe*; 1934/1990 *Ausdruck*) pointing in two directions, NT and CT are simultaneously realized in one and the same segment of the narrative text.

The way CT and NT are represented in text interference can be illustrated with a schematic profile of their features. The first to work with a catalogue of the features in which CT and NT differ was Lubomír Doležel (1958; 1960; 1965; 1967; 1973a; 1993), a disciple of Prague Structuralism. In several publications (Schmid 1973; 2003; 2014a) I have elaborated on the profile of the relevant features and the relationship between them. The main difference is that, unlike Doležel, I do not assume a fixed opposition between an "objective" NT and a "subjective" CT. Instead of constructing an absolute opposition of idealized texts, we will assume that both NT and CT can be endowed to the same extent with the traits of sober object-orientation and subjective listener-orientation and can exercise the expressive function to the same extent. That NT is not necessarily less subjective than CT is sufficiently demonstrated in all European literatures from sentimentalism all the way through to realism. Thus, our schema does not contain features where NT and CT basically form an opposition, but features where, if the two texts are accordingly configured, an opposition *can* exist. If NT and CT do not differ in certain features, we speak of a *neutralization* of their opposition. This neutralization is marked in the tables below by an "x" for both NT and CT.

The features potentially relevant to a schematic profile are (cf. Schmid 2010, 139–148):

1. Thematic features
NT and CT can differ in the *selection* of what is thematized and in characteristic themes.

2. Evaluative or ideological features
NT and CT can differ in the (explicit or implicit) *evaluation* of individual thematic units and in their general *evaluative position*.

3. Grammatical features – person
NT and CT can differ in the use of *grammatical person*, *pronouns*, and *verb forms*. In order to describe the characters in the story, a non-diegetic narrator uses exclusively the pronouns and verb forms of the third person. In CT, the system of three grammatical persons is used: the speaking entity is described in the first person, the character addressed in the second person, and a character under discussion is referred to in the third person. In the case of a diegetic narrator, this

feature loses its differentiating power. Both the narrating self (functioning as a narrator) and the narrated self (functioning as a character) are referred to in the first person.

4. Grammatical features – tense

NT and CT can differ in the use of tense. As a rule, three tiers of tense (present, past, future) are used in CT. In NT, as a rule, the epic preterite or the historical present (functioning as an equivalent) are used to describe the action in the story. (In statements that refer not to the diegesis but to the exegesis, that is, in comments, auto-thematization, apostrophe of the reader, and so on, the narrator can, of course, use all three tenses.)

5. Grammatical features – orientation system

NT and CT can use different orientation systems to describe space and time. The use of chronotopic deictic forms that are oriented around the character's Here-Now-I-system is characteristic of CT, e.g., *today, yesterday, tomorrow, here, there, right, left*. In NT, the deictic terms are replaced with anaphoric orientation terms, such as *on that day, that same morning, the day before, on the day after the events described, in the same place, to the right of the hero*, i.e., expressions that are oriented around statements already made in the text, but that do not presuppose knowledge of the character's chronotopic position.

6. Features of language function

NT and CT can be characterized by different language functions in the sense of Bühler's model (representation, expression, appeal).

7. Stylistic features – lexis

NT and CT can be characterized by the use of different names for one and the same object and by differing lexical repertoires in general, whereby NT is not necessarily literary or stylistically neutral, and CT not necessarily colloquial.

8. Stylistic features – syntax

NT and CT can be characterized by differing syntactic patterns.

In the following we use this schematic profile to differentiate FCN from other patterns (direct discourse, indirect discourse, and FID). We only consider the basic forms that are common in the languages in question, and we exclude potential secondary forms. All the basic types can occur, as a result of differences in axiological and stylistic features, in either a *narratorial* or a *figural* variant. These variants do not form ideal types, but a sliding scale. Narratoriality and figurality are equally gradational, and thus we can distinguish between more or less figural and more or less narratorial variants. The distinction between narratorial and figural variants, however, only makes sense in works that fundamentally differentiate between NT and CT in their axiological and stylistic features. This is usually not the case in texts before the nineteenth century.

Only in the nineteenth century did the characters gradually acquire their own linguistic profile in European literatures, but even in Romantic narrative CT and NT are still not clearly distinguished linguistically from each other or from the author's style. Full linguistic perspectivization did not establish itself in all parameters until the middle of the nineteenth century in the narrative art of realism, which applied the principle of mimetism and perspectivism to the relationship between NT and CT in its quest for an authentic representation of reality and a depiction of human beings as autonomous subjects.

But even in modernity it is possible to have no opposition between NT and CT in the features of lexis and syntax – e.g., if CT is formulated in written language, for which Henry James's novels provide numerous examples, or if, on the other hand, the narrator is a man of the people and narrates colloquially, as is the rule in the Russian skaz of the 1920s. In such cases we can say that the opposition – there is by this time in principle an awareness, or even expectation, of the potential difference between NT and CT – is neutralized.

For establishing the feature matrices, it will be assumed that direct discourse authentically reproduces CT (something which need not always be the case in literary texts). In deciding whether to link features to NT or CT, we will take neutral NT in the example sentences as a starting point. The example sentences, apart from the fourth and final one, are my own.

1. Direct discourse

> She asked herself, "Oh! Why do I have to pitch up to this dumb Christmas party today? After all, Christmas isn't till tomorrow!"

Table 2: Feature Matrix for the Basic Type of Direct Discourse

	1. Theme	2. Evalua- tion	3. Person	4. Tense	5. Orienta- tion sys- tem	6. Lang. function	7. Lexis	8. Syntax
NT								
CT	x	x	x	x	x	x	x	x

2. Indirect discourse

She asked herself why she had to pitch up to this dumb Christmas party today; after all, Christmas wasn't till tomorrow.

Table 3: Feature Matrix for the Basic Type of Indirect Discourse

	1. Theme	2. Evaluation	3. Person	4. Tense	5. Orientation system	6. Lang. function	7. Lexis	8. Syntax
NT			x	x		x		x
CT	x	x			x	x	x	x

3. Free indirect discourse

Oh! Why did she have to pitch up to this dumb Christmas party today? After all, it wasn't Christmas till tomorrow!

Table 4: Feature Matrix for the Basic Type of Free Indirect Discourse

	1. Theme	2. Evaluation	3. Person	4. Tense	5. Orientation system	6. Lang. function	7. Lexis	8. Syntax
NT			x	x				
CT	x	x			x	x	x	x

4. Figurally colored narration

Since FCN is not a representation of speech or thought, the example sentence cannot be converted to this pattern. Instead, we take the first sentence from the example text quoted earlier, Čexov's tale "Rothschild's Violin."

The town was small, more wretched still than a village, and it was filled almost entirely with old folk, who died so seldom that it was a crying shame.

Table 5: Feature Matrix for FCN

	1. Theme	2. Evalua- tion	3. Person	4. Tense	5. Orienta- tion sys- tem	6. Lang. function	7. Lexis	8. Syntax
NT	x		x	x	x	x		x
CT	x	x			x		x	

The narrator selects objects and themes that do occur in the consciousness of the character, but not at the current moment of the story. There is a sense in which the *theme* feature is bound to CT; but the selecting entity remains the narrator. That is why both texts are involved here. The *evaluation* of the selected objects is clearly that of the character. The *grammatical* features of *person* and *tense* are those of NT. The opposition between the texts is neutralized where the *orientation system* is concerned, since there are neither deictics nor anaphoric indications. The immediate beginning with "The town," without expressing where we are, points more to the character as the originator. He knows what town is meant. And the narrator draws us directly into that character's horizon. As to its *representation function* ("Darstellungsfunktion", Bühler), the sentence, on the other hand, points to the narrator. The *lexis* is figural, whereas the *syntax* is narratorial.

3.2   Types of FCN: Contagion and Reproduction

In FCN we can distinguish two modes of the adoption of evaluations and designations from CT. In the first mode, the figural elements of the narrative text reflect evaluations and designations of the character, without these being part of a current act of consciousness on the part of the character. The narrator, so to speak, is *infected* with the figural evaluations and designations. The difference from FID is that in the latter the character's current acts of consciousness are presented, whereas in FCN the content of the narrative statements belongs entirely to the narrator: it is just individual figural evaluations and designations that are adopted. Following Leo Spitzer (1923a), we will call this mode *contagion* or *infection* of NT by CT. An example is the beginning of Čexov's story "The Student" (1894):

Погода вначале была *хорошая*, тихая. Кричали дрозды, и по соседству в болотах *что-то живое* жалобно гудело, точно дуло в пустую бутылку. Протянул один вальдшнеп, и выстрел по нем прозвучал в весеннем воздухе *раскатисто и весело*. Но когда стемнело в лесу, *некстати* подул с востока холодный *пронизывающий* ветер, всё смолкло. По лужам протянулись ледяные иглы, и стало в лесу *неуютно, глухо и нелюдимо*. Запахло зимой. (Čexov, *PSS*, VIII, 306; italics mine – W. Sch.)

At first the weather was *fine* and still. The thrushes were calling, and in the swamps close by *something alive* droned pitifully with a sound like blowing into an empty bottle. A snipe flew by, and the shot aimed at it rang out *with a gay, resounding note* in the spring air. But when it began to get dark in the forest a cold, *penetrating* wind blew *inappropriately* from the east, and everything sank into silence. Needles of ice stretched across the pools, and it felt *cheerless, remote, and lonely* in the forest. There was a whiff of winter. (Chekhov, *ShSt*, 106; italics mine – W. Sch.)

At first it is not clear who is the subject of the perceptions and the originator of the evaluations (italicized in the quotation). Here we can observe a phenomenon typical of FCN in Čexov's stories: before the explicit appearance of a reflector character, the narration is already colored with his or her evaluations and terms. In this way, FCN can prepare the ground for the later appearance of a reflector. The next paragraph introduces the reflector, Ivan Velikopol'skij, a twenty-two-year-old student of the Spiritual Academy, who, on a snipe hunt on Good Friday (!), is disturbed by the evening coolness of spring and consequently comes to negative conclusions about the course of human history. The quoted opening paragraph contains indices for an egocentric person who on the one hand aesthetically perceives the suffering of the creature ("the shot aimed at it rang out with a gay, resounding note in the spring air"), but on the other feels insulted in his bodily sensations by the natural evening coolness of spring ("a cold, penetrating wind blew inappropriately"; for details: Schmid 1997; 2014c). The first paragraph clearly does not contain FID, but it is imbued with the student's evaluations. The whole first paragraph clearly remains in the domain of the narrator, who is, as it were, infected by the hero's evaluative position.

If the figurally colored elements of the narrative discourse reflect not the current situation of the figure at a given moment, as is the case in the example above, but rather the evaluations and terms *typical* of CT, we can speak of a *reproduction* of CT – the second mode, or type, of FCN. This technique is in evidence in the opening of Dostoevskij's tale "A Nasty Anecdote," quoted above (section 2.3). I repeat part of the quotation:

Once in winter, on a cold and frosty evening – very late evening, rather, it being already the twelfth hour – three *extremely distinguished* gentlemen were sitting in a *comfortable*, even sumptuously appointed, room inside a *handsome* two-story house on Petersburg Island and were occupied in *weighty* and *superlative* talk on an *extremely remarkable* topic. (Vološinov 1973, 135; italics are Vološinov's)

The italicized words denote evaluations that stem from the assembled generals' axiology and way of thinking, despite the fact that they could not be considered the current content of the characters' consciousnesses.

Reproduction is often used by narrators to express distance from characters' values. Baxtin/Vološinov also observes this distance in Dostoevskij's tale:

> Those words [italicized in the quotation] might be enclosed in quotation marks as "another's speech," the reported speech of Nikiforov [the host]. But they belong not only to him. After all, the story is being told by a narrator, who would seem to be in solidarity with the "generals," who fawns upon them, adopts their attitude in all things, speaks their language, but nonetheless provocatively overdoes it and thus thoroughly exposes all their real and potential utterances to the author's irony and mockery. (Vološinov 1973, 136)

Both forms, infection as well as reproduction, must be distinguished from quoted figural designation, which is separated from the narrator's discourse by means of graphic indicators. FID, on the other hand, would represent the thoughts of the assembled generals, which is clearly not the case here.

3.3 How Many Voices?

The simultaneously represented texts are associated with the semantic and evaluative positions of their originators. This can lead to a semantic and axiological double structure that has been described by Baxtin (1934/1935) with the term "hybrid construction":

> What we are calling a hybrid construction is an utterance that belongs, by its grammatical (syntactic) and compositional markers, to a single speaker, but that actually contains mixed within it two utterances, two speech manners, two styles, two "languages," two semantic and axiological belief systems. [...] It frequently happens that even one and the same word will belong simultaneously to two languages, two belief systems that intersect in a hybrid construction – and, consequently, the word has two contradictory meanings, two aspects [...]. (Baxtin [1934/1935] 2012, 57; tr. 1981, 304–305)[1]

The phenomenon of the simultaneous presence of two texts in one and the same segment of the narrative text can be called *bitextuality*. But bitextuality does not automatically mean double-voicedness, i.e., conflict between the semantic and axiological positions represented in the two texts. On this point we must disagree with Baxtin.

---

1 For Baxtin's further remarks on linguistic-stylistic hybridity as the basis of the genre of the novel, see Baxtin ([1934/1935] 2012, 113–121; tr. 1981, 358–366.

Since the 1920s there has been a difference of opinion over whether the forms of text interference, most of all FID, serve more to engender empathy or criticism. Arguing against Werner Günther (1928, 83–91), who described FID as a synthetic form, merging the two perspectives of the narrator, the "inner view" immersed in the figure and the distanced "outer view," which thus unites "empathy" and "criticism" in one act, Eugen Lerch (1928, 469–471) states: "FID in itself means only empathy, not also criticism [...]. Through FID, the author can even identify himself, at least for a moment, with characters who are not agreeable to him or whose opinions he does not share at all."

Against Etienne Lorck (1921) and other representatives of "Sprachseelenforschung" ("research on the soul of language"), who saw the achievement of FID primarily in "Einfühlung" ("empathy"), Leo Spitzer (1928) emphasized that FID is "nachahmende Rede" ("imitative speech"), either more "caricaturing," insofar as the reporter does not identify with the speaker, or more "empathetic" speech.

The dispute between the bivocalists (cf. Roy Pascal's [1977] dual-voice position) and the univocalists (Banfield 1982; Paducěva 1996), which is still ongoing today, can be resolved by considering the axiological relationship between NT and CT in any given work. Between single-accented text interference and the double-voiced satirical presentation of the hero's content and expression, a broad spectrum of possible forms with different value relations extends, ranging from empathy to humorous accentuation, critical irony to scathing mockery.

Thus, bitextuality does not necessarily take on a two-voice, double-accented character as postulated by Baxtin/Vološinov, who was fixated with agonal relations. In his interpretation of the passage from Dostoevskij's "A Nasty Anecdote" quoted above (section 2.3), Vološinov argues that the "colorless, banal, insipid epithets," which are italicized in his quotation, originate in the consciousness of the generals and receive ironic and mocking accentuation in the context of the narration.

> Each of these colorless, banal, insipid epithets is an arena in which *two* intonations, *two* points of view, *two* speech acts converge and clash. [...] Thus almost every word in the narrative (as concerns its expressivity, its emotional coloring, its accentual position in the phrase) figures simultaneously in two intersecting contexts, two speech acts: in the speech of the author-narrator (ironic and mocking) and the speech of the hero (who is far removed from irony). [...] We have here a classic instance of a linguistic phenomenon almost never studied – the phenomenon of *speech interference*. (Vološinov 1929; tr. 1973, 135–137)

Vološinov's concept of "speech interference" does not coincide with our concept of text interference. The concept of speech interference assumes a double ideological accentuation of the two discourses. In contrast, text interference is present even when features point to the two texts simultaneously. Text interference does not require a clear-cut difference in the evaluative position of the two texts being realized. Total ideological agreement of the two texts is also possible as a borderline case. So, the concept of text interference used here is wider in scope than Baxtin's/Vološinov's "speech interference" and does not automatically imply those agonal structures that Baxtin and Vološinov place below "double-voiced" structures such as interference and dialogicity.[2]

The decision as to whether a given case of text interference is to be interpreted as simple-voiced or double-voiced is ultimately a matter of interpretation, or more precisely: it depends on how the reader perceives the positions of narrator and hero and how he or she understands the relation of NT and CT in terms of values and ideology.

In Dostoevskij's "A Nasty Anecdote," the difference in values between narrator and protagonists is very pronounced. There is little room for interpretation here.

It will not be possible to determine the value relation between NT and CT so easily at the beginning of "The Student." At first it might seem as if the narrator is empathetic toward his hero. But as soon as the reader experiences the hero's self-centeredness and the prospective clergyman's disinterest in the suffering of other creatures, animal or human, he will add a critical narratorial note to the self-centered figural evaluations.

An even stronger dynamic in the process of reception and evaluation characterizes the story "Rothschild's Violin," which we will therefore consider in more detail. The more Jakov Ivanov's rude behavior toward his wife Marfa and the Jew Rothschild becomes apparent, the more the hero will lose the sympathy of the reader. But when the decisive event of the novella occurs, Jakov's insight and inner transformation on the threshold between life and death, externally expressed by passing the violin, his "orphan," on to the persecuted Jew, the reader will switch to a different value relationship between NT and CT. The climax of Jakov's transformation occurs in the scene by the river, where Jakov laments the losses in his life in an extended free indirect monologue that develops from an indirect representation of his thoughts. This passage will be quoted in detail, as it vividly illustrates the dynamics of the hero's mental change and, in parallel, the dynamics with which the reader's sympathy is guided, and thus also the changing attitude of the narrator toward his hero. We assume here that the reader

---

2 On the difference between speech interference and my text interference, and on Baxtin/Vološinov's concentration on agonal text structures, cf. Schmid 1989.

projects the evolution of his sympathy back onto the narrator by imputing chang-ing attitudes to him.

Он недоумевал, как это вышло так, что за последние сорок или пятьдесят лет своей жизни он ни разу не был на реке, а если, может, и был, то не обратил на нее внима-ния? Ведь река порядочная, не пустячная; на ней можно было бы завести рыбные ловли, а рыбу продавать купцам, чиновникам и буфетчику на станции и потом класть деньги в банк; можно было бы плавать в лодке от усадьбы к усадьбе и играть на скрипке, и народ всякого звания платил бы деньги; можно было бы попробовать опять гонять барки — это лучше, чем гробы делать; наконец, можно было бы разво-дить гусей, бить и зимой отправлять в Москву; небось одного пуху в год набралось бы рублей на десять. Но он прозевал, ничего этого не сделал. Какие убытки! Ах, ка-кие убытки! А если бы всё вместе — и рыбу ловить, и на скрипке играть, и барки го-нять, и гусей бить, то какой получился бы капитал! Но ничего этого не было даже во сне, жизнь прошла без пользы, без всякого удовольствия, пропала зря, ни за по-нюшку табаку; впереди уже ничего не осталось, а посмотришь назад — там ничего, кроме убытков, и таких страшных, что даже озноб берет. И почему человек не может жить так, чтобы не было этих потерь и убытков? Спрашивается, зачем срубили бе-резняк и сосновый бор? Зачем гуляет выгон? Зачем люди делают всегда именно не то, что нужно? Зачем Яков всю свою жизнь бранился, рычал, бросался с кулаками, обижал свою жену и, спрашивается, для какой надобности давеча напугал и оскор-бил жида? Зачем вообще люди мешают жить друг другу? Ведь от этого какие убытки! Какие страшные убытки! *Если бы не было ненависти и злобы, люди имели бы друг от друга громадную пользу.* (Čexov, *PSS*, VIII, 303–304)

He could not fathom how it was that in the last forty or fifty years of his life he had not once been to the river, or if, perhaps, he had been there, then he had not really taken it in. This was a decent river after all, not some measly little stream; he could have set up a fishery here, sold the fish to the merchants, officials, the man at the station buffet, and then taken his money to the bank; he could have rowed from country estate to country estate and played his violin at the houses, and people of all ranks would have paid him money; he could have tried getting the barges afloat again – it would surely have been better than making coffins; and then he could have bred geese, slaughtered them, and sent them in the winter to Moscow, no doubt the down alone would have brought in a good ten roubles a year. Yet he had let all this slip through his fingers, he had not done a thing. What losses! What dreadful losses! If you put it all together – catching fish, playing the violin, sailing barges, slaughtering geese – oh, the capital it would have generated! But nothing of the kind had happened, not even in his dreams. Life had gone by without profit, without any kind of pleasure, it had all been for naught, all in vain. Nothing lay ahead, and if you looked back there were nothing but losses, losses so terrible that they would send a shiver down your spine. Why was it that man could not live free of all this wastage and loss? Why had they chopped down the silver-birch forest and the pine wood? Why was the pasture meadow not put to use? Why did people always have to do the very thing that they ought not to do? Why had Jakov quarreled all his life, growled, flown at people with his fists, upset his wife – and why, oh why, had he just frightened and insulted the Jew? Why can people not live and let live? What losses it caused! What terrible losses! *If there were no hatred or ill will, people could bring each other such phenomenal profit.* (Čexov, *S*, 287–288; tr. rev.)

In this passage, a significant mental event takes place: the transfer of the calculation of profits and losses from the economic sphere, which Jakov has always been thinking of, to the coexistence of human beings. But this inner progress is relativized by the fact that Jakov comes to the absurd conclusion: "Life brings man losses, whereas death brings him profit!" (Čexov, *S*, 288; «От жизни человеку — убыток, а от смерти — польза», Čexov, *PSS*, VIII, 304). To return to the opening sentence of the story: in regressive, accumulative reception, the reader will perceive the figural logic of the economic loss in a narratorially accentuated way, and in this backward movement he or she will hear two voices directed against each other, even if he or she may have initially assumed empathy on the part of the narrator. He or she will not impute satirical mockery to the voice of the narrator, but a slight irony does become apparent in the latter's reproduction of the figure's evaluations.

Thus, we can put an end to the old controversy about how many voices are implied by devices of text interference by turning to the relationship between NT and CT. Everything depends, of course, on how the reader perceives this relationship. We must be prepared for a double dynamic here. On the one hand, the relationship between the two instances in a given work can change, for example when the hero changes his views and values. On the other hand, an interpretation of the relationship between NT and CT can change in the reading history of one and the same reader, depending, for example, on the development of his experience or world view.

3.4 FCN within FID

We have a rather complex case of FCN when a character is infected in his inner speech by the words or evaluations of another character or ironizes elements of another person's discourse. We find an example of this in Jane Austen's *Emma*. The eponymous heroine ponders how she could talk Harriet, whom she has convinced of Mr. Elton's love for her, out of her love for him now that the vicar has turned out to be engaged to someone else.

The passage to be considered occurs in the context of inner speech on Emma's part, presented in FID.

> Could she but have given Harriet her feelings about it all! She had talked her into love; but alas! she was not so easily to be talked out of it. The charm of an object to occupy the many vacancies of Harriet's mind was not to be talked away. (Austen, *Emma*, 147)

The structure becomes more complex when Emma's inner speech contains FCN pointing to the discourse of Harriet Smith. We then have two levels of text interference: on the first level, the text of character A (in this case Harriet) is superimposed with the text of the deliberating character B (Emma), and on the second level, Emma's text is superimposed with the narrator's text.

> Harriet was one of those, who, having once begun, would be always in love. And now, poor girl! she was considerably worse from this re-appearance of Mr Elton. She was always having a glimpse of him somewhere or other. Emma saw him only once; but two or three times a day Harriet was sure *just* to meet with him, or *just* to miss him, *just* to hear his voice, or see his shoulder, *just* to have something occur to preserve him in her fancy, in all the favouring warmth of surprise and conjecture. She was, moreover, perpetually hearing about him; for, excepting when at Hartfield, she was always among those who saw no fault in Mr Elton, and found nothing so interesting as the discussions of his concerns [...]. (Austen, *Emma*, 147; italics in the original)

By visualizing poor Harriet's speech, Emma inwardly distances herself from the young girl's motives, explaining the latter's infatuation as a kind of stubbornness and Harriet's impression of Elton's omnipresence as a tic. This attitude, expressed in Emma's FID, is in turn challenged by the narrator's disapproval – a clear case of text interference.

3.5 Misunderstood Text Interference (Jenninger's Allegedly Scandalous Speech)

It is in the nature of text interference that it can easily be misunderstood, especially if the recipient is not trained in ironic discourse. An extreme and highly political example of catastrophic misunderstanding of text interference is the perception of the speech that the President of the West German Bundestag, Philipp Jenninger, gave on November 10, 1988, on the occasion of the fiftieth anniversary of the so-called Reichskristallnacht, i.e., the November pogroms of 1938. Jenninger's speech was considered a scandal by the majority of the audience, especially by German journalists, and led to the speaker having to resign from his high office. From a narratological perspective, the outrage of the journalists presents itself as a fundamental misreception. But the speaker was not entirely blameless for the fact that his actual point was turned upside-down. In his attempt to fathom and explain the causes of pre-war anti-Semitism, Jenninger reconstructed the widespread prejudices against Jews in Nazi Germany and presented them by employing text interference. After he had made his concerns sufficiently clear at the beginning of his speech, he used the means of FCN and FID to present popular opinion of the 1930s. In the following excerpts, the parts corresponding to FCN are single underlined, the parts in FID are double underlined, and quoted figural designation,[3] which the speaker used extensively but did not sufficiently mark by means of intonation, is dotted underlined:

Für die Deutschen, die die Weimarer Republik überwiegend als eine Abfolge außenpoliti- scher Demütigungen empfunden hatten, musste [der politische Triumphzug Hitlers] wie ein Wunder erscheinen. Und nicht genug damit: aus Massenarbeitslosigkeit war Vollbe- schäftigung, aus Massenelend so etwas wie Wohlstand für breiteste Schichten geworden. Statt Verzweiflung und Hoffnungslosigkeit herrschten Optimismus und Selbstvertrauen. Machte nicht Hitler wahr, was Wilhelm II. nur versprochen hatte, nämlich die Deutschen herrlichen Zeiten entgegenzuführen? War er nicht wirklich von der Vorsehung auserwählt, ein Führer, wie er einem Volk nur einmal in tausend Jahren geschenkt wird?
[…]
Das heißt, Hitlers Erfolge diskreditierten nachträglich vor allem das parlamentarisch ver- fasste, freiheitliche System, die Demokratie von Weimar selbst. Da stellte sich für sehr viele Deutsche nicht einmal mehr die Frage, welches System vorzuziehen sei. Man genoss viel- leicht in einzelnen Lebensbereichen weniger individuelle Freiheiten; aber es ging einem persönlich doch besser als zuvor, und das Reich war doch unbezweifelbar wieder groß, ja, größer und mächtiger als je zuvor. – Hatten nicht eben erst die Führer Großbritanniens, Frankreichs und Italiens Hitler in München ihre Aufwartung gemacht und ihm zu einem weiteren dieser nicht für möglich gehaltenen Erfolge verholfen? Und was die Juden anging: Hatten sie sich nicht in der Vergangenheit doch eine Rolle angemaßt – so hieß es damals – , die ihnen nicht zukam? Mussten sie nicht endlich einmal Einschränkungen in Kauf neh- men? Hatten sie es nicht vielleicht sogar verdient, in ihre Schranken gewiesen zu werden? Und vor allem: Entsprach die Propaganda – abgesehen von wilden, nicht ernstzunehmen- den Übertreibungen – nicht doch in wesentlichen Punkten eigenen Mutmaßungen und Überzeugungen?
[…]
Waren die Juden in früheren Zeiten für Seuchen und Katastrophen, später für wirtschaftli- che Not und „undeutsche" Umtriebe verantwortlich gemacht worden, so sah Hitler in ihnen die Schuldigen für schlechthin alle Übel: sie standen hinter den „Novemberverbrechern" des Jahres 1918, den „Blutsaugern" und „Kapitalisten", den „Bolschewisten" und „Frei- maurern", den „Liberalen" und „Demokraten", den „Kulturschändern" und „Sittenverder- bern", kurz sie waren die eigentlichen Drahtzieher und Verursacher allen militärischen, politischen, wirtschaftlichen und sozialen Unglücks, das Deutschland heimgesucht hatte. Die Geschichte reduzierte sich auf einen Kampf der Rassen; zwischen Ariern und Juden, zwischen germanischen „Kulturspendern" und jüdischen „Untermenschen". Die Rettung für das deutsche Volk und die endgültige Niederwerfung des Menschheitsverderbers konn- ten nur in der Erlösung der Welt vom jüdischen Blut als dem bösen Prinzip der Geschichte liegen.
(https://www.lmz-bw.de/fileadmin/user_upload/Downloads/Handouts/ 2018-06-13-jenninger-rede.pdf)

---

3 I have identified quoted figural designation, which requires quotation marks or comparable graphic markings to be recognized, on the basis of the printed text of the speech.

For the Germans, who had perceived the Weimar Republic predominantly as a succession of foreign policy humiliations, [Hitler's triumphal political rise] <u>must have seemed like a miracle. And that was not all: mass unemployment had turned into full employment, mass misery into something like prosperity for the broadest strata of the population. Instead of despair and hopelessness, optimism and self-confidence prevailed. Didn't Hitler achieve what Wilhelm II had only promised, namely bringing the Germans to glorious times? Was he not indeed chosen by Providence, a leader as is given to a people only once in a thousand years?</u> [...]

<u>In other words, Hitler's successes retrospectively discredited above all the parliamentary, liberal system, the democracy of Weimar itself. For many Germans, the question of which system was preferable no longer even arose. In some areas of life, people may have enjoyed less individual freedom, but personally they were better off than before, and the Reich was undeniably great again, indeed, greater and more powerful than ever before.</u> – <u>Hadn't the leaders of Great Britain, France, and Italy just paid their respects to Hitler in Munich and helped him to another of these successes that were not supposed to be possible?</u> And as for the Jews: <u>had they not in the past presumed a role for themselves</u> – so it was said at the time – <u>that was not theirs to play? Didn't they finally have to accept restrictions? Did they not perhaps even deserve to be put in their place? And above all: did the propaganda – apart from wild exaggerations that were not to be taken seriously – not correspond in essential points to their own assumptions and convictions?</u>

[...]

Whereas in earlier times the Jews were held responsible for epidemics and catastrophes, and later for economic hardship and "un-German" activities, Hitler saw them as the culprits behind all evils: they were behind the "November criminals" of 1918, the "bloodsuckers" and "capitalists," the "Bolsheviks" and "Freemasons," the "liberals" and "democrats," the "desecrators of culture" and "spoilers of morals," in short, <u>they were the real masterminds and perpetrators of all the military, political, economic, and social misfortunes that had befallen Germany.</u>

History was reduced to a racial struggle; between Aryans and Jews, between Germanic "cultural donors" and Jewish "subhumans." <u>The salvation of the German people and the final defeat of the corrupter of humanity could only lie in the redemption of the world from Jewish blood as the evil principle of history.</u>

Of course, it is not Jenninger's authentic voice that sounds in the marked sections, but a voice that is shifted in perspective to the object of the speech. The speaker places himself in the axiological position of the anti-Semitically minded Germans and reconstructs their questions and arguments. However, he neglects to place signs of distancing in his reproduction of the collective discourse. Without such signals, text interference is axiologically highly ambiguous and can also be understood as an expression of empathic agreement.[4] The *Süddeutsche Zei-*

---

4 This was also the case with Flaubert's *Madame Bovary*. The presentation of the adulteress's sinful thoughts in the form of text interference directed the moral indignation of contemporaries

tung, for example, gained the calamitous impression that "the President of the Bundestag had made the language of the Nazi criminals his own" (*SZ*, November 11, 1988, 1).

The form of an oral speech offered the possibility of using intonation to differentiate between one's own voice and that of others in such a way that listeners could pick up on the differing evaluations. Jenninger, however, did not do this. He reckoned with an audience familiar with his techniques for rendering speech and thought. This assumption was mistaken.

Thus, the causes of the misunderstanding can be found on both sides. The speaker did not sufficiently mark opinions opposite to his own as such, and his audience did not register the perspective shift due to inattention or unfamiliarity with the phenomenon. It is just a surprise that so many journalists, who one would assume to be familiar with various forms of rendering speech and opinion, fell prey to misjudgment and joined in the indignation about this alleged Nazi sympathizer.[5]

against the author, who was supposedly speaking in his own name: the use of text interference triggered a court case for violation of morality (see LaCapra 1982).

5 On Jenninger's speech and its misunderstanding, see the convincing analyses by the Japanese Germanist Yasushi Suzuki 1991 (with a preliminary remark by Franz Stanzel 1991) and Holger Siever (2001); cf. http://buecher.hagalil.com/lang/jenninger.htm [February 10, 2021].

4 Functions and Areas of Application

FCN has a different role in the construction of a work from FID. While the latter represents the current content of a person's consciousness, we find FCN in passages where the normal functions of a narrator are fulfilled. These include describing a situation, depicting a landscape, characterizing a figure, or telling a life story. Very often, FCN is used to give an overview of a longer period of time or to present flashbacks.

In the following, various functions and areas of application of FCN are considered. The comprehensiveness and step-by-step nature of the analysis is justified in light of the fact that the device has been so widely neglected in narratology.

4.1 Introducing a Story

4.1.1 Anton Čexov, "The Bride"

In the passages quoted above (sections 1.2 and 3.2) from Čexov's stories "Rothschild's Violin" and "The Student," we have seen how a character, his circumstances, and his character traits are introduced by a figurally colored description that cannot be read as being presented in FID but must be attributed to the narrator and is thus to be understood as being presented in FCN. (The term *narration* in "FCN" is used in a broad sense that includes description.)

A similar but more complex role is played by FCN in Čexov's last story, "The Bride" (also "The Betrothed"; Russian: Nevesta, 1903). The passage at issue is not in the first paragraph of the narrative but in its second:

> В саду было тихо, прохладно, и темные покойные тени лежали па земле. Слышно было, как где-то далеко, очень далеко, должно быть, за городом, кричали лягушки. Чувствовался май, милый май! Дышалось глубоко и хотелось думать, что не здесь, а где-то под небом, над деревьями, далеко за городом, в полях и лесах, развернулась теперь своя весенняя жизнь, таинственная, прекрасная, богатая п святая, недоступная пониманию слабого, грешного человека. И хотелось почему-то плакать. (Čexov, *PSS*, X, 202)

> In the orchard it was quiet and cool, and dark tranquil shadows lay across the ground. From some distant, faraway place, most likely outside of town, came the sound of frogs croaking. The orchard was filled with a feeling of May, dear May! The air came in deep breaths and it was tempting to think that not here, but somewhere else, between the treetops and the sky, in the fields and forests far beyond the town, spring had begun its mysterious, beautiful,

https://doi.org/10.1515/9783110763102-005

rich, sacred life, inaccessible to the understanding of weak and sinful human beings. For some reason, it brought on a feeling close to tears. (Tr. by Carol Apollonio in Čexov, *S*, 481)

It is not stated in this passage who is the subject of perception and emotion, who has these impressions, makes the exclamation "dear May!" and has the idea of the "mysterious, beautiful, rich, sacred life of spring, inaccessible to the understanding of weak and sinful human beings." In the first paragraph almost all the persons of the story are mentioned, but they are mentioned as objects of the perception of the heroine Nadja, who is looking from the orchard through the window into the parlor:

> Было уже часов десять вечера, и над садом светила полная луна. В доме Шуминых только что кончилась всенощная, которую заказывала бабушка Марфа Михайловна, и теперь Наде — она вышла в сад на минутку — видно было, как в зале накрывали на стол для закуски, как в своем пышном шелковом платье суетилась бабушка; отец Андрей, соборный протоиерей, говорил о чем-то с матерью Нади, Ниной Ивановной, и теперь мать при вечернем освещении сквозь окно почему-то казалась очень молодой; возле стоял сын отца Андрея, Андрей Андреич, н внимательно слушал. (Čexov, *PSS*, X, 202)

> It was already ten in the evening, and a full moon shone over the orchard. In the Šumin household the vespers service ordered by Nadja's grandmother Marfa Mixajlovna – or Granny as she was known at home – had just ended. Nadja had stepped outside, and now, looking in through the window, she could see all the activity in the parlor. The table was being set for refreshments; Granny was bustling around in her puffy silk dress; and Father Andrej, the archpriest from the cathedral, was talking with Nadja's mother, Nina Ivanovna, who for some reason looked very young now in the evening light. Father Andrej's son Andrej Andreič stood next to them, listening attentively. (Tr. by Carol Apollonio in Čexov, *S*, 481; tr. rev.)

In the first paragraph's description of the family, which in the Russian original is structured as an indirect representation of perception by the title heroine, "Nadja ... could see how ..." («Наде ... видно было, как ...»), the figures are outlined in essential features of their future roles, which gives the description a certain narratorial touch despite its figural coloring: the dominant grandmother, who is not by chance mentioned first, in her piety and activity; the mother immersed in conversation with the clergyman, perhaps on theological or philosophical topics; and finally the groom Andrej Andreič, who listens attentively to the words of his father, Father Andrej. (It is no accident that the father's first name, Andrej, is doubled in the obedient son.) In the traits observed, there is a reversal in the roles of the three women: the most active figure is the grandmother, who is busy looking after both the spiritual and the physical well-being of the family. And it is not the youngest of the three women, the bride, who is wearing a "puffy silk dress,"[1] but the grandmother. The mother, engrossed in conversation with Father Andrej, probably needing orientation in life, is perceived through the window by the daughter as "very young" in the evening light. The youngest woman, however, is assigned the role of age, of observation.

Nadja's role as an observer in the first paragraph allows the impressions offered in the second paragraph to be seen as originating in her as the bride of the title, all the more so as the bride is the focus of the third paragraph, which begins with the words:

Ей, Наде, было уже 23 года; с 16 лет она страстно мечтала о замужестве, и теперь наконец она была невестой Андрея Андреича, того самого, который стоял за окном [...]. (Čexov, *PSS*, X, 202)

> She, Nadja, was already twenty-three; since the age of sixteen she had dreamed passionately of marriage, and now at last she was engaged; she was to marry Andrej Andreič, that man standing just inside the window [...]. (Tr. by Carol Apollonio in Čexov, *S*, 481)

In this sentence, which is clearly FCN, it is striking that Andrej Andreic is not referred to more specifically than with a simple qualification of his position in the room: "that man standing just inside the window" («того самого, который стоял за окном»).

Despite the contextual indications of the dominant perspective, it is important to note that the second paragraph, quoted above, does not name a subject that could clearly function as the originator of the impressions and emotions conveyed. In her commentary, the editor of the new Norton critical edition of Čexov's *Selected Stories*, Cathy Popkin, notes on Carol Apollonio's translation:

> The [second] paragraph conveys the sounds, sights, and feelings of May through Nadya's perspective but never names her as the perceiving subject; it concludes with the impersonal construction "And for some reason felt like crying" (А почему-то хотелось плакать), perfectly natural in Russian but impossible to render in English without indicating a subject. Here and throughout, Apollonio avoids bringing a person into such passages wherever possible. Hence her formulation in the final sentence – "it brought on a feeling close to tears"; Nadya does not make an unauthorized appearance in the paragraph, and we feel that the May night itself might break down and cry [...]. (Čexov, *S*, 481)

---

1 The adjective *pyšnyj* ("puffy") is omitted in the Apollonio translation, but it is important because it gives the grandmother's dress a touch of the inappropriate. Whom does she want to please? Perhaps her God, whom she is devoted to serving?

These remarks seem very apposite. The second paragraph is clearly FCN. It is neither FID nor free indirect perception. It does not convey an interior monologue but belongs to the narrator. Spoken from the spatial perspective of the heroine, the paragraph is colored with her mood and formulated in her lexis and syntax; but it is the narrator's discourse.

The new Norton edition by Cathy Popkin gives some examples of the second paragraph in other translations:

Ronald Hingley ("A Marriageable Girl")[2]

May, lovely May, was in the air. Nadya could breathe freely, and liked to fancy that there was another place – beneath the sky, above the trees, far beyond town, in fields and woods – where springtime had generated a secret life of its own: a life wonderful, right and hallowed . . . a life beyond the understanding of weak, sinful man. She felt rather like crying. (Čexov, *S*, xlvii)

Hingley dissolves the impersonal constructions of the original and relates the actions and emotions to Nadja as subject. This disambiguation destroys the specific effect of FCN, transforming a highly complex reproduction of the interference between two voices into a simple consciousness report.

Robert Payne ("The Bride")[3]

There was a feeling of May, sweet May, in the air. You found yourself breathing deeply, and you imagined that somewhere else, somewhere beneath the sky and above the treetops, somewhere in the open fields and the forests far from the town – somewhere there the spring was burgeoning with its own mysterious and beautiful life, full of riches and holiness, beyond the comprehension of weak, sinful man. And for some reason you found yourself wanting to cry. (Čexov, *S*, xlvi)

Payne's solution to the problem, namely replacing the impersonal expressions with a generalized "you," is also not satisfying, because it gives the wrong impression of a conversation situation. The generalized "you" does not adequately reflect the impersonal structure of the original.

---

2 Ronald Hingley, *The Oxford Chekhov*. Vols. 5–9. London: Oxford UP, 1965–1978.
3 Robert Payne, *The Image of Chekhov. Forty Stories by Anton Chekhov in the Order in Which They Were Written*. New York: Alfred A. Knopf, 1963. Reprinted as Forty Stories, New York: Vintage, 1991.

Constance Garnett ("The Betrothed")[4]

> There was a feeling of May, sweet May! One drew deep breaths and longed to fancy that not here but far away under the sky, above the trees, far away in the open country, in the fields and the woods, the life of spring was unfolding now, mysterious, lovely, rich and holy beyond the understanding of weak, sinful man. And for some reason one wanted to cry [...] (Čexov, *S*, xlvi)

The time-honored translation by Constance Garnett replaces the impersonal sentences with a "one"-construction, which is less personal than Payne's version but still misses the original. In the competition between the translations, Carol Apollonio's version is the clear winner.

The impersonal FCN in the second paragraph generalizes the state of joyful expectation that is characteristic of a bride. But the expectation is not that suggested by some naive or submissive Soviet interpreters, who hear a longing for the Revolution here. As with all the illusionary euphoric upswings of the heroes in Čexov's works, the narrator presents the joyful expectation of spring, of the "mysterious, beautiful, rich, sacred" spring, with a good dose of irony. The narrator's distance is only too justified if one considers the end of the story, the last sentence, which the author changed decisively in the galley proof at the last moment (cf. Wächter 1992, 260–263).

In the fair copy, the story of the bride who has given her bridegroom the slip closes with her leaving the small town and setting off for a new, active life in St. Petersburg:

> Она пошла к себе наверх укладываться, а на другой день утром уехала. (Čexov, *PSS*, VIII, 320)

> *She went upstairs to pack, and the next morning she left.

In the galley proof, the author made an addition that questions the finality of the departure and keeps the possibility open that the bride will not be able to escape the spell of repetition that dominates the world she is leaving. The insertion by no means says that she will return; it leaves the answer to the question of the future open. Let us look at the last sentence with the insertion in the final Russian original and in the translations:

---

4 Constance Garnett, *201 Stories by Anton Chekhov*.
www.ibiblio.org/eldritch/ac/jr/201.htm [accessed September 21, 2020].

Она пошла к себе наверх укладываться, а на другой день утром простилась со своими, и живая, веселая, покинула город — как полагала, навсегда. (Čexov, *PSS*, VIII, 220)

She went upstairs to pack, and the next morning she said her farewells and alive, happy, left the town behind – as she thought, forever. (Tr. Carol Apollonio in Čexov, *S*, xlvii)

She went upstairs to her own room to pack, and the next morning said good-bye to her family, and left the town. She was full of life and high spirits, and she expected never to return. (Tr. Robert Payne in Čexov, *S*, xlvi)

She went upstairs to her own room, to pack, and the next morning said good-bye to her family, and full of life and high spirits left the town – as she supposed for ever. (Tr. Constance Garnett in Čexov, *S*, xlvi)

She went to her room to pack. Next morning she said good-bye to the family. Vigorous, high-spirited, she left town: for ever, presumably. (Tr. Ronald Hingley in Čexov, *S*, xlvii)[5]

It is typical of Čexov, who as a writer never departs from the doctor's scientific stance, that he always depicts only temporary moments in the characters' psychological processes, refraining from speculative prognoses. The represented mental states are only valid for the present moment and do not allow any extrapolations about the future. When interpreting the addition inserted by the author, it should be remembered that it refers to a moment in which the young woman is "full of life and high spirits." The sobering relativization of the finality of the departure makes an ironic narratorial intonation very likely in the euphoria expressed in the second paragraph.

4.1.2 Saul Bellow, "Looking for Mr Green"

In the critical literature on Saul Bellow's short story "Looking for Mr Green" (1968), one reads that it "is mostly written from Grebe's [i.e., the protagonist's] point of view in free indirect discourse."[6] This impression seems to be confirmed by the beginning of the text, which we will look at a little more closely:

Hard work? No, it wasn't really so hard. He wasn't used to walking and stair-climbing, but the physical difficulty of his new job was not what George Grebe felt most. He was delivering

---

5 Hingley's translation shifts the roles. While in the original the narrator assigns the conjecture to the character, in Hingley's translation the narrator himself is the one making the conjecture.
6 David Dowling (www.encyclopedia.com/arts/encyclopedias-almanacs-transcripts-and-maps/looking-mr-green-saul-bellow-1968 [accessed July 26, 2021]).

Relief checks in the Negro district, and although he was a native Chicagoan this was not a part of the city he knew much about – it needed a depression to introduce him to it. No, it wasn't literally hard work, not as reckoned in foot-pounds, but yet he was beginning to feel the strain of it, to grow aware of its peculiar difficulty. He could find the streets and numbers, but the clients were not where they were supposed to be, and he felt like a hunter inexperienced in the camouflage of his game. It was an unfavorable day, too – fall, and cold, dark weather, windy. But, anyway, instead of shells in his deep trench coat pocket he had the cardboard of checks, punctured for the spindles of the file, the holes reminding him of the holes in player-piano paper. And he didn't look much like a hunter, either; his was a city figure entirely, belted up in this Irish conspirator's coat. He was slender without being tall, stiff in the back, his legs looking shabby in a pair of old tweed pants, gone through and fringy at the cuffs. With this stiffness, he kept his head forward, so that his face was red from the sharpness of the weather; and it was an indoors sort of face with gray eyes that persisted in some kind of thought and yet seemed to avoid definiteness of conclusion. He wore sideburns that surprised you somewhat by the tough curl of the blond hair and the effect of assertion in their length. He was not so mild as he looked, nor so youthful; and nevertheless there was no effort on his part to seem what he was not. He was an educated man; he was a bachelor; he was in some ways simple; without lushing, he liked a drink; his luck had not been good. Nothing was deliberately hidden. (Bellow, *Mr Green*, 260)

At first it really seems as if we have entered the hero's inner monologue or – better – inner dialogue with himself, but soon it becomes clear that we are in the objective narration of a non-diegetic (i.e., third-person) narrator. Once we have entered the description of the hero from the point of view of an outside observer, there is no way in this first paragraph to work our way from the description of Grebe by the narrator to his consciousness. We conclude from this that the figural fragments of the beginning belong to the omniscient narrator's discourse, which reproduces the hero's inner speech.

4.2 Concluding a Story: Anton Čexov, "The Student"

We have already observed FCN at the beginning of Čexov's story "The Student" (see above, section 3.2). We concluded that the narrator is infected by the thoughts and feelings of the hero, the twenty-two-year-old student of the Spiritual Academy Ivan Velikopol'skij. The budding clergyman, who is snipe-hunting on Good Friday, shows a somewhat narcissistic character in the first paragraph: he disregards the plaintive cries of a bird ("something alive droned pitifully with a sound like blowing into an empty bottle") and perceives the shot only aesthetically ("the shot aimed at it rang out with a gay, resounding note in the spring air"). Faced with the chilly evening, he appears a little self-pitying and personally offended, as if it was not supposed to get chilly in Russia on Good Friday night.

In the actual story, freezing and hungry, he encounters two women, mother and daughter, to whom he tells the Twelve Gospels read on Holy Thursday. The version he tells is less related to Christ's suffering than to Peter's suffering and his own suffering from cold and hunger (Schmid 2014c). Observing the reactions of his listeners, he misinterprets the mother's tears and the daughter's numbness as their interest in what happened to Peter two thousand years ago. Against the background of the student taking the signs of remorse and silent suffering of the women as the point of departure for his abstract and exhilarating conclusions, the last, very long sentence of the story's text is revealing. It consists of two parts. The first contains an indirect representation of thought:

> А когда оп переправлялся на пароме через реку и потом, поднимаясь на гору, глядел на свою родную деревню и на запад, где узкою полосой светилась холодная багровая заря, то думал о том, *что правда и красота, направлявшие человеческую жизнь там, в саду и во дворе первосвященника, продолжались непрерывно до сего дня и, по-видимому, всегда составляли главное в человеческой жизни и вообще па земле* [...]. (Čexov, *PSS*, VIII, 309; italics mine – W. Sch.)

> And when ferrying across the river and later climbing the hill he gazed at his native village and to the west of it, where a narrow strip of cold, crimson twilight still shone, he kept thinking *of how the truth and beauty guiding human life back there in the garden and the high priest's courtyard carried on unceasingly to this day and had in all likelihood and at all times been the essence of human life and everything on earth* [...]. (Tr. Michael Henry Heim in Čexov, *S*, 293; italics mine – W. Sch.)

Here again some skepticism about the content of the student's thoughts is appropriate. To what extent does the story of Peter and his betrayal of Christ demonstrate the triumph of truth and beauty? Is the student not simply repeating a philosophical commonplace of his epoch, the nineteenth-century longing for a combination of the ethical and the aesthetic?

Although these thoughts are unambiguously marked as an indirect representation of thought («думал о том, что»; "he kept thinking of"), their content is attributed by many readers and interpreters to the author himself, and authorial optimism is inferred from them.[7] Indeed, the rendering of the student's thoughts is not very figural. Lexis and syntax correspond entirely to the style of the narrator's text. Therefore, the indirect representation can easily be traced back to the narrator and be understood as the narrator's discourse. Only insofar as – i.e., only

---

7 On Russian and Western readings that argue for authorial optimism, see Schmid 1998, 278-279, note 3.

if – the words can be ascribed to the narrator, can anything akin to FCN be identified here. But the evaluation, of course, remains figural.

The second part of the concluding sentence and paragraph is as follows:

> [...] и чувство молодости, здоровья, силы, — ему было только 22 года, — и невыразимо сладкое ожидание счастья, неведомого, таинственного счастья овладевали пм мало-помалу, и жизнь казалась ему восхитительной, чудесной и полной высокого смысла. (Čexov, *PSS*, VIII, 309)

> [...] and a feeling of youth, health, strength – he was only twenty-two – and an ineffably sweet anticipation of happiness, unknown and mysterious, gradually took possession of him, and life appeared wondrous, marvelous, and filled with lofty meaning. (Tr. Michael Henry Heim in Čexov, *S*, 293)

The second part of the long final sentence contains an account of the student's various emotions: first, his "feeling of youth, health, strength"; second, the inexpressibly sweet expectation of an unknown mysterious happiness; and third, his conception of life as "wondrous, marvelous, and filled with lofty meaning." Although the narrator obviously names the figural emotions reliably, he is infected by the student's exuberance in enumerating them. Emphasizing the youthful age of the student, he seeks to awaken understanding for the student's naive view of the world, which he cannot but articulate ironically. We have here a clear case of text interference: the character's evaluations, the narrator's linguistic design. But the interference is double-voiced. Misjudgment of the distancing accentuation in the story's concluding words is the reason why the majority of readers and interpreters perceive the narrator as a wholehearted sympathizer of the aspiring clergyman.

4.3 Flashbacks

4.3.1 Jurij Trifonov, *The Long Goodbye*

In Thomas Mann's *Death in Venice* we encountered the presentation of a backstory. Čexov's tale "Rothschild's Violin" introduced the external and internal situation of the coffinmaker Jakov Ivanov with FCN in its first paragraph. The following section of Jurij Trifonov's novel *The Long Goodbye* (Dolgoe proščanie,

1971), one of his Moscow novels, serves as an introduction and overview of the plot setting.[8]

> Когда приехали в Саратов, все было вначале очень скверно: поселились в плохой гостинице, стояла жара, публика не ходила, все как-то разладилось, актеры болели, и Сергей Леонидович, не выносивший жары и плохих гостиниц, укатил в Москву, оставив вместо себя Смурного. Этот Смурный пришел в театр года два назад и сразу, как заметила Ляля, «положил на нее глаз». Но она отвергла его без колебаний, потому что прошел слух, что он интригует против Сергея Леонидовича, хочет занять его место, а это казалось Ляле чудовищной подлостью. Подлых людей она терпеть не могла. Правда, она не знала в точности размеров подлости Смурного и как именно он интригует против Сергея Леонидовича, но люди говорили, что подлость имеет место, и Ляля каким-то особым чутьем, которому привыкла доверять, этим слухам поверила. (Trifonov, *Sobr. soč.*, II, 131–132)

> Things were pretty miserable when the company first arrived in Saratov. They were lodged in a bad hotel, the heat didn't let up, and no one came to the theater. Everything seemed to go wrong: the actors began getting sick, and Sergej Leonidovič, who couldn't stand either hot weather or bad hotels, took off for Moscow, leaving Smurnyj in charge. Smurnyj had joined the theater two years ago and right away had started "giving Ljalja the eye," as she noticed. She had rejected his advances without hesitation since it was rumored that he was scheming against Sergej Leonidovič, trying to take his place. This struck Ljalja as despicable and mean, and she couldn't stand mean people. True, she didn't know exactly how he was scheming against Sergej Leonidovič or to what lengths he would be willing to go, but people said that something underhanded was going on, and with some special instinct which she had learned to rely on, Ljalja believed the rumors. (Trifonov, *LG*, 204)

There is an unmistakable figural coloring to this flashback. But no figure has yet been named that could be the bearer of perspective. Only with the appearance of the first woman's name, in the affectionate form, does the reader find a figure to which he can attach the memories. And this figure is presented as perceptive: "as she noticed" («как заметила Ляля»). Even if Ljalja is mentioned as observing and registering, the text remains the responsibility of the narrator, who asserts his authorship through repeated narratorial representations of consciousness ("Ljalja [...] believed the rumors"; «этим слухам [Ляля] поверила»). However, there can be no question of FID.

---

[8] Trifonov was the leading representative of the Russian Urban Prose of the 1970s, which made a decisive contribution to the replacement of Socialist Realism and the renewal of narrative prose. A specific trait of this movement was reflection on the inner man and the thematization of his contradictory consciousness. Trifonov was considered a candidate for the Nobel Prize until his death on March 28, 1981.

With his figuralization of the narrative text, Trifonov paved the way in Russian literature of the 1970s for a rehabilitation of the techniques for depicting consciousness that were frowned upon in Socialist Realism (cf. Schmid 1979).

4.3.2 Katherine Mansfield, "The Daughters of the Late Colonel"

The narratives of the New Zealand short-story writer Katherine Mansfield, already mentioned in sections 1.3 and 2.8, offer some examples of more or less clear FCN. Among the stories that may contain FCN is the narrative "The Daughters of the Late Colonel" (1921).

Colonel Pinner, the tyrannical father of Josephine and Constantia, has died. When the daughters went to say goodbye to their dying father, Nurse Andrews did not leave his bedside, so they were unable to discuss anything private. They invited the Nurse to stay for a week after their father's death, but now resent her for her excessive eating. The review of the scene where they part company can be conceived as figural in some features, with sprinklings of the daughters' FID, but ultimately the reader will settle on FCN, i.e., an account by the narrator reproducing the daughters' reactions. The following quotation forms the entire third microchapter of the story:

> But, after all, it was not long now, and then she'd be gone for good. And there was no getting over the fact that she had been very kind to father. She had nursed him day and night at the end. Indeed, both Constantia and Josephine felt privately she had rather overdone the not leaving him at the very last. For when they had gone in to say good-bye Nurse Andrews had sat beside his bed the whole time, holding his wrist and pretending to look at her watch. It couldn't have been necessary. It was so tactless, too. Supposing father had wanted to say something – something private to them. Not that he had. Oh, far from it! He lay there, purple, a dark, angry purple in the face, and never even looked at them when they came in. Then, as they were standing there, wondering what to do, he had suddenly opened one eye. Oh, what a difference it would have made, what a difference to their memory of him, how much easier to tell people about it, if he had only opened both! But no – one eye only. It glared at them a moment and then ... went out. (Mansfield, *Stories*, 214–215)

A hint of irony on the part of the narrator shimmers through in the reproduction. The distance from the daughters' thinking and feeling becomes most obvious as the text continues. The daughters feel guilty for having had their father buried; they could have kept him in their flat for a time, at least tentatively. Microchapter 5 ends with Josephine's speech:

> "[...] one thing's certain" – and her [Josephine's] tears sprang out again – "father will never forgive us for this – never!" (Mansfield, *Stories*, 217)

Microchapter 6 then begins with the words:

> Father would never forgive them. That was what they felt more than ever when, two mornings later, they went into his room to go through his things. (Mansfield, *Stories*, 217)

The narrator's distance from the girls' thinking becomes clearer when he visualizes the rules established by their father:

> It had been a rule for years never to disturb father in the morning, whatever happened. And now they were going to open the door without knocking even ... Constantia's eyes were enormous at the idea; Josephine felt weak in the knees. (Mansfield, *Stories*, 217)

While the first two sentences of this last quotation can be interpreted as FCN, the two-part third sentence seems more likely to belong to the narrator's text. At any event, the figural evaluation is much less prominent.

4.3.3 Dieter Wellershoff, "The Normal Life"

A flashback in FCN often develops out of a figural act of remembering modeled in FID. An example is the second paragraph of Dieter Wellershoff's story "The Normal Life" (Das normale Leben, 2004):

> Nebenan sprang der Motor des Kühlschranks an. Und jetzt wusste er es wieder: Er war in seinem Apartment in Ahrenshoop an der Ostsee, das er vor elf Jahren, noch zusammen mit Dagmar, seiner zweiten Frau, in einem letzten Versuch, die bröckelnde Ehe zu retten, erworben hatte. Es war allerdings ein vergeblicher Rettungsversuch gewesen, denn die beiden Male, die sie in der Enge des Zweizimmerapartments eine Woche zusammen verbrachten, hatten den Trennungsprozeß nur beschleunigt. Zuerst hatte er vorgehabt, das wenige Jahre nach der Wende sehr günstig gekaufte Apartment wieder abzustoßen, aber damit gewartet, weil die Preise stiegen. Und inzwischen hatte er sich daran gewöhnt, zwei- oder dreimal im Jahr herzukommen, um sich von der Stadtluft zu erholen und meistens auch, um etwas zu schreiben, einen Artikel, eine Kritik oder einen seiner Vorträge für eine Reihe mit dem Titel „Die Wissenschaft des Lebens", mit denen er sich seit seiner Pensionierung als Rundfunkredakteur noch einen späten Namen gemacht hatte. Eine Auswahl davon war vor zwei Jahren als Buch erschienen, und der Verlag plante einen weiteren Band mit neuen Arbeiten, diesmal unter dem Obertitel „Das Glück". Darüber, vor allem über die Spannung von „Glück haben" und „glücklich sein", oder luck and happiness, fortuna und beatitudo, hatte er in den letzten Tagen vor großen Auditorien gesprochen. Es war ein Erfolg gewesen, der ihn belebt und bestätigt hatte. Doch was gewöhnlich danach folgte – die Interviews, die Einladungen zum Abendessen, die nicht enden wollenden Gespräche mit den verschiedensten Leuten –, hatte ihn mehr als früher angestrengt. Noch kurz vorher war er im Krankenhaus gewesen und hatte erwogen, die Reise abzusagen, hatte sich dann aber anders entschieden. Und das war auch die richtige Entscheidung gewesen. Er hatte die drei

Auftritte in Osnabrück, Bremen und Lübeck so gut geschafft, wie er es sich nur wünschen konnte. Nun wollte er sich erholen. (Wellershoff, *NL*, 129–130)

*Next door, the refrigerator motor started. And now he knew again: he was in his apartment in Ahrenshoop on the Baltic Sea, which he had acquired eleven years ago, still together with Dagmar, his second wife, in a last attempt to save their crumbling marriage. It had been a futile attempt, however, because the two times they spent a week together in the cramped conditions of the two-room apartment had only accelerated the separation process. At first he had intended to sell the apartment, which he had bought at a very low price a few years after the fall of the Berlin Wall, but had waited because prices were rising. And in the meantime he had gotten used to coming here two or three times a year to recover from the city air and usually also to write an article, a review, or one of his lectures for a series entitled "The Science of Life," with which he had made a late name for himself since his retirement as a radio editor. A selection of these had been published as a book two years ago, and the publishing house was planning another volume with new works, this time under the title "Happiness." In the last few days he had spoken about this, especially about the tension between "having luck" and "being happy," or luck and happiness, fortuna and beatitudo, in front of large audiences. It had been a success that had revived and confirmed him. But what usually followed – the interviews, the dinner invitations, the never-ending conversations with all kinds of people – had strained him more than before. He had been in hospital shortly before and had considered canceling the trip, but had then changed his mind. And that had been the right decision. He had managed the three appearances in Osnabrück, Bremen, and Lübeck as well as he could have wished for. Now he wanted to recover.

Wellershoff is a master in the depiction of inner worlds and, according to serious critics, he occupies a leading position in the genre of consciousness prose in postwar German literature. In his novels and stories, FID naturally plays an important role. The quoted passage, however, only amounts to a representation of the current content of the hero's consciousness at its beginning and end: "And now he knew again: he was in his apartment in Ahrenshoop on the Baltic Sea" ("Und jetzt wusste er es wieder: Er war in seinem Apartment in Ahrenshoop an der Ostsee") – "Now he wanted to recover" ("Nun wollte er sich erholen"). In between, the passage contains his backstory, and there is no indication that this is conveyed by the figure's acts of remembering. The facts that he bought the apartment eleven years ago, and that he made the purchase together with Dagmar, who was his second wife, are so clear to the hero that he does not need to engage in an act of painstaking recollection. This is information that the narrator gives his reader to make the hero's story understandable. The other facts are not transmitted in FID either, but as elements of the happenings selected by the narrator. Once again, there is no indication that the backstory unfolds in an act of the character's consciousness.

4.4 Characterizing Figures:
Ernest Hemingway, "Up in Michigan"

FCN often serves to characterize the figures expressing themselves in the designations and evaluations. We observe such a function in the example from Dickens's *Little Dorrit* quoted by Baxtin to illustrate the intrusion of another's speech into narrative discourse (see above, section 2.3). Mr. Merdle's manner of thinking is expressed in the somewhat ceremonious epic tone of the italicized words.

The collision with the authentic narrative style throws an ironic light on Merdle's way of thinking and expressing himself. The result is a satirical effect that is fundamental to Dickens's novel.

Ernest Hemingway's early story "Up in Michigan," written in Paris in 1921/22 and published in 1923 in the collection *Three Stories and Ten Poems*, describes the sexual encounter of a young girl, Liz, with a blacksmith, Jim, on the planks of a dock. Although the girl takes a liking to the young man, she tries to stop him when he, drunk, begins to explore her body. After the sex act, he falls asleep and she begins to cry. Covering the fast-asleep man neatly and carefully with her jacket, she goes indoors. She is deeply disappointed. Since the story was first published, readers have differed in their opinions about whether the sex act was rape.

Susan Swartzlander ([1989] 1992) observes in her subtle analysis of the story that the narrative voice adopts the speech rhythms and syntax of the characters. As all of the characters share the same idiomatic English, she argues, diction alone is no index of the prevailing point of view. It must of course be objected that evaluation is an important factor when it comes to determining perspective. Without it, it is relatively uncertain to which instance a given index points.

The description of Liz's crush on Jim is strongly affected by Liz's modes of perception, evaluation, and expression:

> Liz liked Jim very much. She liked the way he walked over from the shop and often went to the kitchen door to watch for him to start down the road. She liked it about his mustache. She liked it about how white his teeth were when he smiled. She liked it very much that he didn't look like a blacksmith. She liked it how much A. J. Smith and Mrs. Smith liked Jim. One day she found that she liked it the way the hair was black on his arms and how white they were above the tanned line when he washed up in the washbasin outside the house. Liking that made her feel funny. (Hemingway, *Michigan*, 34)

Sheldon Norman Grebstein (1973, 79–80) notes "the simplicity, the one-thing-at-a-time quality, yet also the obsessiveness of Liz's perceptions." We can add to this the stereotypical expression "She liked it ..."

The narrative style changes noticeably when Liz's perception of the nature of Charlevoix Bay is described:

> A steep sandy road ran down the hill to the bay through the timber. From Smith's back door you could look out across the woods that ran down to the lake and across the bay. It was very beautiful in the spring and summer, the sky blue and bright and usually whitecaps on the lake beyond the point from the breeze blowing in from Charlevoix and Lake Michigan. From Smith's back door Liz could see ore barges way out in the lake going toward Boyne City. When she looked at them they didn't seem to be moving at all but if she went in and dried some more dishes and then came out again they would be out of sight beyond the point. (*Michigan*, 34–35)

Despite the somewhat more sophisticated description, we observe a certain stereotypy. Thus, the road "runs down" and the woods "run down." It is not surprising that the sky is blue and bright in spring and summer. The apparent motionlessness of the ore barges is seen from a child's perspective. Nevertheless, current mental activity of the figure is not being represented here, so we cannot speak of free indirect perception. Here, it is clearly the impersonal narrator who represents not a current but an iterative perception of nature by the heroine. Thus, FCN is present here.

The narrative style is different when Jim is described. The choice of the things mentioned is completely adapted to the limited horizon of the hero. In it, the things that satisfy Jim's physical needs play a major role:

> Jim began to feel great. He loved the taste and the feel of whiskey. He was glad to be back to a comfortable bed and warm food and the shop. He had another drink. (*Michigan*, 37)

The interpretation by Swartzlander, according to which the bay is presented "in all its idyllic serenity," which reflects "Liz's excessive romanticism," can hardly be followed. Swartzlander is right, however, in that the bright image of the bay presented through the perception of Liz in love is replaced by the dark image presented to Liz when she is deeply disappointed:

> Liz started to cry. She walked over to the edge of the dock and looked down to the water. There was a mist coming up from the bay. She was cold and miserable and everything felt gone. (*Michigan*, 38–39)

Cold and lightlessness are also associated with the last sentence of the story: "A cold mist was coming up through the woods from the bay" (*Michigan*, 39).

4.5 Characterizing a Collective

The text that is taken up by the narrator is often not limited to a single character but can represent groups of people. We had such a case of a FCN referring to a collective in the example from Katherine Mansfield's "Garden Party" given by Franz Stanzel for the device he called "reflectorization of the narrator" (see section 2.8).

We will call this form of FCN, which is not related to a single figure but to a group of persons, *collective FCN*. We thus have a simple descriptive category, which nonetheless seems to be more appropriate than the figuralization from an "empty deictic center" brought into play by Fludernik (1996, 143–155), drawing on Banfield (1987). Moreover, one is spared Fludernik's intuition-defying distinction between reflectorization and figuralization (see section 2.9), which can be sacrificed to Occam's razor.

4.5.1 Charles Dickens, *Little Dorrit*

Let us examine some of the instances of collective FCN that Baxtin (2012, 55–61) cites in his study of Dickens's *Little Dorrit* as examples of heteroglossia in the English comic novel.

> In a day or two it was announced to all the town, that Edmund Sparkler, Squire, son-in-law of the eminent Mr Merdle of worldwide renown, was made one of the Lords of the Circumlocution Office, and proclamation was issued, to all true believers, that this admirable *appointment was to be hailed as a graceful and gracious mark of homage, rendered by the graceful and gracious Decimus, to that commercial interest, which must ever in a great commercial country – and all the rest of it, with blast of trumpet.* So, bolstered by this mark of Government homage, the *wonderful* Bank and all the other *wonderful* undertakings went on and went up; and gaspers came to Harley Street, Cavendish Square, only to look at the house where the golden wonder lived. (Dickens, *Dorrit*, book 2, ch. 12; quoted after Baxtin 2012, 56; here and in the rest of this section, Baxtin's italics)

Baxtin (2012, 56–57) notes for this example that in the italicized passages the indirect discourse that presents "another's speech in another's language" is surrounded by the "hidden, diffused speech of another." In our context, it should be noted that the evaluations following the indirect discourse (twice "wonderful") are not those of an individual figure but represent the mindset of a collective.

The parodistic traits of the double-voiced reproduction emerge even more clearly in the following passage:

It was a dinner to provoke an appetite, though he had not had one. The rarest dishes, sumptuously cooked and sumptuously served, the choicest fruits, the most exquisite wines; marvels of workmanship in gold and silver, china and glass, innumerable things delicious to the senses of taste, smell, and sight, were insinuated into its composition. *O, what a wonderful man this Merdle, what a great man, what a master man, how blessedly and enviably endowed* – in one word, what a rich man! (Dickens, *Dorrit*, book 2, ch. 12)

The ironic reproduction of the collective glorification of the successful banker ends with a narrative naming of the real reason for Mr. Merdle's miracles – his wealth. We have here a complicated interweaving of narrator's text and characters' text, which prompts Baxtin to introduce his notion of *hybrid construction* (see above section 2.3).

Baxtin considers pseudo-objective motivation to be characteristic of novel style in general and of comic style in particular. He finds another example of this in Dickens's novel in the following passage:

As a vast fire will fill the air to a great distance with its roar, so the sacred flame which the mighty Barnacles had fanned caused the air to resound more and more with the name of Merdle. It was deposited on every lip, and carried into every ear. There never was, there never had been, there never again should be, such a man as Mr Merdle. Nobody, as foresaid, knew what he had done, but *everybody knew him to be the greatest that had appeared*. (*Dorrit*, book 2, ch. 13)

In the given examples of ironic-parodic reproduction, the characters' text is formed from the social doxa, the common opinion. What is generally accepted as true undergoes an unmistakable relativization through the overlaying of narrative irony. This can be taken as the general tendency of collective FCN, a tendency that not infrequently results in a satirical function, as we see in Dickens.

4.5.2 Jane Austen, *Emma*

We find indirect FCN that characterizes a collective in Jane Austen's *Emma*. Philip Elton, the young vicar of Highbury, mistakenly believing that Emma Woodhouse, the beautiful, high-spirited, intelligent woman of twenty years, is in love with him, proposes to her. When Emma reveals she believed him attached to Harriet Smith, a beautiful but unsophisticated young girl, he is outraged, considering Harriet socially inferior. After being rejected by Emma, Elton goes to Bath and returns with a pretentious vulgar wife, Augusta Elton, formerly Miss Hawkins.

Mr Elton returned, a very happy man. He had gone away *rejected and mortified – disappointed* in a very sanguine hope, after a series of what appeared to him strong encouragement; and not only losing the *right lady*, but finding himself debased to the level of a *very wrong one*. He had gone away *deeply offended* – he came back engaged to another – and to *another as superior, of course, to the first*, as under such circumstances what is gained always is to what is lost. He came back gay and self-satisfied, eager and busy, *caring nothing for Miss Woodhouse, and defying Miss Smith*. (Austen, *Emma*, 145; italics mine – W. Sch.)

This paragraph is entirely attuned to Mr. Elton's horizon. In the italicized segments, one hears the voice of the rejected wooer returning triumphantly with a better bride. This is FCN related to a character.

If we look at the preceding paragraph, the picture is different. The bride's outstanding qualities are not only represented from the vicar's point of view, but in their naming the evaluation by the collective of the town of Highbury is also reflected:

A week had not passed since Miss Hawkins's name was first mentioned in Highbury, before she was, by some means or other, discovered to have *every recommendation of person and mind*; to be *handsome, elegant, highly accomplished, and perfectly amiable*: and when Mr Elton himself arrived to triumph in his *happy prospects*, and *circulate the fame of her merits*, there was very little more for him to do, than to tell her Christian name, and say whose music she principally played. (Austen, *Emma*, 144–145; italics mine – W. Sch.)

When the narrator sums up Elton's courtship in the moves that are important to the hero, the discourse becomes double-voiced, ironic in relation to Elton, his wife, the very quick success – and to the Highbury public that is to be impressed by Elton's triumph:

The *charming* Augusta Hawkins, in addition to all the usual advantages of *perfect beauty and merit*, was in possession of an independent fortune, of so many thousands *as would always be called ten*; a point of some dignity, as well as some convenience: the story told well; *he had not thrown himself away* – he had *gained a woman of 10,000 l. or thereabouts*; and *he had gained her with such delightful rapidity* – the first hour of introduction had been so very soon followed by distinguishing notice; the history which he had to give Mrs Cole of the rise and progress of the affair was *so glorious* – the *steps so quick*, from the accidental rencontre, to the dinner at Mr Green's, and the party at Mrs Brown's – smiles and blushes rising in importance – with consciousness and agitation richly scattered – the lady had been so easily impressed – so sweetly disposed – had in short, to use a most intelligible phrase, been so very ready to have him, that vanity and prudence were equally contented. (Austen, *Emma*, 145; italics mine – W. Sch.)

The narrator marks the ironic relationship to Elton's successful courtship with the words "to use a most intelligible phrase."

4.5.3 Thomas Mann, "Tristan"

In Thomas Mann's story "Tristan," Franz Stanzel (1979, 233–238; tr. 1984, 180–184) detects two narrators, or a narrator with different perspectives, at work: on the one hand, an omniscient "authorial narrator" who introduces the reader to the scene of the action as befits his "narrative situation," and on the other hand, a narrator who assumes the cognitive and linguistic perspective of a reflector figure fixed in time and place. The reflectorized teller-character introduces the story's hero, the writer Detlev Spinell, without mentioning his name:

> Was für Existenzen hat „Einfried" nicht schon beherbergt! Sogar ein Schriftsteller ist da, ein exzentrischer Mensch, der den Namen irgendeines Minerals oder Edelsteines führt und hier dem Herrgott die Tage stiehlt ... (Mann, VIII, 217)

> The characters whom Einfried has sheltered! Even a writer is here, an eccentric person, who bears the name of some kind of mineral or precious stone and who fritters the Lord's days away here. (Tr. after Stanzel 1984, 182)[9]

When the narrator describes the impression the new patient, Herr Klöterjahn's wife, makes on the Einfried residents, he again introduces the writer. Again he mentions the writer as if he did not know him:

> Ein Schriftsteller, der seit ein paar Wochen in „Einfried" seine Zeit verbrachte, ein befremdender Kauz, dessen Name wie der eines Edelsteins lautete, verfärbte sich geradezu, als sie [Gabriele Klöterjahn] auf dem Korridor an ihm vorüberging, blieb stehen und stand noch immer wie angewurzelt, als sie schon längst entschwunden war. (Mann, VIII, 220–221)

> A writer who had for a few weeks been passing his time in Einfried, – an odd fish with a name reminiscent of some kind of precious stone – positively changed color when she [Gabriele Klöterjahn] passed him in the corridor: he stopped short and was still standing as if rooted to the spot long after she had disappeared. (Mann, *Death in Venice*, 97)

With its evaluative accents betraying a disdain for writing, this statement reflects the culture-averse mindset of the sanatorium residents. At the same time, the attention to the change in the color of the writer's face and his stiffness shows the readiness of the sanatorium residents to participate in the weaving of new stories, possibly even a "novel."

---

9 The translation by H. T. Lowe-Porter in this case erases the exclamation, a feature of the characters' text, and arrives at a neutral propositional sentence: "All sorts and kinds of people have received hospitality at Einfried" (Mann, *Tristan*, 86).

The still anonymous "writer" is encountered a third time when he finds Herr Klöterjahn doing something incorrect:

Dass [Herr Klöterjahn] auch anderen irdischen Freuden nicht grundsätzlich abhold war, bewies er an jenem Abend, als ein Kurgast von „Einfried," ein Schriftsteller von Beruf, ihn auf dem Korridor in ziemlich unerlaubter Weise mit einem Stubenmädchen scherzen sah, – ein kleiner, humoristischer Vorgang, zu dem der betreffende Schriftsteller eine lächerlich angeekelte Miene machte. (Mann, VIII, 222)

[Herr Klöterjahn] was also not altogether averse to certain other worldly pleasures, as was made evident one evening when one of the patients at Einfried, a writer by profession, saw him flirting rather disgracefully with a chambermaid in the corridor – a trifling, humorous incident to which the writer in question reacted with a quite ludicrous grimace of disapproval. (Mann, *Death in Venice*, 98–99)

The evaluation of the writer's reaction corresponds to the horizon of the residents: for them, such "humorous" incidents certainly lighten up the monotony of their existence, and they do not readily agree with the writer's disdain for them.

The fourth introduction of the writer is given by the "authorial narrator," who names him for the first time, albeit haltingly. This narratorial introduction does not occur until the beginning of the fourth section:

Spinell hieß der Schriftsteller, der seit mehreren Wochen in „Einfried" lebte, Detlev Spinell war sein Name, und sein Äußeres war wunderlich. (Mann, VIII, 223)

The name of the writer who had been living in Einfried for several weeks was Spinell – Detlev Spinell, and his appearance was rather extraordinary. (Mann, *Death in Venice*, 99)

From whose point of view was the very first introduction given? Stanzel resorts to the somewhat unfortunate construct of a "reflectorized narrator" (see above, section 2.8). We would say, on the contrary, that the narrator takes on the perspective of the characters, namely the collective of the residents of the sanatorium. For us, the first introduction is a clear case of collective FCN with a slightly ironic note.

The narration of Gabriele Klöterjahn's life and illness history is highly stylized, composed entirely of other people's words, in which her own voice hardly figures at all. The history of her life and illness is dominated by the voice of the successful wholesaler Klöterjahn, who, downplaying his wife's lung disease, loudly and good-humoredly tells his wife's story to anyone who shows an interest in it.

Another passage that Stanzel deals with is the scene in which Herr Klöterjahn's wife plays the Liebestod motif from *Tristan und Isolde* on the piano in the conversation room of the sanatorium. The scene, one of the deepest inwardness and wordless communion of souls, is suddenly interrupted by the entrance of a patient:

> Plötzlich geschah etwas Erschreckendes. Die Spielende brach ab und führte ihre Hand über die Augen, um ins Dunkle zu spähen, und Herr Spinell wandte sich rasch auf seinem Sitze herum. Die Tür dort hinten, die zum Korridor führte, hatte sich geöffnet, und herein kam eine finstere Gestalt, gestützt auf den Arm einer zweiten. (Mann, VIII, 246–247)

> At this point there was a startling interruption. The pianist suddenly stopped playing and shaded her eyes with her hand to peer into the darkness; and Herr Spinell swung round on his chair. At the far side of the room the door that led into the passage had opened, and a shadowy figure entered, leaning on the arm of a second figure. (Mann, *Death in Venice*, 119)

As the narrator immediately explains, the woman who enters is the demented pastor with the name Höhlenrauch (meaning "cave smoke"). Does the failure to recognize the old woman not contradict the assumption that the narrator is relating the perception of the residents of the sanatorium? The widow Höhlenrauch must be well known to the patients. In the quoted scene, the eerie lady is obviously perceived and portrayed from Detlev Spinell's perceptual perspective. The newcomer Spinell is not yet familiar with the ghostly appearances of Pastorin Höhlenrauch and can only perceive the entrant as a "shadowy figure." The quoted passage thus contains a classic case of free indirect perception, from Detlev Spinell's point of view.

Stanzel's construct of a "reflectorization of the teller-character" can thus be broken down on the one hand into collective FCN, on the other hand into the protagonist's free indirect perception.

4.5.4 Fëdor Dostoevskij, "A Nasty Anecdote"

The device that Baxtin/Vološinov called "anticipated and disseminated reported speech" could also involve the text of a collective, as in the thinking of the generals gathered in a cozy atmosphere on a winter evening in St. Petersburg in Dostoevskij's novella "A Nasty Anecdote" (Skvernyj anekdot, 1862).

The story must be understood as a satire of the half-hearted or hypocritical humanitarianism of the Russian liberals of the 1860s. It describes the extremely embarrassing experiences of the real State Councilor Ivan Pralinskij. At a gentlemen's evening, Pralinskij, more of a vain chatterbox than a liberal or even a revolutionary, passionately espouses before his skeptically reticent colleagues the new ideas of humanity that the liberal regime of Alexander II has awakened in

Russia. Irritated by the skepticism of his guest Nikiforov ("We won't hold out") and inspired by the unaccustomed alcohol, Pralinskij on his way home decides to honor the wedding celebration of Pseldonimov, one of the minor clerks in his office, with his presence, so as to surprise the common people with his unpretentiousness and magnanimity and to prove to the whole world what moral greatness he is capable of. The visit turns out quite differently than Pralinskij had imagined. His appearance causes consternation in the hitherto cheerfully exuberant gathering. None of the humane speeches and popular gestures he has thought up succeeds. To avoid further embarrassment, he sticks to drinking. The unfortunate party ends with the drunken state councilor, insulted by a radical, trying to go home, stumbling, falling lengthwise, and immediately falling asleep on the floor. The next morning Pralinskij finds himself in the most miserable situation. After a week of shameful seclusion, he dares to return to his office. One of his first acts is to approve the transfer request of poor Pseldonimov. When he again fails to make a popular gesture, he vows to be extremely strict with his subordinates in the future.

Text interference plays a major role in Dostoevskij's satirical narrative.[10] Particular importance is attached to FCN. We have already noted above that Baxtin substantiates his definition of this procedure in the book published under Vološinov's name with a quotation from "A Nasty Anecdote." Above we quoted from

---

10 There is a detailed presentation of the various patterns of text interference in Schmid ([1973] 1986, 197–206). It is not irrelevant to the representation of consciousness that the hero's way of thinking is presented in long direct interior monologues (of 45, 105, 22, and 17 lines in length). The narrator precedes the second monologue with an explanation that is revealing regarding Dostoevskij's problems with the representation of consciousness: «Известно, что целые рассуждения проходят иногда в наших головах мгновенно, в виде наких-то ощущений, без перевода на человеческий язык, тем более на литературный. Но мы постараемся перевесть все эти ощущения героя нашего и представить читателю хотя бы только сущность этих ощущений, так сказать то, что было в них самое необходимое и правдоподобное. Потому что ведь многие из ощущений наших, в переводе на обыкновенный язык, покажутся совершенно неправдоподобными. Вот почему они никогда и на свет не являются, а у всякого есть. Разумеется, ощущения и мысли Ивана Ильича были немного бессвязны. Но ведь вы знаете причину» (*PSS*, V, 12–13). "It is known that whole trains of thought sometimes pass instantly through our heads, in the form of certain feelings, without translation into human language, still less literary language. But we shall attempt to translate all these feelings of our hero's and present the reader if only with the essence of these feelings, with what, so to speak, was most necessary and plausible in them. Because many of our feelings, when translated into ordinary language, will seem perfectly implausible. That is why they never come into the world, and yet everybody has them. Naturally, Ivan Il'ič's feelings and thoughts were a bit incoherent. But you know the reason why" (Dostoevskij, *Nasty Anecdote*, 15).

the translation in the English version of Vološinov's book (1973). Now the same passage, which is preceded by the opening sentence of the story, is presented in the translation by Richard Pevear and Larissa Volokhonsky.

> This nasty anecdote occurred precisely at the time when, with such irrepressible force and such touchingly naive enthusiasm, the regeneration of our dear fatherland began, and its valiant sons were all striving toward new destinies and hopes. Then, one winter, on a clear and frosty evening, though it was already past eleven, three extremely respectable gentlemen were sitting in a comfortably and even luxuriously furnished room, in a fine two-storied house on the Petersburg side, and were taken up with a solid and excellent conversation on a quite curious subject. These three gentlemen were all three of general's rank. They were sitting around a small table, each in a fine, soft armchair, and as they conversed they were quietly and comfortably sipping champagne. (Dostoevskij, *Nasty Anecdote*, 3)

The first sentence contains a clear example of collective FCN. It ironically reproduces the mindset of the patriotically tuned higher circles of Russian society.

The point of reference changes with the second sentence. Here, FCN serves to satirically expose the minds preoccupied with comfortable living and the cozy complacency of the respectable gentlemen of general's rank gathered in the scene. The text from which the stereotypical designations and evaluations are taken is a collective text that expresses the social self-image of the higher bureaucracy of the official city of St. Petersburg.

The ironic reproduction of the collective characters' text is described by Baxtin/Vološinov as follows:

> [...] the story is being told by a narrator, who would seem to be in solidarity with the "generals," who fawns upon them, adopts their attitudes in all things, speaks their language, but nonetheless provocatively overdoes it and thoroughly exposes all their real and potential utterances to the author's irony and mockery. By each of these banal epithets, the author, through his narrator, makes his hero ironic and ridiculous. (Vološinov [1929] 1973, 136)

We will see below (section 4.6.1) how FCN focuses on the figure of the actual State Councilor Pralinskij as the narrative progresses.

4.5.5 Ernest Hemingway, "Up in Michigan"

We find FCN that characterizes a collective, the inhabitants of Hortons Bay, in the beginning of Hemingway's story "Up in Michigan," when Jim is introduced:

> Jim Gilmore came to Hortons Bay from Canada. He bought the blacksmith shop from old man Horton. Jim was short and dark with big mustaches and big hands. He was a good

horseshoer and did not look much like a blacksmith even with his leather apron on. He lived upstairs above the blacksmith shop and took his meals at A. J. Smith's. (Hemingway, *Michigan*, 34)

Here the perception of the hero from the outside dominates, with the information accessible to the inhabitants of Hortons Bay and the designations they have ("old man Horton"). Without the designation "old man Horton," the beginning of the narrative would be considered a normal introduction to the situation by the narrator.

4.6 Characterizing a Milieu through Colloquialisms

A wide-ranging aspect of FCN is the incorporation of expressions from the simple vernacular of the people into narrative discourse. This use of FCN is especially common in Russian literature. In the nineteenth century, the contagion of narrative discourse with the vernacular was strongly prominent in Nikolaj Leskov's narratives, in which skaz also played a distinctive role (on skaz see Schmid 2014e). FCN and skaz began to converge, and the two types were not always clearly distinguishable. Let us have a look at the first sentence of the short novel *The Life of a Peasant Woman* (Žitie odnoj baby, 1863) by Nikolaj Leskov:

Маленький мужичонко был рюминский Костик, а злющий был такой, что упаси господи! (Leskov, *Sobr. soč.*, I, 109)

*Rjumin Kostik was a small man, but when he got angry … may God have mercy!

The opening words of the diegetic narrator, when considered in their full context, introduce a skaz narrative, but taken on their own, they can just as easily be seen as FCN.

In the 1920s, when Russian prose emphatically depicted the life and language of the people, the narrative text was remarkably often stylized following the vernacular (cf. the careful studies by Koževnikova 1971, 1994). A strong opposing current of the time was poetic, ornamental prose, which developed in individual authors, even on the basis of skaz stylization. FCN was heavily involved in these stylistic trends.

4.6.1 Boris Pil'njak, *The Naked Year*

The curious blending of the mutually exclusive stylistic principles of ornamentalism and skaz in Boris Pil'njak's non-novel *The Naked Year* (Golyj god, 1922)[11] can be demonstrated by two examples.

Chapter 1 begins with the heading:

Здѣсь продаются пѣмадоры (Pil'njak, *Izbr. pr.*, 51)

The headline is untranslatable. It is the text of a notice that refers to the sale of tomatoes. This notice is located just opposite the sign *Department of People's Protection of the Ordyn Council of Deputies*. The point is twofold: first, tomatoes are obviously such a scarce commodity that they can only be obtained in the building of the Soviet People's Protection Department. Second, the sign contains a vernacular corruption of the Russian word for tomatoes. Instead of *pomidory* it says *pĕmadory*, the latter being written with the letter *jat'* (ѣ), which was abolished in 1918, suggesting that *pĕmadory* is a word existing already in documents. This is one of the author's numerous sideswipes at the lack of education of Soviet officials. For us, the text of the notice is an indication that the language of the people even penetrates into the headings via FCN.

Chapter 4 is headed with the strange text:

Кому — таторы, а кому — ляторы (Pil'njak, *Izbr. pr.*, 121)

*Some are given tators and others lators.

The following text resolves the confusion: in Moscow a person is standing in front of a store sign that says *Commutators, Accumulators*. He reads: "Some ... are given tators and ... others ... lators ...," understanding the first components of the technical expressions unknown to him as datives of the Russian distributive pronoun *kto ... kto*, i.e., as *komu ... komu* ("some ... the others"), and he says: "You see, here too they cheat the common people!"

One can imagine that Pil'njak did not make friends with the Soviet authorities with this alignment with the thinking of the common people.

---

11 Immediately after the novel was published in Berlin, that is, in *tamizdat* (literature of the Soviet Union published abroad), the question of the unity of the work was raised in view of the profusion of voices and styles. Cf. Jensen (1979).

4.6.2 Lev Tolstoj, "The Forged Coupon"

Long before the experimental 1920s, in classical Russian realism we can find sprinklings of simple folk language in narrative discourse outside the stylization of skaz. Lev Tolstoj would never be described as avant-garde, and he works much less with voices than Dostoevskij, which is why Baxtin contrasts him with the dialogic, polyphonic Dostoevskij as a monologic, homophonic author (cf. Emerson 1984). Nevertheless, we can find instances of FCN in his work. In 1880 he began the story "The Forged Coupon" (Fal'šivyj kupon), which he interrupted in 1904 and did not complete. In some places, the narrative discourse is interspersed with expressions drawn from the vocabulary of the people.

> И Иван, протрезвившись, вспомнил, что ему советовал мастеровой, с которым он пил вчера, и решил идти к *аблакату* жаловаться. (Tolstoj, *Povesti*, I, 372; italics mine – W. Sch.)

> *And Ivan, sobered up, remembered what he had been advised by the foreman with whom he had drunk yesterday, and decided to go to the *ablakat* to complain.

Regardless of whether the corruption of the word *advokat* goes back to the foreman or is used by Ivan himself, the word *ablakat* is included by the narrator in his discourse to characterize the speech of the uneducated common people. In the next paragraph, the narrator speaks in his own language and uses the word *advokat*.

Two pages further on, the narrator speaks of *odëža* ("clothing"), using the original East Slavic form (which became the vernacular variant) instead of the South Slavic form *odežda*, which entered the Russian written language. The colloquial *odëža* comes from the lexicon of the common-man hero.

4.7 Satirical Description

4.7.1 Fëdor Dostoevskij, "A Nasty Anecdote"

FCN is often found in passages where narrators describe their characters. Not infrequently, the narrator ironically accentuates the words and evaluations that correspond to the characters' texts.

The ironic or satirical description of a character with the help of FCN occurs extremely frequently in Dostoevskij's early works *The Double* (Dvojnik, 1846) and "Mr. Proxarčin" (Gospodin Proxarčin, 1846). Since the satirical description of a character for these two works has already been described in detail,[12] we turn to works from Dostoevskij's middle period (1859–1866).

The narrator of Dostoevskij's story "A Nasty Anecdote" includes in his narrative discourse phrases taken from the characters' speech. Thus, when describing the habits of the host Stepan Nikiforovič Nikiforov, he uses three times in a row the phrase "he could not bear" («терпеть не мог»):

> [...] *терпеть не мог* хватать с неба звезды [...] был очень не глуп, но *терпеть не мог* выказывать свой ум [...] смолоду *терпеть не мог* гостей у себя. (*PSS*, V, 5–6; italics mine – W. Sch.)

> [...] he *could not bear* having stars in his eyes [...] he was far from stupid, but *could not bear* to display his intelligence [...] from his youth he *could not bear* to receive guests. (*Nasty Anecdote*, 4; tr. rev.; italics mine – W. Sch.)

As it continues, the narrative account is frequently colored by the text of the hero Pralinskij.

The infection of the narrative report by Pralinskij's text and the reproduction of the character's text become conspicuous wherever the narrative report contains evaluations that cannot be attributed to the narrator, who is seeking to expose Pralinskij's hypocrisy and show solidarity with the innocent Pseldonimov. This includes all the attributes that put Pralinskij in an honorable light or make the wedding guests look contemptible.

With ironic intention, the narrator reproduces individual phrases of the characters, such as the phrase "more often than he should have" («чаще, чем бы следовало»):

> Иван Ильич [Пралинский] горячился и в жару воображаемого спора *чаще, чем бы следовало*, пробовал из своего бокала. Тогда Степан Никифорович брал бутылку и тотчас же добавлял его бокал, что, неизвестно почему, начало вдруг обижать Ивана Ильича, тем более что Семен Иваныч Шипуленко, которого он особенно презирал и, сверх того, даже боялся за цинизм и за злость его, тут же сбоку прековарно молчал и *чаще, чем бы следовало, улыбался*. (*PSS*, V, 8; italics mine – W. Sch.)

> Ivan Il'ič was getting excited and in the heat of the imagined dispute sampled from his glass *more often than he should have*. Then Stepan Nikiforovič would take the bottle and top up his glass at once, which, for no apparent reason, suddenly began to offend Ivan Il'ič, the more so in that Semen Ivanyč Šipulenko, whom he particularly despised and, moreover, even feared on account of his cynicism and malice, was most perfidiously silent just beside

---

12 Schmid [1973] 1986, 134–141 (on FCN in *The Double*), 163–168 (on FCN in "Mr. Proxarčin"). On the latter work cf. also Tunimanov 1971.

him, and smiled *more often than he should have*. (*Nasty Anecdote*, 7–8; italics mine – W. Sch.)

The most conspicuous and frequent of the attributes derived from the character's text is *malignant* (*zlokačestvennyj*). The narrator uses this epithet for various characters and for various behaviors. It remains open whether he is reproducing a unique figural evaluation again and again or whether he is infected each time anew by the stereotypically thinking hero.

On its first occurrence, the epithet is still embedded in an indirect representation of the hero's perception, so it can still be considered a marked presentation of CT.

Ивану Ильичу показалось даже, что в глазах его [Пселдонимова]есть что-то холодное, затаенное, даже что-то себе на уме, особенное, *злокачественное*. (*PSS*, V, 20; italics mine – W. Sch.)

It even seemed to Ivan Il'ič that there was in his eyes something cold, secretive, even something kept to himself, peculiar, *malignant*. (*Nasty Anecdote*, 26; italics mine – W. Sch.)

But then the epithet appears independently of indirect representation, in a narratorial context:

[...] явилась одна *злокачественная* женская фигура. (*PSS*, V, 30)

[...] there appeared a *malignant* female figure [...]. (*Nasty Anecdote*, 41)

Другие вели себя с какою-то небрежною, *злокачественною* независимостью. (*PSS*, V, 29)

The others behaved with a certain nonchalant, *malignant* independence [...]. (*Nasty Anecdote*, 40)

Не прошло десяти минут, после того как молодых заперли одних в зале, как вдруг послышался раздирающий крик, не отрадный крик, а самого *злокачественного* свойства. (*PSS*, V, 40; italics mine – W. Sch.)

Ten minutes had not passed since the young couple was shut in the drawing room, when a rending cry was suddenly heard, a cry not of joy, but of a most *malignant* quality. (56–57; italics mine – W. Sch.)

After the embarrassing happenings in which Pralinskij cut such a pathetic figure, he imagines how he will be received in his office:

С ужасом убеждался он, что непременно услышит за собою двусмысленный шепот, увидит двусмысдленные лица, пожнет *злокачественнейшие* улыбки. (*PSS*, V, 44; italics mine – W. Sch.)

He was convinced to his horror, that he was sure to hear ambiguous whispers behind his back, to see ambiguous faces, to reap the most *malignant* smiles. (*Nasty Anecdote*, 62; italics mine – W. Sch.)

The denser the FCN appears, the more the narrative discourse loses the character of the narrator's speech and approaches free indirect perception. We have here a similar relationship of narrator's text and character's text as in *The Double*, but with the difference that there the figural view becomes increasingly unreal due to the hero's mental illness (see below, sections 4.9.1 and 4.10.1), whereas in "A Nasty Anecdote" what is perceived by the hero is quite real.

It is revealing how translations treat contagion and reproduction. The remarks that follow are based on German translations, for Dostoevskij's stories (and works of Russian literature in general) have been translated into no other language more frequently than into German. Two tendencies can be observed that contradict each other and yet can occur within one and the same translation.

On the one hand, figural designations in narrative discourse are emphasized by quotation marks. While such a redaction may be guided by the understandable desire to clearly identify the segments that have been identified as figural, it nevertheless distorts the text and disregards the ambiguity intended by Dostoevskij. Contagion or reproduction, forms of the covert presentation of consciousness, become quoted figural designations, which are modifications of direct speech.

Even more inappropriate is another treatment of FCN, in which the stereotypical nature of the designations attributed by translators to the author is stylistically "softened" by the introduction of synonyms, as if Dostoevskij were in need of stylistic correction. This treatment of FCN betrays a serious misunderstanding of Dostoevskij's poetics of multiple voices. (The English translation by Pevear and Volokhonsky used here is free of such flaws.)

To believe that Dostoevskij's style must be improved is to succumb to the legend that the author wrote somewhat uncontrollably in a wild or holy furor, paying little attention to style. Even the literary pope of the Germans, Marcel Reich-Ranicki, has declared on television that in the opinion of specialists Dostoevskij's style is somewhat careless. The truth is that among the authors of world literature Dostoevskij stands out as the master of voices. Voices are embodied in stylistic peculiarities. The many-voicedness of Dostoevskij's narrative texture can give the impression of stylistic imbalance. Even the young Dostoevskij was annoyed by the fact that the Russian audience chalked up stylistic weaknesses to him as the author and not to the speaking or writing characters. In a letter to his brother Mixail of February 1, 1846, the fledgling author writes:

Не понимают, как можно писать таким слогом. Во всем они привыкли видеть рожу сочинителя; я же моей не показывал. (*PSS*, XXVIII/1, 117)

*People don't understand how one can write in such a style. They're used to seeing the writer's mug in everything; but I haven't shown mine.

4.7.2 Fëdor Dostoevskij, Crime and Punishment

In Dostoevskij's novel *Crime and Punishment* (Prestuplenie i nakazanie, 1866), Rodion Raskol'nikov's sister Dunja, fleeing from the advances of her employer Svidrigajlov, decides to marry the Court Councilor Petr Lužin. Raskol'nikov sees the connection with the well-heeled man as a self-sacrifice on the part of his sister for the financial well-being of the family, as a means of enabling his further studies, and reacts to the marriage plans with indignation. At the first meeting with the fiancé, Raskol'nikov looks at him attentively and with special interest:

Действительно, в общем виде Петра Петровича поражало как бы что-то особенное, а именно, нечто как бы оправдывавшее название «жениха», так бесцеремонно ему сейчас данное. Во-первых, было видно и даже слишком заметно, что Петр Петрович усиленно поспешил воспользоваться несколькими днями в столице, чтоб успеть принарядиться и прикраситься в ожидании невесты, что, впрочем, было весьма невинно и позволительно. Даже собственное, может быть даже слишком самодовольное, собственное сознание своей принятой перемены к лучшему могло бы быть прощено для такого случая, ибо Петр Петрович состоял на линии жениха. Всё платье его было только что от портного, и всё было хорошо, кроме разве того только, что всё было слишком новое и слишком обличало известную цель. Даже щегольская, новехонькая, круглая шляпа об этой цели свидетельствовала: Петр Петрович как-то уж слишком почтительно с ней обращался и слишком осторожно держал ее в руках. Даже прелестная пара сиреневых, настоящих жувеневских, перчаток свидетельствовала то же самое, хотя бы тем одним, что их не надевали, а только носили в руках для параду. В одежде же Петра Петровича преобладали цвета светлые и юношественные. На нем был хорошенький летний пиджак светло-коричневого оттенка, светлые легкие брюки, таковая же жилетка, только что купленное тонкое белье, батистовый самый легкий галстучек с розовыми полосками, и что всего лучше: всё это было даже к лицу Петру Петровичу. Лицо его, весьма свежее и даже красивое, и без того казалось моложе своих сорока пяти лет. Темные бакенбарды приятно осеняли его с обеих сторон, в виде двух котлет, и весьма красиво сгущались возле светловыбритого блиставшего подбородка. Даже волосы, впрочем чуть-чуть лишь с проседью, расчесанные и завитые у парикмахера, не представляли этим обстоятельством ничего смешного или какого-нибудь глупого вида, что обыкновенно всегда бывает при завитых волосах, ибо придает лицу неизбежное сходство с немцем, идущим под венец. Если же и было что-нибудь в этой довольно красивой и солидной физиономии действительно неприятное и отталкивающее, то происходило уж от других причин. Рассмотрев без церемонии господина Лужина, Раскольников ядовито улыбнулся, снова опустился на подушку и стал по-прежнему глядеть в потолок. (Dostoevskij, *PSS*, VI, 113–114)

Indeed, there was some striking peculiarity, as it were, in Petr Petrovič's general appearance – namely, something that seemed to justify the appellation of "fiancé" just given him so unceremoniously. First, it was evident, and even all too noticeable, that Petr Petrovič had hastened to try to use his few days in the capital to get himself fitted out and spruced up while waiting for his fiancée – which, incidentally, was quite innocent and pardonable. Even his own, perhaps all too smug awareness of his pleasant change for the better could be forgiven on such an occasion, for Petr Petrovič did indeed rank as a fiancé. All his clothes were fresh from the tailor and everything was fine, except perhaps that it was all too new and spoke overly much of a certain purpose. Even the smart, spanking-new top hat testified to this purpose: Petr Petrovič somehow treated it all too reverently and held it all too carefully in his hands. Even the exquisite pair of lilaccolored, real Jouvain gloves testified to the same thing, by this alone, that they were not worn but were merely carried around for display. In Petr Petrovič's attire, light and youthful colors predominated. He was wearing a pretty summer jacket of a light brown shade, lightcolored summer trousers, a matching waistcoat, a fine, newly purchased shirt, a little tie of the lightest cambric with pink stripes, and the best part was that it all even became Petr Petrovič. His face, very fresh and even handsome, looked younger than his forty-five years to begin with. Dark side-whiskers pleasantly overshadowed it from both sides, like a pair of mutton chops, setting off very handsomely his gleaming, clean-shaven chin. Even his hair, only slightly touched with gray, combed and curled by the hairdresser, did not thereby endow him with a ridiculous or somehow silly look, as curled hair most often does, inevitably making one resemble a German on his way to the altar. And if there was indeed something unpleasant and repulsive in this rather handsome and solid physiognomy, it proceeded from other causes. Having looked Mr Lužin over unceremoniously, Raskol'nikov smiled venomously, sank onto the pillow again, and went back to staring at the ceiling. (*CaP*, 145–146)

The description of the fiancé has an unmistakably figural coloring. But the question is which figure this coloring is based on. According to the evaluative accents that can be found in the quotation, three evaluative instances can be distinguished. Such multi-voicedness is characteristic of Dostoevskij's poetics. Disparaging evaluations are most likely to be attributed to Raskol'nikov, who views the conceited fiancé critically. Certain remarks, however, are more likely to be attributed to the narrator. But then there are a lot of positive accents, which refer to the newly acquired clothes and the beautifully arranged appearance of the fiancé . These evaluations probably come directly from the text of Petr Petrovič himself. It is not likely that the critical Raskol'nikov perceives the details of the outfit of his sister's fiancé in such detail as is offered here. Thus, in one and the same passage of the narrative text, the narrator and the figure Raskol'nikov, who is used as an observer, as well as the object of observation, the fiancé, are presented with their respective evaluations. It is this form of multi-voicedness for which one can most readily accept Baxtin's (1929) controversial concept of "polyphony." Even at the risk of leveling out the ambiguity and oscillation of the text interference, I have tried to mark the voices in the text passage: Raskol'nikov's voice with single underlining and the voice of the fiancé Petr Petrovič with double underlining.

I am well aware that this division into voices will be controversial and in general does not take into account the ambiguous character of the text interference. The intention is simply to show how in FCN a seemingly purely narratorial narrative text can reflect the evaluative positions not only of one, but also of several figures.

The quoted passage has to be understood in terms of double-voicedness in two different dimensions. Satirical accents become noticeable where the vain fiancé is concerned; the narrator smugly enumerates his fashionable, foppish new clothes in all their detail. And a slight ironic hue, or coloring, which, however, does not cancel out the critical evaluation of the fiancé, becomes apparent in relation to Raskol'nikov, who observes him with disdain.

4.8 Empathetic Description

4.8.1 Fay Weldon, "Weekend"

The counterpart of satirical description is empathetic description, which is associated with sympathy for a suffering being. An example of a text with empathetic FCN is Fay Weldon's narrative "Weekend" (1978).[13]

Martha is on her way to the weekend cottage with her husband and three children:

> Weekend! Only two hours' drive down to the cottage on Friday evenings: three hours' drive back on Sunday nights. The pleasures of greenery and guests in between. They reckoned themselves fortunate, how fortunate! (Weldon, *Weekend*, lines 10–13)

What one might at first think to be FID with Martha's inner speech because of the emphatic use of "Weekend! Only two hours drive," proves on closer inspection to be not so clear in perspective. Should the heroine of the narrative be so happy about the total of five hours of driving on the weekend? And the "guests in between" will not make the few hours of the stay in the cottage any more relaxing for Martha. The final sentence with the sobering "They reckoned themselves" and

---

13 I owe the reference to this story to Fludernik (1996, 141–143), where it is treated as a case of "reflectorization."

the emphatic assessment "fortunate, how fortunate" certainly does not reflect Martha's authentic view. We have something else here, the narrator's account of the unpleasant life of Martha, wife and mother, exploited by her husband Martin. This life is portrayed with empathy. Here we have a case of empathetic FCN with the narrator's ironic accentuation of the evaluations.

The next paragraph, which at first could be taken for a résumé in Martha's inner speech, is probably better interpreted as summary information provided by the narrator, who orients himself on Martha's horizon, speaking in her language and with her intonation, and thus as FCN.

> On Fridays Martha would get home on the bus at six-twelve and prepare tea and sandwiches for the family: then she would strip four beds and put the sheets and quilt covers in the washing machine for Monday: take the country bedding from the airing basket plus the books and the games, plus the weekend food – acquired at intervals throughout the week, to lessen the load – plus her own folder of work from the office, plus Martin's drawing materials (she was a market researcher in an advertising agency, he a freelance designer) plus hairbrushes, jeans, spare T-shirts, Jolyon's antibiotics (he suffered from sore throats), Jenny's recorder, Jasper's cassette player and so on – ah, the so on! – and would pack them, skilfully and quickly, into the boot. (*Weekend*, lines 14–25)

That Martha, who does not complain, becomes aware of all her duties on the way to the cottage and also gives herself the explanations in parentheses, is unlikely. In this respect there is little to support FID as an explanation of the passage's structure, which remains FCN.

In the further course of the narrative, the presentation of Martha's troublesome life is detached from the guiding frame of the narrator's discourse and seems to pass into interior monologue of the heroine. There are passages in which pure interior monologue in FID, with its characteristic features such as exclamations, questions to oneself, appeals to oneself, is present and where even the grammatical boundary to – however unmarked – direct discourse is crossed:

> Martin likes slim ladies. Diet. Martin rather likes his secretary. Diet; Martin admires slim legs and big bosoms. How to achieve them both? Impossible. But try, oh try, to be what you ought to be, not what you are. Inside and out. (*Weekend*, lines 147–150)

But the context in such cases does not allow a clear assignment and speaks more for FCN than for FID. The following passage offers a clear example of the uncertainty, the oscillation between the narrator's empathetic discourse and Martha's interior monologue:

> "I wish *you'd* wear scent," said Martin to Martha, reproachfully. Katie wore lots. Martha never seemed to have time to put any on, though. Martin bought her bottle after bottle.

Martha leapt out of bed each morning to meet some emergency – miaowing cat, coughing child, faulty alarm clock, postman's knock – when was Martha to put on scent? It annoyed Martin all the same. She ought to do more to charm him. (*Weekend*, lines 362–367; italics in the original)

In this passage, several voices overlap: Martin with his request to Martha, either spoken directly or realized by Martha, Martin with his expectation of stronger erotic stimulation, which Martha is obviously becoming aware of, Martha's self-defensive visualization of the demands occurring simultaneously in the morning. It is unclear whether Katie is being referred to by Martin or whether Martha herself is thinking of Katie always being strongly perfumed. The multiplicity of voices and intentions is tied together by the narrator, who presents the points of view in a large-scale FCN form, with unmistakable empathy for Martha.

4.8.2 No FCN in Children's Literature

When considering the function of empathy, one must also look at children's literature. FID is widely used in this genre. For Russian, where children's literature is strongly developed and its authors are held in high esteem, Ljudmila Sokolova (1968, 212–215) has noted a strong presence of FID in works by children's authors. But she is not aware of FCN and consequently does not give attention to the phenomenon. But this might not be the only reason for her neglect of FCN.

While reading German stories to my grandchildren, I detected FID at every turn, but found no FCN. This has a fundamental reason. Children need characters in stories with whom they can identify. In FCN, the figure who colors the narrative is usually not named and often remains undefined. This puzzles children, and they reject it. FCN withholds from them the homeliness, the familiarity, that they need in stories.

Even more distant for children than empathetic contagion is double-voiced reproduction. Children have no understanding of voice interference, and irony is difficult for them to comprehend. This also sheds light on literature for adults. It is not by chance that the masters of multiple voices and their interference – Dostoevskij, James Joyce, Virginia Woolf – are considered difficult writers.

4.9 Feigning a Motivation:
Fëdor Dostoevskij, *The Eternal Husband*

"*The Eternal Husband* [Večnyj muž, 1870], the most perfect and polished of all Dostoevsky's shorter works" (Frank 1995, 394), is a serious variation of the classic love triangle between husband, lover, and wife. In our context, what is of interest is the depiction of the mental process through which a forgotten and repressed action makes its way into consciousness.

The story begins with unclear mental upheaval on the part of the hero Vel'čaninov (derived from Russian *velikij* "big"):

> Пришло лето — и Вельчанинов, сверх ожидания, остался в Петербурге. Поездка на юг России расстроилась, а делу и конца не предвиделось. Это дело — тяжба по имении — принимало предурной оборот. Еще три месяца тому назад оно имело вид весьма несложный; но как-то вдруг всё изменилось. «Да и вообще всё стало изменяться к худшему!» – эту фразу Вельчанинов с злорасдством и часто стал повторять про себя. (*PSS*, IX, 5)

> Summer came – and Vel'čaninov, beyond all expectation, stayed in Petersburg. His trip to the south of Russia fell through, and there was no end to his case in sight. This case – a lawsuit over an estate – was taking a most nasty turn. Three months earlier it had looked quite uncomplicated, all but indisputable, but everything had changed somehow suddenly. "And generally everything has begun to change for the worse!" – Vel'čaninov began repeating this phrase to himself gloatingly and frequently. (Dostoevskij, *Eternal Husband*, 65)

In the wider context, however, there are indications that Vel'čaninov's interventions not only do not promote the progress of the case but actually hinder it. His lawyer complains about his unhelpful intrusions and urges him to go to the country. But Vel'čaninov cannot make up his mind to leave the town.

> Пыль, духота, белые петербургские ночи, раздражающие нервы, — вот чем наслаждался он в Петербурге. (*PSS*, IX, 5)

> The dust, the stuffiness, the white nights of Petersburg, which chafed his nerves – this was what he enjoyed in Petersburg. (*Eternal Husband*, 66)

Puzzled by this unconvincing reasoning, the reader begins to suspect that Vel'čaninov is deliberately delaying his court case in order to have an alibi for his presence in Petersburg. This presence the hero feels is necessary for entirely different motives that he cannot admit to himself.

We discover two levels of consciousness, or two voices, in the hero, a split that is typical of Dostoevskij's psychology. On one level Vel'čaninov is deeply concerned at having encountered someone, on the other he tries to conceal his concern from himself with flimsy explanations (cf. Schmid 1968). The disquieting experience, as various time references in the second chapter suggest, is the unexpected reappearance of Trusockij (from Russian *trus* "coward"), the husband of Vel'čaninov's former and now long-forgotten lover. With his violent reactions, his insults and curses, and by spitting in front of Trusockij, who is allegedly a stranger to him, Vel'čaninov reveals that he has recognized the stranger. But on the other level of consciousness, with his other voice, he represses and fights this realization. He explains the rising unpleasant memories and the bad conscience associated with them as "hypochondria."

> Квартира его была где-то у Большого театра, недавно нанятая им, и тоже не удалась; «всё не удавалось!» Ипохондрия его росла с каждым днем; но к ипохондрии он уже был склонен давно. (*PSS*, IX, 5)

> His apartment, recently rented, was somewhere near the Bol'šoj Theater, and this, too, had not worked out; "nothing works out!" His hypochondria was increasing day by day, but he had long been inclined to hypochondria. (*Eternal Husband*, 66)

Only at the beginning of the third chapter is it reported that Vel'čaninov recognizes the stranger. This apparent contradiction can be resolved in such a way that Vel'čaninov's recognition of Trusockij in the third chapter takes place on a different level of consciousness than the spontaneous recognition on their first encounter, which obviously triggered the hero's "hypochondria." Subconsciously, Vel'čaninov recognized Trusockij immediately, but the act of recognition reaches a fully articulable state of awareness only in Vel'čaninov's confrontation with Trusockij at the beginning of the third chapter.

The narrator intervenes in the battle of voices raging in Vel'čaninov's consciousness by giving textual realization above all to the appeasing voice that explains the deep inner disquiet, the emergence of a guilty conscience with "hypochondria," "illness," or "old age." The first chapters of the narrative are characterized by a grand-scale form of FCN. What sounds like an objective report by the narrator turns out to be a covert rendition of the hero's belittling, placating voice. There are smooth transitions between narrative discourse and the representation of the character's interior speech in direct discourse. What is stated in the mode of FCN is confirmed in direct discourse:

> как-то вдруг всё изменилось. «Да и вообще всё стало изменяться к худшему!»

> everything had changed somehow suddenly. "And generally everything has begun to change for the worse!"

> Квартира [...] тоже не удалась; «всё не удавалось!»

His apartment [...] had not worked out; "nothing works out!"

The narrator must be thought of as a critical instance that adds an ironic intonation to designations and evaluations of the character. This is indicated by the numerous instances of quoted figural designation, where the quotation marks serve as signals of the critical narrator's distance from his hero.

After the introductory paragraph already examined, we come across the following description of Vel'čaninov in the second paragraph:

> Это был человек много и широко поживший, уже далеко не молодой, лет тридцати восьми или даже тридцати девяти, и вся эта «старость» — как он сам выражался — пришла к нему «совсем почти неожиданно» [...]. (PSS, IX, 5)

> This was a man who had lived much and broadly, now far from young, about thirty-eight or even thirty-nine, and all this "old age" – as he himself put it – had come upon him "almost quite unexpectedly" [...]. (*Eternal Husband*, 66)

In this case, the narrator explicitly points to the figural origin of the term "old age." However, such hints are generally missing in what follows.

> [...] этот «здоровенный» был жестоко поражен ипохондрией. (PSS, IX, 6)

> [...] this "hale fellow" was cruelly afflicted with hypochondria. (*Eternal Husband*, 66)

The quoted figural designation "hale fellow" reflects the judgment of the environment, whereas the words "cruelly afflicted," which are not marked as figural, reflect the hero's own evaluation of his condition.

> [Его тщеславие] стало вырождаться в какое-то особого рода тщеславие, которого прежде не было: стало иногда страдать уже совсем от других причин, чем обыкновенно прежде, — от причин неожиданных и совершенно прежде немыслимых, от причин «более высших» [...]. (*PSS*, IX, 6)

> [His vanity] began to degenerate into some peculiar sort of vanity, which had not been there before, he began to suffer sometimes from entirely different causes than usual before – from unexpected causes, entirely unthinkable before, from "more higher" causes than previously [...]. (*Eternal Husband*, 67)

Further on, the mention of "higher reasons," by which Vel'čaninov means the remorse rising in him, appears in quotation marks. Quoted figural designation occurs even within the direct inner speech of Vel'čaninov himself:

> «Итак, всё это только болезнь, всё это "высшее" одна болезнь, и больше ничего!» (*PSS*, IX, 7)

"And so all this is just an illness, all this 'higher' is just an illness and nothing more!" (*Eternal Husband*, 69)

Vel'čaninov uses the language, the terms of the belittling voice, to make fun of his own increasingly distressed conscience.

Characteristic of the ironic storytelling are the phrases that appear in several places in quotation marks, taken from everyday language, such as "God knows why" and "out of the blue." These phrases are used in connection with the unpleasant memories that arise in Vel'čaninov:

> В сущности, это были всё чаще и чаще приходившие ему на память, *«внезапно и бог знает почему»*, иные происшествия из его прошедшей и давно прошедшей жизни, но приходившие каким-то особенным образом. (*PSS*, IX, 7; italics mine – W. Sch.)

> Essentially, it was certain events from his past and long-past life that returned more and more often to his memory, *"suddenly and God knows why,"* but that returned in some special way. (*Eternal Husband*, 69; italics mine – W. Sch.)

Vel'čaninov's memories become more and more depressing. He has no explanation for the action of his mind and invokes the formula of coincidence "out of the blue" («ни с того ни с сего»):

> Вдруг, например, *«ни с того ни с сего»* припомнилась ему забытая — и в высочайшей степени забытая им — фигура добренького одного старичка чиновника, седенького и смешного, оскорбленного им когда-то, давным-давно, публично и безнаказанно и единственно из одного фанфаронства, чтоб не пропал даром один смешной и удачный каламбур [...]. (PSS, IX, 8; italics mine – W. Sch.)

> Suddenly, for instance, *"out of the blue"* he remembered the forgotten – and forgotten by him in the highest degree – figure of one kindly little official, gray-haired and ridiculous, whom he had insulted once, long, long ago, publicly and with impunity and solely from braggadocio: only so as not to lose a funny and fortunate quip [...]. (*Eternal Husband*, 70; italics mine – W. Sch.)

From a certain point in his memories, Vel'čaninov recalls long-forgotten details and is overcome with remorse:

> И когда теперь припомнил *«ни с того ни с сего»* Вельчанинов о том, как старикашка рыдал и закрывался руками как ребенок, то ему вдруг показалось, что как будто он никогда не забывал этого [...]. (*PSS*, IX, 8; italics mine – W. Sch.)

> And now, when Vel'čaninov remembered *"out of the blue"* how the old fellow had wept, covering his face with his hands like a child, it suddenly seemed to him that he had never forgotten it. And, strangely, all this had seemed very funny to him at the time, but now – quite the contrary [...]. (*Eternal Husband*, 71; italics mine – W. Sch.)

In the epilogue of the story, which describes the state of the hero after two years, the struggle of voices in Vel'čaninov is completely at rest. The hero is cured of all hypochondria and attacks of guilty conscience. In the mode of FCN, the narrator presents Vel'čaninov's inner state in his triumphant second voice:

> Не вдаваясь в подробности, ограничимся лишь замечанием, что он сильно переродился, или, лучше сказать, исправился, в эти последние два года. От разных «воспоминаний» и тревог — последствий болезни, — начавших было осаждать его два года назад в Петербурге, во время неудававшегося процесса, — уцелел в нем лишь некоторый потаенный стыд от сознания бывшего малодушия. [...] Причиною всех этих выгодных и здравых перемен к лучшему был, разумеется, выигранный процесс. [...] он смотрел теперь совсем другим человеком в сравнении с тем «хомяком», которого мы описывали за два года назад и с которым уже начинали случаться такие неприличные истории, — смотрел весело, ясно, важно. (*PSS*, IX, 106–107)

> Without going into details, we shall limit ourselves to pointing out that he had regenerated, or, better to say, improved greatly over the two last years. Of the former hypochondria almost no traces remained. All that remained to him of various "memories" and anxieties – the consequences of illness – which had begun to beset him two years ago in Petersburg during the time of his then unsuccessful lawsuit – was some hidden shame from the awareness of his former faintheartedness. [...] The reason for all these beneficial and sensible changes for the better was, naturally, the winning of the lawsuit [...] he now looked like a totally different man compared with that "marmot" we described two years ago, with whom such indecent stories were beginning to happen – he looked cheerful, bright, imposing. (*Eternal Husband*, 221–223)

It is not very plausible that the reason for the change, supposedly for the better, was winning the case. Note the hero's immediate reaction to the happy outcome: Vel'čaninov remained completely indifferent.

In the mode of FCN, the narrator presents Vel'čaninov's second voice, which suppresses the truth. The reader is challenged to reconstruct a version of the actual inner events to set against the figurally colored narrative account.

4.10 Parodying a Character

4.10.1 Fëdor Dostoevskij, *The Double*

Fëdor Dostoevskij's short novel (*povest'*) *The Double* contains a form of FCN that can be regarded as a parody. We can observe parodistic FCN in two very different variants. The first of them determines the beginning of the fourth chapter and extends over three printed pages of the Russian original with a total of 1,223 words. This is the highly rhetorical description of the feast at State Councilor

Berendeev's house, which he gives on the occasion of the birthday of his daughter Klara Olsuf'evna and to which the hero of the novel, Mr. Goljadkin, is not invited. (The following quotation includes only 15% of the description of the feast.)[14]

День, торжественный день рождения Клары Олсуфьевны, единородной дочери статского советника Берендеева, в оно время благодетеля господина Голядкина, — день, ознаменовавшийся блистательным, великолепным званым обедом, таким обедом, какого давно не видали в стенах чиновничьих квартир у Измайловского моста и около, — обедом, который походил более на какой-то пир вальтасаровский, чем на обед, — который отзывался чем-то вавилонским в отношении блеска, роскоши и приличия, с шампанским-клико, с устрицами и плодами Елисеева и Милютиных лавок, со всякими упитанными тельцами и чиновною табелью о рангах, — этот торжественный день, ознаменовавшийся таким торжественным обедом, заключился блистательным балом, семейным, маленьким, родственным балом, но все-таки блистательным в отношении вкуса, образованности и приличия. Конечно, я совершенно согласен, такие балы бывают, но редко. Такие балы, более похожие на семейные радости, чем на балы, могут лишь даваться в таких домах, как например дом статского советника Берендеева. Скажу более: я даже сомневаюсь, чтоб у всех статских советников могли даваться такие балы. О, если бы я был поэт! — разумеется, по крайней мере такой, как Гомер или Пушкин; с меньшим талантом соваться нельзя — я бы непременно изобразил вам яркими красками и широкою кистью, о читатели! весь этот высокоторжественный день. (Dostoevskij, *PSS*, I, 128)

The day, the birthday festivity of Klara Olsuf'evna, the only-begotten daughter of State Councillor Berendeev, once Mr Goljadkin's benefactor – the day, marked by a splendid, magnificent dinner party, a dinner party such as had not been seen for a long time within the walls of officials' apartments by the Izmajlovskij Bridge and roundabouts – a dinner more like some sort of Balshazzar's feast than a dinner – which had something Babylonian in it with regard to splendor, luxury, and decorum, with Clicquot champagne, with oysters and fruit from Eliseevs' and Miljutin's shops, with various fatted calves and the official table of ranks – this festive day, marked by such a festive dinner, concluded with a splendid ball, a small, intimate, family ball, but splendid all the same with regard to taste, good breeding, and decorum. Of course, I agree completely, such balls do take place, but rarely. Such balls, more like family rejoicings than balls, can be given only in such houses as, for example, the house of State Councillor Berendeev. I say more: I even doubt that all state councillors can give such balls. Oh, if I were a poet! – to be sure, at least such a poet as Homer or Puškin; you can't butt into it with less talent – I would unfailingly portray for you with bright colors and sweeping brushstrokes, O readers! all of that highly festive day. (Dostoevskij, *Double*, 30)

---

14 The revised 1866 version of the novel does not differ significantly in this passage from the original 1846 version.

In its alogical traits and involuntary comedy, this solemn-declamatory style is reminiscent of the rhetorical skaz in some of Nikolai Gogol's works (see the minute linguistic analysis of Vinogradov [1922]).

Gogol' is recalled, among other things, by the formula *x, which is more like y than x*, which appears seven times on the three pages of the description of the ball. In the passage quoted, it occurs twice:

> обед[ом], который походил более на какой-то пир вальтасаровский, чем на обед
>
> a dinner more like some sort of Balshazzar's feast than a dinner,
>
> балы, более похожие на семейные радости, чем на балы
>
> balls, more like family rejoicings than balls.

Significantly, the similarity is found in Gogol's "Diary of a Madman" (Zapiski sumasšedšego, 1835; entry for 11 November), a work that inspired Dostoevskij's *The Double* in some other respects as well:

> ее платье, больше похожее на воздух, чем на платье. (Gogol', *Sobr. soč*, III, 190)
>
> *her dress looking more like air than a dress.

There is also another Gogol' formula in the passage quoted from the description of the ball: *x happens, rarely, but it happens*:

> Конечно, я совершенно согласен, такие балы бывают, но редко.
>
> *Of course, I agree completely, such balls do take place, but rarely.

We find the origin of this formula in Gogol's tale "The Nose" (Nos, 1836). At the end of his improbable story about the nose of Collegiate Assessor Kovalëv, which its owner saw walking around Petersburg in the uniform of a state councilor in broad daylight , the narrator assures us in good faith:

> Кто что ни говори, а подобные происшествия бывают на свете, — редко, но бывают. (Gogol', *Sobr. soč*, III, 73)
>
> *Whatever may be said to the contrary, such cases occur – rarely, it is true, but they occur.

In our context, however, the intertextual reference to Gogol' is less relevant than the intratextual relationship of the declamatory narrative skaz to the expressions of the hero.

The use of the rhetorical *figura praeteritionis* in the description of the ball is widespread, with the emphasis on forced omissions and the associated lamenta-

tion about the weakness and dullness of the pen and ignorance of the secrets of
the exalted, solemn style:

> Нечего уже и говорить, что перо мое слабо, вяло п тупо для приличного изображения
> бала, импровизированного необыкновенною любезностью седовласого хозяина. Да
> и как, спрошу я, как могу я, скромный повествователь весьма, впрочем, любопыт-
> ных в своем роле приключений господина Голядкина, — как могу я изобразить эту
> необыкновенную и благопристойную смесь красоты, блеска, приличия, веселости,
> любезной солидности и солидной любезности, резвости, радости, все эти игры и
> смехи всех этих чиновных дам, более похожих на фей, чем на дам, — говоря в выгод-
> ном для них отношении, — с их лилейно-розовыми плечами и личиками, с их воз-
> душными станами, с их резво-игривыми, гомеопатическими, говоря высоким сло-
> гом, ножками? (Dostoevskij, *PSS*, I, 130)

> Needless to say, my pen is too weak, sluggish, and dull for a proper portrayal of the ball
> improvised by the extraordinarily obliging gray-haired host. And how, may I ask, can I, the
> humble narrator of the adventures of Mr Goljadkin – highly curious adventures in their
> way, however – how can I portray this extraordinary and decorous mixture of beauty, bril-
> liance, decency, gaiety, amiable solidity and solid amiability, friskiness, joy, all the games
> and laughter of all these official ladies, more like fairies than ladies – speaking in a sense
> advantageous to them – with their lily-and-rose shoulders and faces, their airy waists, and
> their friskily playful, homeopathic (speaking in high style) little feet? (Dostoevskij, *Double*,
> 33)

With such rhetorical figures and modesty topoi, the ironic narrator parodies
Goljadkin's striving for higher language and entry into higher society. The double
Goljadkin Junior, who moves unscrupulously and extremely successfully in the
spheres of higher society, is nothing more than the embodiment of the wishes of
Goljadkin Senior. The junior is what the senior wants to be but is not able to be.

Mr Goljadkin has two voices, which correspond to his division into the existence to which he aspires and the being he actually is. On the one hand, he expresses himself in stilted, often hyperbolic qualifications of the facts he observes
or thinks about, in a style that must be understood as inadequate for the matter;
but on the other hand, his language is aphatic and defective (cf. Lachmann 1971).
His sentences are full of repetitions and break off again and again, thus becoming
ellipses. He observes his speech and thematizes it, varies and modifies certain
phrases, moving in a circle of tautology. Thematically, his inner speech revolves
around his ego, his autonomy and independence (cf. Schmid 1973, 100–113). The
narrator imitates and parodies this second style immediately after his rhetorically
strained description of the ball, while retaining features of the high style:

> На всё это, как уже выше имел я честь объяснить вам, о читатели! недостает пера
> моего, и потому я молчу. Обратимся лучше к господину Голядкину, единственному,
> истинному герою весьма правильной повести нашей.

Дело в том, что он находится теперь в весьма странном, чтоб не сказать более, положении. Он, господа, тоже здесь, то есть не на бале, но почти что на бале; он, господа, ничего; он хотя и сам по себе, но в эту минуту стоит на дороге не совсем-то прямой; стоит он теперь — даже странно сказать — стоит он теперь в сенях, на черной лестнице квартиры Олсуфья Ивановича. Но это ничего, что он тут стоит; он так себе. Он, господа, стоит в уголку, забившись в местечко хоть не потеплее, но зато потемнее, закрывшись отчасти огромным шкафом и старыми ширмами, между всяким дрязгом, хламом п рухлядью, скрываясь до времени и покамест только наблюдая за ходом общего дела в качестве постороннего зрителя. Он, господа, только наблюдает теперь; он, господа, тоже ведь может войти … почему же не войти? Стоит только шагнуть, и войдет, и весьма ловко войдет. (Dostoevskij, *PSS*, I, 131)

For all this, as I have already had the honor of explaining to you above, O readers! my pen is inadequate, and therefore I keep silent. Better let us turn to Mr Goljadkin, the real, the only hero of our quite truthful story.

The thing is that he now finds himself in a quite strange, to say the least, position. He, ladies and gentlemen, is also here, that is, not at the ball, but almost at the ball; never mind him, ladies and gentlemen; he is his own man, but at this moment he is standing on a path that is not entirely straight; he is now standing – it is even strange to say it – he is now standing in the hallway to the back stairs of Olsufij Ivanovič's apartment. But never mind that he is standing there; he is all right. He is standing, ladies and gentlemen, in a little corner, huddled in a place not so much warm as dark, hidden partly by an enormous wardrobe and some old screens, among all sorts of litter, trash, and junk, hiding for a time and meanwhile only observing the general course of events in the capacity of an external onlooker. He, ladies and gentlemen, is only observing now; he may also go in, ladies and gentlemen … why not go in? He has only to take a step, and he will go in, and go in rather adroitly. (Dostoevskij, *Double*, 34)

At the end of this description in Goljadkin's language, the narrator approaches the consciousness of the hero, and FCN turns into FID.

Dostoevskij's parodistic imitation of the Goljadkin style was also performed outside of *The Double*. In his letter to his brother Mixail about the state of his work on the new short novel, the author falls into the tone of his hero, imitating his second voice and parodying the aphatic tendency resulting from the eternal repetitions, retractions, and terminations:

Яков Петрович Голядкин выдерживает свой характер вполне. Подлец страшный, приступу нет к нему; никак не хочет вперед идти, претендуя, что еще ведь он не готов, а что он теперь покамест сам по себе, что он ничего, ни в одном глазу, а что, пожалуй, если уж на то пошло, то и он тоже может, почему же и нет, отчего же и нет? Он ведь такой, как и все, он только так себе, а то такой, как и все. Что ему! Подлец, страшный подлец! Раньше половины ноября никак не соглашается окончить карьеру. Он уж теперь объяснился с его превосходительством и, пожалуй, (отчего же нет) готов подать в отставку. А меня, своего сочинителя, ставит в крайне негодное положение. (Dostoevskij, *PSS*, XXVIII/1, 113)

Jakov Petrovič Goljadkin maintains his character quite well! He is utterly base, and I posi-
tively can't manage him. He won't move a step, for he always maintains that he isn't ready;
that he's mere nothingness as yet, but could, if it were necessary, show his true character;
then why won't he? And after all, he says, he's no worse than the rest. He's like everybody
else, he's just like himself, or he's like everybody else. Oh, a terribly base fellow! In no case
can he bring his career to a finish before the middle of November. He has already had an
interview with His Excellency, and is not disinclined to take his leave – as, indeed, he well
may. Me, his author, he is putting in a very bad position. (Dostoevskij, *Letters*, 25; tr. rev.)

4.10.2 Thomas Mann, "Tristan"

The narrator of Thomas Mann's "Tristan" uses a sinuous, stilted, precious style
in some passages. This is not his authentic narrator's text, and a trace of ironic
distance is unmistakable in it.

Was Fräulein von Osterloh betrifft, so steht sie mit unermüdlicher Hingabe dem Haushalte
vor. (Mann, VIII, 216)

As for Fräulein von Osterloh, she manages all domestic matters here, and does so with tire-
less devotion. (Mann, *Death in Venice*, 93)

[Frau Klöterjahn] war aus Bremen gebürtig, was übrigens, wenn sie sprach, an gewissen
liebenswürdigen Lautverzerrungen zu erkennen war, und hatte dortselbst vor zwiefacher
Jahresfrist dem Großhändler Klöterjahn ihr Jawort fürs Leben erteilt. (Mann, VIII, 221)

[Frau Klöterjahn] had been born in Bremen, a fact in any case attested by certain charming
little peculiarities of her speech; and there, some two years since, she had consented to
become the wedded wife of Herr Klöterjahn the wholesale merchant. (Mann, *Death in Venice*, 97)

Er [Spinell] war ungesellig und hielt mit keiner Seele Gemeinschaft. Nur zuweilen konnte
eine leutselige, liebevolle und überquellende Stimmung ihn befallen, und das geschah je-
desmal, wenn Herr Spinell in ästhetischen Zustand verfiel, wenn der Anblick von irgend
etwas Schönem, der Zusammenklang zweier Farben, eine Vase von edler Form, das vom
Sonnenuntergang bestrahlte Gebirge ihn zu lauter Bewunderung hinriss. (Mann, VIII, 224)

He [Spinell] was unsociable and kept company with no one. Only occasionally was he
seized by a mood of affability and exuberant friendliness, and this always happened when
his aesthetic sensibilities were aroused – when the sight of something beautiful, a harmo-
nious combination of colors, a vase of noble shape or the light of the setting sun on the
mountains, transported him to articulate expressions of admiration. (Mann, *Death in Venice*, 100)

The narrative style unmistakably bears the signature of Spinell, a writer who expresses himself with stilted and splayed words, and the narrator accentuates this

ironically. The novella is written in a large-scale form of double-voiced FCN. The taste of the "aesthete" Spinell is not unproblematic. The novel he has been working on for years is written "in elaborate typography with every letter looking like a Gothic cathedral" ("mit Buchstaben, von denen ein jeder aussah wie eine gotische Kathedrale"), and the action takes place

> in mondänen Salons, in üppigen Frauengemächern, die voller erlesener Gegenstände waren, voll von Gobelins, uralten Meubles, köstlichem Porzellan, unbezahlbaren Stoffen und künstlerischen Kleinodien aller Art. (Mann, VIII, 224).

> in fashionable drawing-rooms and luxurious boudoirs full of exquisite *objets d'art*, full of Gobelin tapestries, very old furniture, priceless porcelain, rare materials, and artistic treasures of every sort (Mann, *Death in Venice*, 100)

As critically illuminated as Spinell's character may be, he is definitely close to the author in his writerly hardships. When he writes in his fateful letter to Herr Klöterjahn that "words come to [him] in such a rush that they would choke [him] if [he] could not unburden [himself] of them in this letter..." (*Death in Venice*, 123; "ihm die Worte mit einer solchen Heftigkeit zuströmen, dass er an ihnen ersticken würde, dürfte er sich ihrer nicht in dem Brief entlasten," VIII, 250), the narrator corrects him:

> Die Worte schienen ihm durchaus nicht zuzuströmen; für einen, dessen bürgerlicher Beruf das Schreiben ist, kam er jämmerlich langsam von der Stelle, und wer ihn sah, musste zu der Anschauung gelangen, dass ein Schriftsteller ein Mann ist, dem das Schreiben schwerer fällt als anderen Leuten. [...] Andererseits muss man zugeben, dass das, was schließlich zustande kam, den Eindruck der Glätte und Lebhaftigkeit erweckte, wenn es auch inhaltlich einen wunderlichen, fragwürdigen und oft sogar unverständlichen Charakter trug. (VIII, 251)

> Rushing was the very last thing his words seemed to be doing; indeed, for one whose profession and social status it was to be a writer, he was making miserably slow progress, and no one could have watched him without reaching the conclusion that a writer is a man to whom writing comes harder than to anyone else. [...] On the other hand it must be admitted that what he finally produced did give the impression of smooth spontaneity and vigor, notwithstanding its odd and dubious and often scarcely intelligible content. (*Death in Venice*, 123)

Thomas Mann used similar words to characterize his own laborious writing. In a letter from December 1946, he admits: "Writing has become more and more difficult for me than for others, all lightness is a sham there" ("Das Schreiben wurde mir immer schwerer als anderen, alle Leichtigkeit ist da Schein"; letter to Gottfried Kölwel, dated December 10, 1946).

Detlev Spinell, parodied by the narrator in his sinuous style, thus becomes recognizable as an ironic self-portrait of the author.

4.11 Creating an Illusory Reality

4.11.1 Fëdor Dostoevskij, *The Double*

In *The Double*, Dostoevskij uses yet another function of FCN, the creation of an illusory, chimerical perception of reality. In the narrative, it becomes clear only at the end that the double is not a Romantic figure autonomous in his own right or an illusorily reinterpreted colleague of Goljadkin, but rather a pure fantasy product of the hero, a spawn of his desire to be more than he can be. The split in consciousness is not an illness that strikes the hero undeservedly, but arises from his character defect, from the conflict between wanting to be and being able to be. In this context, it is revealing that Dostoevskij, in his revision of the work (1866), deleted early references to Goljadkin's inclination toward paranoid ideas and narcissistic fantasies of salvation and only at the very end of the story set out the hero's mental illness. Up to this point, Goljadkin's delusion is presented as objective reality.

When the hero's inner speech resounds in the presentation, we are dealing with FID; when the hero's conscious activity is involved in the representation of illusory reality, we can speak of free indirect perception. Goljadkin's reaction to his discovery, for example – his realization that the resemblance of the stranger he has invited to himself is not such an unusual business as it first appeared to him – is shaped in FID:

Всё было так натурально! И было от чего сокрушаться, бить такую тревогу! Ну, есть, действительно есть одно щекотливое обстоятельство, — да ведь оно не беда; оно не может замарать человека, амбицию его запятнать п карьеру его загубить, когда не виноват человек, когда сама природа сюда замешалась. К тому же гость просил покровительства, гость плакал, гость судьбу обвинял, казался таким незатейливым, без злобы и хитростей, жалким, ничтожным и, кажется, сам теперь совестился, хотя, может быть, и в другом отношении, странным сходством лица своего с хозяйским лицом. (Dostoevskij, *PSS*, I, 156)

It was all so natural! And what cause was there to lament, to raise such an alarm? Well, there is, there actually is this ticklish circumstance – but there's no harm in that: it can't besmirch a man, if nature itself has mixed into it. Besides, the guest asked for protection, the guest wept, the guest blamed fate, he seemed so artless, without malice or cunning, pathetic, insignificant, and, it seemed, was now ashamed himself, though perhaps in another connection, of the strange likeness of his own and his host's face. (Dostoevskij, *Double*, 68)

The following quotation can be assigned to the pattern of free indirect perception in those parts that are embedded in a strongly figuralized context (single underlining). Goljadkin meets his double for the first time:

> Думать-то и ощущать, впрочем, некогда было: <u>прохожий уже был в двух шагах</u>. Господин Голядкин тотчас, по всегдашнему обыкновению своему, поспешил принять вид совершенно особенный, — вид, ясно выражавший, что он, Голядкин, сам по себе, что он ничего, что дорога для всех довольно широкая и что ведь он, Голядкин, сам никого не затрогивает. Вдруг он остановился, как вкопанный, как будто молнией пораженный, и быстро потом обернулся назад, <u>вслед прохожему, едва только его минувшему</u>, — обернулся с таким видом, как будто что его дернуло сзади, как будто ветер повернул его флюгер. (Dostoevskij, *PSS*, I, 140)

> However, there was no time for thinking and feeling; <u>the passerby was two steps away</u>. Mr Goljadkin hastened at once, as was his wont, to assume a completely special air, an air which showed clearly that he, Goljadkin, was his own man, that he was all right, that the way was wide enough for everybody, and that he, Goljadkin, was not offending anybody. Suddenly he stopped as if rooted, as if struck by lightning, and then quickly turned to look <u>at the man who had just walked past him</u> – turned as if something had pulled him from behind, as if the wind had whirled his weathervane. (Dostoevskij, *Double*, 46–47)

The identification of the doppelgänger by Goljadkin is also made in alternating FID (single underlining) and free indirect perception (double underlining). The unknown passer-by goes ahead of Goljadkin to his house:

> [Господин Голядкин] <u>тотчас же увидал своего интересного спутника, на минуту потерянного.</u> [...] Господин Голядкин почти совсем нагонял его; даже раза два или три подол шинели незнакомца ударил его по носу. Сердце в нем замирало. <u>Таинственный человек остановился прямо против дверей квартиры господина Голядкина, стукнул</u> [...]. Вне себя вбежал в жилище свое герой нашей повести; не снимая шинели и шляпы, прошел он коридорчик и, словно громом пораженный, остановился на пороге своей комнаты. <u>Все предчувствия господина Голядкина сбылись совершенно. Всё, чего опасался он и что предугадывал, совершилось теперь наяву.</u> Дыхание его порвалось, голова закружилась. <u>Незнакомец сидел перед ним, тоже в шинели и в шляпе, на его же постели, слегка улыбаясь, и, прищурясь немного, дружески кивал ему головою.</u> Господин Голядкин хотел закричать, но не мог, — протестовать каким-нибудь образом, но сил не хватило. Волосы встали на голове его дыбом, и он присел без чувств на месте от ужаса. Да и было от чего, впрочем. <u>Господни Голядкин совершенно узнал своего ночного приятеля. Ночной приятель его был не кто иной, как он сам, — сам господин Голядкин, другой господин Голядкин, но совершенно такой же, как и он сам, — одним словом, что называется, двойник его во всех отношениях.</u> (Dostoevskij, *PSS*, I, 143)

> [Mr Goljadkin] <u>at once saw his interesting companion, whom he had lost for a moment.</u> [...] Mr Goljadkin almost caught up with him completely; the skirt of the stranger's overcoat even struck him on the nose once or twice. His heart was sinking. <u>The mysterious man</u>

stopped right in front of the door to Mr Goljadkin's apartment, knocked [...]. Beside himself, the hero of our narrative also ran into his lodgings; not taking off his overcoat and hat, he went down the little corridor and, as if thunderstruck, stopped on the threshold of his room. All of Mr Goljadkin's forebodings had come perfectly true. All that he had feared and anticipated had now become reality. His breath broke off, his head spun. The stranger sat before him, also in his overcoat and hat, on his own bed, smiling slightly, narrowing his eyes a little, nodding to him amicably. Mr Goljadkin wanted to cry out but could not – to protest in some way, but had no strength. His hair stood on end, and he slumped down where he was, insensible from horror. With good reason, however. Mr Goljadkin had perfectly well recognized his night companion. His night companion was none other than himself – Mr Goljadkin himself, another Mr Goljadkin, but perfectly the same as himself – in short, what is known as his double in all respects. (Dostoevskij, *Double*, 50)

Besides FID and free indirect perception, the text of *The Double* is also characterized by the abundant use of FCN. This is basically the device to be found in all those passages in which the doppelgänger is portrayed from an apparently objective point of view as an autonomous being, without figural perception being particularly marked. At these points, the evaluation of the represented objects as autonomous and objectively existent is certainly figural, even if no particular stylistic features of Goljadkin's speech are present.

In the passage quoted above, which we have taken to be free indirect perception, Goljadkin's consciousness is still clearly involved. In the following quotation, however, the doppelgänger is portrayed in an apparently narratorial presentation as an objective appearance of reality:

Прохожий быстро исчезал в снежной метелице. Он тоже шел торопливо, тоже, как и господин Голядкин, был одет и укутан с головы до ног и, так же как и он, дробил и семенил по тротуару Фонтанки частым, мелким шажком, немного с притрусочкой. [...] Вдруг, сквозь завывания ветра и шум непогоды, до слуха его долетел опять шум чьих-то весьма недалеких шагов. Он вздрогнул и открыл глаза. Перед ню, опять, шагах в двадцати от него, чернелся какой-то быстро приближавшийся к нему человечек. Человечек этот спешил, частил, торопился: расстояние быстро уменьшалось. Господин Голядкин уже мог даже совсем разглядеть своего нового запоздалого товарища, — разглядел и вскрикнул от изумления и ужаса; ноги его попкосились. Это был тот самый знакомый ему пешеход, которого он, минут с десять назад, пропустил мимо себя и который вдруг, совсем неожиданно, теперь опять перед ним появился. [...] Незнакомец остановился действительно, так — шагах в десяти от господина Голядкина, и так, что свет близ стоявшего фонаря совершенно падал на всю фигуру его, — остановился, обернулся к господину Голядкину II с нетерпеливо-озабоченным видом ждал, что он скажет. [...] Незнакомец молча и с досадою повернулся и быстро пошел своею дорогою, как будто спеша нагнать потерянные две секунды с господином Голядкиным. (Dostoevskij, *PSS*, I, 141)

The passerby was quickly vanishing into the snowy blizzard. He, too, was walking hastily, he, too, like Mr Goljadkin, was dressed and wrapped from head to foot and, just like him, pattered and minced down the sidewalk of the Fontanka with scurrying little steps, trotting slightly. [...] Suddenly, through the howling of the wind and the noise of the storm, there again came to his ears the noise of someone's footsteps quite close by. He gave a start and opened his eyes. Before him again, some twenty paces away, was the black shape of a little man quickly approaching him. This man was hurrying, flurrying, scurrying; the distance was quickly diminishing. Mr Goljadkin could even thoroughly examine his new late-night comrade – examined him and cried out in astonishment and terror; his legs gave way under him. This was that same walker he knew, the one whom he had let pass by some ten minutes earlier and who now had suddenly, quite unexpectedly, appeared before him again. [...] The stranger actually stopped some ten paces from Mr Goljadkin, and so that the light of a nearby streetlamp fell full on his whole figure – stopped, turned to Mr Goljadkin, and, with an impatiently preoccupied air, waited for what he would say. [...] The stranger said nothing, turned in vexation, and quickly went on his way, as if hurrying to make up the two seconds lost on Mr Goljadkin. (Dostoevskij, *Double*, 47–48)

It must be conceded, however, that the subjectivity of the observing hero is manifested in the gaps between the passages in FCN: in the narrative representation of Goljadkin's consciousness, in direct speech, and in FID. In this respect, the condition that non-current consciousness processes have to be involved for FCN to pertain must be relativized. It remains the case, however, that in the passages in FCN the ontological autonomy of the doppelgänger and the objectivity of his portrayal are affirmed. The wavering of the reader between assuming objectivity of the representation and suspecting figural illusion is precisely the effect to which the text interference lends itself.

The objectivity of the depiction of the doppelgänger seems to increase when Goljadkin Junior threatens to outdo the older Goljadkin in front of his superiors and colleagues:

В кучке молодых окружавших его сослуживцев вдруг, и, словно нарочно, в самую тоскливую минуту для господина Голядкина, появился господин Голядкин-младший, веселый по-всегдашнему, с улыбочкой по-всегдашнему, вертлявый тоже по-всегдашнему, одним словом: шалун, прыгун, лизун, хохотун, легок на язычок и на ножку, как и всегда [...] втершись он в кучку чиновников, тому пожал руку, этого по плечу потрепал, третьего обнял слегка [...] пятого, и, верятно, своего лучшего друга. чмокнул в самые губки [...]. (Dostoevskij, *PSS*, I, 194–195)

In the bunch of young colleagues surrounding him, suddenly and, as if on purpose, at the most anguished moment for him, Mr Goljadkin Jr. appeared, cheerful as always, with a little smile as always, also fidgety as always – in short, a prankster, a leaper, a smoocher, a tittler, light of tongue and foot, as always [...]. He wormed his way into the bunch of clerks, shook hands with one, patted another on the shoulder, embraced a third slightly [...] gave the fifth, probably his best friend, a smacking kiss right on the lips [...]. (Dostoevskij, *Double*, 121).

The illusory nature of this apparently figural perception becomes clear when the narrator mentions that "in short, it all happened exactly as in Mr Goljadkin Sr.'s dream" (*Double* 121; «одним словом, всё происходило точь-в-точь как во сне господина Голядкина старшего», *PSS*, I, 195). But the objectivity of the representation is restored when the shameless behavior of the junior to the senior is described. Before this, the senior had solemnly taken the extended hand of the one he called his mortal enemy:

> Но каково же было изумление, исступление и бешенство, каков же был ужас и стыд господина Голядкина-старшего, когда неприятель и смертельный враг его, неблаго-родный господин Голядкин-младший, заметив ошибку преследуемого, невинного и вероломно обманутого им человека, без всякого стыда, без чувств, без сострадания и совести, вдруг с нестерпимым нахальством и с грубостию вырвал свою руку из руки господина Голядкина-старшего; мало того, — стряхнул свою руку, как будто за-марал ее через то в чем-то совсем нехорошем; мало того, — плюнул на сторону, со-провождая всё это самым оскорбительным жестом; мало того, — вынул платок свой и тут же, самым бесчиннейшим образом, вытер им все пальцы свои, побывавшие на минутку в руке господина Голядкина-старшего. Действуя таким образом, господин Голядкин-младший, по подленькому обыкновению своему, нарочно осматривался кругом, делал так, чтоб все видели его поведение, заглядывал всем в глаза и, оче-видно, старался о внушении всем всего самого неблагоприятного относительно гос-подина Голядкина. (Dostoevskij, *PSS*, I, 195)

> But what was the amazement, the fury, and the rage, what was the horror and shame of Mr Goljadkin Sr., when his adversary, his mortal enemy, the ignoble Mr Goljadkin Jr., noticing the mistake of the innocent and persecuted man whom he had perfidiously deceived, with-out any shame, without feeling, without compassion and conscience, suddenly, with insuf-ferable impudence and rudeness, tore his hand from Mr Goljadkin Sr.'s hand; what's more, he shook his hand as if he had dirtied it in something quite unsavory; what's more, he spat to the side, accompanying it all with a most insulting gesture; what's more, he took out his handkerchief and right there, in the most outrageous fashion, wiped all the fingers that had rested for a moment in Mr Goljadkin Sr.'s hand. Acting in this way, Mr Goljadkin Jr. delib-erately looked around, as was his mean custom, making sure that everyone had seen his conduct, looked everyone in the eye, and obviously tried to instill in everyone all that was most unfavorable regarding Mr Goljadkin. (Dostoevskij, *Double*, 122)

In this passage it becomes clear not only how the delusion of the sick hero is presented as objective reality, but also how the narrator combines highly subjective figural perception with parody of the character's language. The rhetoric of the passage is characterized by the tendency of Goljadkin's discourse toward high style, overblown formulation, repetition, and empty amplification.

4.11.2   Katherine Mansfield, "The Daughters of the Late Colonel"

In Katherine Mansfield's story "The Daughters of the Late Colonel," we observed (see above, section 4.3.2) passages of FCN bound to Josephine and Constantia, the two daughters of the tyrannical father. Weary from searching his room, the two drink hot water and consider sending something from their father's legacy to their brother Benny in Ceylon, but fear that the shipment might be lost. There is no mail there, only runners. They imagine how a messenger would deliver it:

> Both paused to watch a black man in white linen drawers running through the pale fields for dear life, with a large brown-paper parcel in his hands. Josephine's black man was tiny; he scurried along glistening like an ant. But there was something blind and tireless about Constantia's tall, thin fellow, which made him, she decided, a very unpleasant person indeed. ... On the veranda, dressed all in white and wearing a cork helmet, stood Benny. His right hand shook up and down, as father's did when he was impatient. And behind him, not in the least interested, sat Hilda, the unknown sister-in-law. She swung in a cane rocker and flicked over the leaves of the *Tatler*. (Mansfield, *Stories*, 220)

The vision is not announced as such, nor is its reality content signaled. It is presented like a description of real impressions. The figural imagination seems to be narratorially authenticated reality.

4.12 Presenting Dreams as Reality

Another function of FCN that we can list here is closely related to the representation of illusions. These are the dreams of a protagonist, the content of which is presented by the narrator as objective events, without being marked as a construct of the character. The figural element in this form of text interference is the evaluation of the depicted happenings as real, even if the language is not figurally colored.

4.12.1 Aleksandr Puškin, "The Coffinmaker"

Dream worlds experienced as reality are a frequent motif in Romantic literature. We find a sophisticated post-Romantic variant of this device in Aleksandr Puškin's story "The Coffinmaker" (Grobovščik, 1831).

The Moscow coffinmaker Adrijan Proxorov moves with his coffins and belongings from Razguljaj Square to Nikita Street. As he approaches the new house that has captured his imagination for so long, and that he has bought for a considerable sum, he senses to his amazement that his heart is not rejoicing. Several circumstances prevent the expected joy from materializing. In the decrepit little cottage he leaves, everything had been arranged in the strictest order for eighteen years. In contrast to it, in the new house utter "confusion" (*sumatoxa*) prevails.[15] In addition, the old merchant's widow Trjuxina has been on the verge of death for about a year and Proxorov is afraid that her heirs, despite their promise, will not take the trouble to send for him from Razguljaj Square to such a distant place, and will make arrangements with an undertaker nearby. During these gloomy reflections there is knocking at the door and Proxorov is invited to the silver wedding anniversary celebration of his new neighbor, the German shoemaker Schulz. When at the feast, which is attended mainly by the German craftsmen around the Nikita Gate,[16] a toast is made: "To the health of those we work for, *unserer Kundleute*" (Puškin, *Prose*, 89; «За здоровье тех, на которых мы работаем, *unserer Kundleute*!», Puškin, *PSS*, VIII, 91) and Proxorov is prompted: "And how about you? Drink, brother, to the health of your corpses" (*Prose*, 90; «Что же? пей, батюшка, за здоровье своих мертвецов», *PSS*, VIII, 92), all break out in spontaneous laughter. The Germans are obviously exhilarated by the paradox exposed in the coffinmaker's profession. But Proxorov is deeply offended. "In what way is my profession less honorable than others? [...] What are the infidels laughing about?" (*Prose*, 90; «чем ремесло мое нечестнее прочих? [...] чему смеются басурмане», *PSS*, VIII, 92). Coming home drunk and angry, he decides to invite to his housewarming party not the unbelieving neighbors, but those for whom he works, the "Orthodox dead" (*mertvecov pravoslavnyx*). The right faith is for him his faith that the dead are alive, living in the houses he builds for them (Schmid 2013, 245–279). In fact, before going to bed he invites his "benefactors" to come to feast at his house the following evening. After that he goes to sleep and starts snoring immediately.

---

15 The prosaic coffinmaker shares the initials A. P. (in the draft: A. S. P.) with his author and begins the production of his "works" (*proizvedenija*) in 1799, the year of Puškin's birth. Bethea and Davydov (1981, 16–18), who interpret the story as a metapoetic autobiography on the basis of these parallels, argue as follows: Puškin was in the eighteenth year of his work in 1830, and Russian prose was a house "managed according to the strict order of romantic, sentimental, or moralistic canons" (1981, 17).

16 This Moscow quarter was inhabited at this time not by German craftsmen but by Russian noblemen. For the metapoetic dimension of the narrative it is not insignificant that Puškin's real-life bride Natal'ja Gončarova lived on Nikita Street, in the immediate vicinity of Schulz, and that Puškin's wedding was to take place in the Church of the Ascension, which the coffinmaker passes when returning home from the funeral service for the deceased Trjuxina to the nightmare awaiting him.

It is still dark outside when Proxorov is roused from his sleep. Trjuxina has died during the night, and her steward has sent a special emissary on horseback to bring Proxorov the news. The coffinmaker immediately takes a cab, drives to the house of the deceased, and arranges everything necessary for the funeral. He spends the whole day riding back and forth between Razguljaj Square and the Nikita Gate, and settles everything by evening. Approaching his house, he sees people disappearing through the wicket. At first he thinks of thieves or of lovers sneaking in to his daughters. But one of the figures looks familiar to him. And now it seems to him that people are walking around in his rooms. Thinking of demonic activity, he enters and sees with horror that his house is full of dead people who were buried through his efforts.

Despite all the fantasy, however, the world remains as prosaic as before and its social order is completely preserved. Whatever horrifying image the moonlight falling through the window may illuminate, "yellow and blue faces, gaping mouths, murky half-closed eyes and protruding noses..." (*Prose*, 91), Proxorov continues to see the dead as the living. All of them, male and female, surround the coffinmaker with bows and salutations. All are properly dressed, each according to his or her sex, occupation, and rank. However, the plot develops a crisis when a small skeleton approaches Proxorov and reveals himself as retired Sergeant of the Guards Petr Petrovič Kuril'kin, the person to whom the coffinmaker sold his first coffin in 1799, pretending it was oak even though it was pine. Proxorov must hear a serious reproach in his words, which are clearly meant as nothing more than a reminder of his first customer. However, the construction material is hardly irrelevant for the coffinmaker, who thinks of the dead as living in the coffins he builds. Kuril'kin, however, does not seem to have any bad intentions as he tries to pull the coffinmaker into his bony embrace. Proxorov does not share the joy of having met his first customer, but pushes Kuril'kin's skeleton back so that it crumbles into a thousand pieces. A murmur of indignation rises among the corpses; they all stand up in defense of their fellow's honor and harass Proxorov with threats. Their host, deafened by their shouts and almost crushed by the throng, loses his presence of mind, collapses on Kuril'kin's bones, and faints.

When the coffinmaker wakes up, he is – unlike many of his literary predecessors – by no means relieved. With horror he remembers all the events of the previous day. Of course, that for him means not the reality of the day before with the silver wedding anniversary celebrations, but the funeral and the housewarming party, which take a whole day more in his oneiric calendar. This whole day proves to be a dream only when Proxorov's servant corrects his reference to the dead Trjuxina as an illusion of his alcoholic intoxication. There remains not the slightest sign that refers to the reality of the dreamed day. In contrast to many Romantic narratives, which use material evidence to identify a phantasmagorical event,[17] at first thought to be a dream by the awakened hero, as reality, here there is striking proof against the reality of the narrative: Trjuxina has not died. Only now is Proxorov "much gladdened." Only now does he rise from the dead – not only from the death that almost overtook him in the dream, but also from that death-like state that his life with the coffins[18] and his faith in the living dead meant. Easily getting over the business loss that would have saddened him yesterday, he turns to life, to his new neighbors, who have already knocked on his door, and to his daughters, whom he invites – obviously for the first time – to drink tea with him.

The reader believes the reality of the dream no less than the dreamer. There is not the slightest sign of a change in ontology or perspective at the interface between reality and dream. We are dealing here with a special form of FCN. The narrative text takes over the character's text only in the *ontological evaluation* feature, i.e., in the evaluation of the oneiric happenings as real, but remains completely narratorial in style.

However, there is a subtle sign that ominously suggests the reality of the dream. These are the more or less overt correspondences between dream and reality. The unreal premises of the invitation spoken in drunkenness and anger become true in the macabre housewarming party. But there is no direct connection between Proxorov's waking and dreaming consciousness that is accessible to the dreamer. The coffinmaker does not remember anything about his blasphemous words in the dream. Of the numerous correspondences, the following are particularly distinctive:

---

17 Two examples Puškin alludes to: In A. A. Pogorel'skij-Perovskij's narrative "The Poppy-Seed-Cake Woman of the Lafertovo Quarter" (Lafertovskaja makovnica, 1825), the young Maša, waking after the night of horror, believes that she has had a bad dream, until the key hanging from her neck undeniably testifies to the "truth" of all that she has seen. In A. A. Bestužev-Marlinskij's "Evening in a Caucasian Spa in 1824" (Večer na Kavkazskix vodax v 1824 godu, 1830), the hero has to convince himself of the reality of the nighttime events, which he, awakening on the divan, at first thinks to be a dream, by the money won in a bet.

18 Proxorov actually lives in the new house like in a coffin, belonging more to death than to life. He has left the kitchen and the living room to the coffins, which pile up and tower in the corner where the icons hang in a Russian house. Proxorov sits by the window for hours, lonely and drinking his tea. Sunk in gloomy thoughts of his business losses, he obviously does not look once at the street, at the people, or at the house across the street where the friendly shoemaker Schulz lives. When his daughters, who live in the house like prisoners, look out the window at the passers-by, he scolds them for staring clumsily.

1. In the dream, the two wishes that Proxorov nurtured in reality are fulfilled: he is commissioned to bury old Trjuxina, and the dead prove that they live in the houses that the coffinmaker builds for them. The brigadier explains in the name of the assembled guests that the only people who were invited but stayed "at home" (*doma*) are those who have completely fallen to pieces and are no more than bones without skin.
2. In the dream, Proxorov, handling the burial of Trjuxina, repeats the move to his new house, which required four trips from Razguljaj Square to the Nikita Gate.
3. At the housewarming party, only a "poor man," who was recently buried for free, stands humbly in the corner. (We recognize in him the "poor dead man" from Proxorov's lament to the shoemaker about the "dead man who has nothing and takes the coffin for free").
4. Proxorov's dishonesty and his guilty conscience penetrate from reality into the dream, where they appear in numerous motifs.
5. While the fantasy of dark romanticism, for example in Perovskij's *Poppy-Seed-Cake Woman of the Lafertovo Quarter*, still appears as an autonomous reality that cannot be psychologically relativized, the "devil's work" (*d'javol'ščina*) that horrifies and threatens Proxorov comes entirely from his consciousness and also obeys its logic.
6. Kuril'kin and the other guests generated by the dream consciousness can, however, act independently of Proxorov's anticipations and thus prove an autonomy that seems to ironically confirm Proxorov's speaking and thinking about the dead as living in his coffins. They pose a threat to his existence only to the extent that they are able to demonstrate their independent life in the dream.
7. The decisive plot equivalence, however, is formed by the two festivities, the silver wedding celebration and the housewarming party. Both celebrations end with a scandal that leads to peripeteia, to a shocking development that is based on a misunderstanding: at the silver wedding Proxorov imagines himself to be offended and invites the Orthodox dead instead of his German neighbors; at his housewarming party he thinks the dead are accusing him and pushes Kuril'kin's skeleton away so violently that it falls apart completely. We have to understand this last reaction, the killing of one of the dead, as a reversal of the invitation and as Proxorov's turning away from the realm of the skeletons.

The housewarming party and its turbulent events are reported by the impassive narrator with the character's ontological evaluation in a grand style of FCN.

4.12.2   Fëdor Dostoevskij, *Crime and Punishment*

The German literary scholar Horst-Jürgen Gerigk ([2006] 2013, 23–27) has interesting, but also problematic theses about the phenomenon of dream world experienced as reality. He describes the process as the "thought play" ("Gedankenspiel") of a narrated character and, in relation to the author, as "delegated fantasizing" ("delegiertes Phantasieren"): "the author delegates his poetic work to a figure of fiction – and without warning" (Gerigk [2006] 2013, 41). Gerigk's master example, with which he presents the procedure, is Aleksandr Puškin's story "The Snowstorm" (Metel', 1831). The provocative thesis is that everything that according to its presentation by the narrator seems to happen in the snowstorm and afterwards, in reality only takes place in the imagination of the heroine. The dream or thought play realizes the young girl's unconscious desires. Gerigk explains the reality that underlies the girl's fantasy with a psychological construction that is based on "the fear of individuation" ("Scheu vor der Individuation"; [2006] 2013, 23).

The thesis must be rejected in the case of the "Snowstorm" and other works by Puškin, such as *The Queen of Spades*, to which Gerigk applies his concept. There are simply too few textual clues in the works to support such far-reaching constructions, neither in the story depicted nor in the narrator's text. The most important argument is that Gerigk's conclusions, which repeatedly amount to the realization of dreams, contradict intuition, impoverish the narrative works, and deprive them of their multifaceted significance. So it is no accident that Gerigk, an otherwise highly respected scholar, stands alone in the large community of Puškin interpreters with his dream theses.

In a more recent book, available in German (2013) and Russian (2016), Gerigk has applied his concept of "delegated fantasy" to Dostoevskij's novel *Crime and Punishment*. Gerigk declares the entire plot of the novel a dream that begins with Raskol'nikov's – supposed but according to Gerigk not actual – awakening immediately before the crime:

> *Everything that happens after the clock strikes seven is a dream, including the epilogue. Raskol'nikov only wakes up for the first time when the novel is already finished. But the text says nothing about that. The happenings that begin with chapters 1 to 6 of part 1 are thought through to the end by Raskol'nikov in a dream, fantasized to the end – in a restless state between night dream and day dream. (Gerigk 2013, 93).

This is a thesis that, however suggestively it may be presented, is completely unacceptable in its radicality and in the scope of its claim to validity.

For some of the novel's motifs, however, Gerigk's thesis that the author presents the hero's dreams as real is not entirely out of the question. Gerigk notes that the dream the author dreams for Raskol'nikov has a narcissistic character because the dream makes the whole world, i.e., all the important protagonists of the novel, including the examining magistrate, make a pilgrimage up four stairs into Raskol'nikov's narrow attic. This pilgrimage is, indeed, not a very realistic storyline and corresponds to the sujet of a narcissistic dream.

Gerigk postulates two different kinds of reader to explain whether "delegated fantasy" is recognized. The naive reader is not deprived of the pleasure of adhering to the narrative; however, Dostoevskij shows his hand to the thinking reader by sending signals that the narrative is the fruit of the hero's imagination.

Even if one rejects Gerigk's general thesis that a large part of the novel's plot is a mental game, one will accept that Raskol'nikov's dreams play a major role in the novel and that, in addition to the pilgrimage mentioned above, there is a motif in the novel whose reality even the less sophisticated reader can question. It is about the student's speech that Raskol'nikov overhears by chance while visiting a tavern.

Let us reconstruct the situation. In the first chapter of part 1 we see Raskol'nikov visiting the house of the old pawnbroker Alëna Ivanovna in order to carry out a "trial." We do not yet know what this trial is about. With anxious attention, Raskol'nikov inspects the pawnbroker's apartment. As he leaves, he is seized by an outburst of disgust at his plan, which has already occupied him for a month but whose nature we do not yet understand. In the following chapters we learn from Raskol'nikov's fragmentary thoughts that he intends to kill the pawnbroker. He interprets the fact that her half-sister will not be home the next evening, which he learns by chance, as a hint of fate. The narrator points out that Raskol'nikov has lately become superstitious and tends to attach special importance to coincidences, to see in them something special and mysterious, the result of hidden influences and circumstances. As an example the narrator mentions Raskol'nikov's encounter with the student who talked about the murder of "his" pawnbroker. About a month and a half ago, Raskol'nikov made his first visit to the old woman he had learned about by chance, and on his way back he stopped at a rather wretched tavern. At a table next to him sat a student unknown to him, who told his interlocutor about a pawnbroker, Alëna Ivanovna, *his* pawnbroker. Raskol'nikov was deeply moved:

Это уже одно показалось Раскольникову как-то странным: он сейчас оттуда, а тут как раз про нее же. Конечно, случайность, но он вот не может отвязаться теперь от одного весьма необыкновенного впечатления, а тут как раз ему как будто кто-то подслуживается: студент вдруг начинает сообщать товарищу об этой Алёне Ивановне разные подробности. (Dostoevskij, *PSS*, VI, 53)

That in itself seemed somehow strange to Raskol'nikov: he had just left her, and here they were talking about her. By chance, of course; but just then, when he had not rid himself of a certain quite extraordinary impression, it was as if someone had come to his service: the student suddenly began telling his friend various details about this Alëna Ivanovna. (Dostoevskij, *CaP*, 63)

When the student jokingly exclaims that he could murder and rob this wicked old woman without the slightest pang of conscience, Raskol'nikov shrugs: "How strange it was!" («Как это было странно!», 65/54).[19] Raskol'nikov is obviously thinking again of an act of Providence. When the student presents his "arithmetic" of harm and benefit, he presents, without knowing it, Raskol'nikov with a social-utilitarian motive for murder, which harmonizes beautifully with Raskol'nikov's concern for young women forced into prostitution. The student argues:

Я сейчас, конечно, пошутил, но смотри: с одной стороны, глупая, бессмысленная, ничтожная, злая, больная старушонка, никому не нужная и, напротив, всем вредная, которая сама не знает, для чего живет, и которая завтра же сама собой умрет. [...] С другой стороны, молодые, свежие силы, пропадающие даром без поддержки, и это тысячами, и это всюду! Сто, тысячу добрых дел и начинаний, которые можно устроить и поправить на старухины деньги, обреченные в монастырь! Сотни, тысячи, может быть, существований, направленных на дорогу; десятки семейств, спасенных от нищеты, от разложения, от гибели, от разврата, от венерических больниц, - и всё это на ее деньги. [...] как ты думаешь, не загладится ли одно, крошечное преступленьице тысячами добрых дел? За одну жизнь — тысячи жизней, спасенных от гниения и разложения. Одна смерть и сто жизней взамен — да ведь тут арифметика! (Dostoevskij, *PSS*, VI, 54)

I was joking just now, but look: on the one hand you have a stupid, meaningless, worthless, wicked, sick old crone, no good to anyone and, on the contrary, harmful to everyone, who doesn't know herself why she's alive, and who will die on her own tomorrow. [...] On the other hand, you have fresh, young forces that are being wasted for lack of support, and that by the thousands, and that everywhere! A hundred, a thousand good deeds and undertakings that could be arranged and set going by the money that old woman has doomed to the monastery! Hundreds, maybe thousands of lives put right; dozens of families saved from destitution, from decay, from ruin, from depravity, from the venereal hospitals – all on her money. Kill her and take her money, so that afterwards with its help you can devote yourself to the service of all mankind and the common cause: what do you think, wouldn't thousands of good deeds make up for one tiny little crime? For one life, thousands of lives saved

---

19 The first number refers to the translation by Pevear and Volokhonsky, the second to the original in *PSS*, VI.

from decay and corruption. One death for hundreds of lives – it's simple arithmetic! (Dostoevskij, *CaP*, 65)

This abstract speech, in which the student, so he claims, is ultimately only concerned with "justice" and from which he naturally draws no consequences for himself, makes a deep impression on Raskol'nikov. His thoughts on the control of destiny by a mysterious power, on "predestination" and an "indication," are articulated in FID:

> Раскольников был в чрезвычайном волнении. Конечно, всё это были самые обыкновенные и самые частые, не раз уже слышанные им, в других только формах и на другие темы, молодые разговоры и мысли. Но почему именно теперь пришлось ему выслушать именно такой разговор и такие мысли, когда в собственной голове его только что зародились ... *такие же точно мысли*? И почему именно сейчас, как только он вынес зародыш своей мысли от старухи, как раз и попадает он на разговор о старухе? ... Странным всегда казалось ему это совпадение. Этот ничтожный, трактирный разговор имел чрезвычайное на него влияние при дальнейшем развитии дела: как будто действительно было тут какое-то предопределение, указание ... (Dostoevskij, *PSS*, VI, 55; italics in the original)

> Raskol'nikov was greatly agitated. Of course, it was all the most common and ordinary youthful talk and thinking, he had heard it many times before, only in different forms and on different subjects. But why precisely now did he have to hear precisely such talk and thinking, when ... *exactly the same thoughts* had just been conceived in his own head? And why precisely now, as he was coming from the old woman's bearing the germ of this thought, should he chance upon a conversation about the same old woman? ... This coincidence always seemed strange to him. This negligible tavern conversation had an extreme influence on him in the further development of the affair; as though there were indeed some predestination, some indication in it ... (Dostoevskij, *CaP*, 66; italics in the original)

With the student's argument, Dostoevskij parodies the utilitarian mentality of progressively minded circles in Russia.

The social-utilitarian argument of the student regarding the arithmetic of harm and benefit seems to have played a not inconsiderable role in the genesis of the novel. Raskol'nikov has now, so it seems, received from the student a motivation for the murder on which he has already settled. And he mentions this motivation among the various reasons for the murder in his confession to Sonja Marmeladova. Faced with the skepticism of his listener, however, he withdraws the philanthropic motivation again:[20]

---

20 When the novel was being written, philanthropic motivation was initially conceived as the final justification for the crime. In an exposé of the planned short novel for the publisher of the

[...] я захотел, Соня, убить без казуистики, убить для себя, для себя одного! Я лгать не хотел в этом даже себе! Не для того, чтобы матери помочь, я убил — вздор! Не для того я убил, чтобы, получив средства и власть, сделаться благодетелем человечества. Вздор! Я просто убил; для себя убил, для себя одного [...]. (Dostoevskij, *PSS*, VI, 321–322)

[...] I wanted to kill without casuistry, Sonja, to kill for myself, for myself alone! I didn't want to lie about it even to myself! It was not to help my mother that I killed – nonsense! I did not kill so that, having obtained means and power, I could become a benefactor of mankind. Nonsense! I simply killed – killed for myself, for myself alone [...]. (Dostoevskij, *CaP*, 419)

At first sight it might seem that Raskol'nikov has taken over the student's motif of *arithmetic*. But in reality, Raskol'nikov had the motive and the word *arithmetic* in his mind even before the chance encounter with the student. This becomes clear from Raskol'nikov's interior monologue that takes place before he hears the student:

Пусть, пусть даже нет никаких сомнений во всех этих расчетах, будь это всё, что решено в этот месяц, ясно как день, справедливо как арифметика. Господи! Ведь я всё же равно не решусь! (Dostoevskij, *PSS*, VI, 50)

Suppose, suppose there are even no doubts in all those calculations, suppose all that's been decided in this past month is clear as day, true as arithmetic! Lord! Even so, I wouldn't dare! I couldn't endure it, I couldn't ... (Dostoevskij, *CaP*, 59)

The unlikely coincidence that Raskol'nikov, coming from the pawnbroker, encounters in the tavern that he enters for the first time someone who tells about precisely this woman, using Raskol'nikov's motif and word of *arithmetic*, suggests that the student's speech could be a fantasy construct by the hero. This is

---

Russian Herald (Russkij vestnik), Mixail Katkov, the murder was based on "simple arithmetic." The poor student decided to kill and rob the "stupid, deaf, sick and greedy old woman" in order to save himself, his sister, and his mother, to finish his studies, and then to become an "honest man, unwavering in the performance of his duty toward humanity," which of course "makes up for the crime, if one can even call the murder of the old woman, who herself does not know why she is living in the world and who might have died a month later, a crime" (Dostoevskij, *PSS*, VII, 310–311). In a second version, which Dostoevskij began after burning the early drafts (cf. his letter of February 18, 1866; Dostoevskij, *PSS*, XXVIII/2, 150), a philanthropic motif appeared: "I take power, I gain strength [...] not for the sake of evil, but to bring good fortune." Raskol'nikov prays: "Lord! If the attack on the blind, dull old woman who is not needed by anyone is a sin, [...] accuse me. I have sat in stern judgment upon myself, not vanity..." (quoted after Belov 1979, 18). Only in the third phase was the idea of the "extraordinary man" and the separation of mankind into "rulers" and "trembling creatures" formulated.

not contradicted by the fact that Raskol'nikov himself is deeply surprised by the coincidence. Raskol'nikov himself thinks of a hint of fate, of predestination:

> Странным всегда казалось ему это совпадение. Этот ничтожный, трактирный разговор имел чрезвычайное на него влияние при дальнейшем развитии дела: как будто действительно было тут какое-то предопределение, указание … (Dostoevskij, *PSS*, VI, 55)

> This coincidence always seemed strange to him. This negligible tavern conversation had an extreme influence on him in the further development of the affair; as though there were indeed some predestination, some indication in it … (Dostoevskij, *CaP*, 66)

When Raskol'nikov himself introduces a hint of destiny, he is only trying to suppress his own construction of the student's argument, and thus ultimately the fact that the motif of *arithmetic* originated in his own head.

There is a small hint that the student's speech may originate in Raskol'nikov's mind. The first sentence in the above quotation can clearly be assigned to the narrator ("This coincidence always seemed strange to him"), but a character's evaluation is unmistakable in the subsequent designation of the conversation as a "negligible tavern conversation." These words are therefore FCN. But here we are concerned not with this particular point but with the macrostructure that is indicated in it. The whole episode with the student, or at least his speech, is told by the narrator in categories and with evaluations that do not correspond to him, i.e., the narrator, but to the character.

The figural origin of the episode is very indirectly hinted at by the narrator. When Raskol'nikov visits the "wretched tavern" after his first visit to the pawnbroker, when he has taken a seat and ordered tea, the narrator reports: "He fell into deep thought" (*CaP*, 63; «крепко задумался», *PSS*, VI, 53).

> Странная мысль наклевывалась в его голове, как из яйца цыпленок, и очень, очень занимала его. (Dostoevskij, *PSS*, VI, 53)

> A strange idea was hatching in his head, like a chicken from an egg, and occupied him very, very much. (Dostoevskij, *CaP*, 63)

To what else can the figural expression "strange idea" refer than to the following argument of the student? According to this, the chicken hatching from the egg would be the construction of the arithmetic of the harm and benefit of the murder, which comes from Raskol'nikov's mind. Thus, the macrostructure of FCN appears in an essential motif of the novel.

4.13 Triggering a Mood: Shirley Jackson, "The Lottery"

When Shirley Jackson published the short story "The Lottery" in *The New Yorker* in 1948, a storm of outrage erupted. The newspaper and the author were inundated with letters, mostly of shock, anger, confusion. No other story in *New Yorker* history evoked so many letters. Jackson responded in the *San Francisco Chronicle* (July 22, 1948):

> Explaining just what I had hoped the story to say is very difficult. I suppose, I hoped, by setting a particularly brutal ancient rite in the present and in my own village to shock the story's readers with a graphic dramatization of the pointless violence and general inhumanity in their own lives.

The story is about a ritual in which on June 27 each year the three hundred inhabitants of an unnamed village gather in the square. Each villager, regardless of gender and age, draws a lot. All the lots except one are unmarked. Whoever has the misfortune to draw the only marked lot is stoned to death. This year, the lot falls on Tessie Hutchinson, the mother of three young children, among them little Davy. After the drawing of the lots has been completed quickly, the procedure begins:

> The children had stones already. And someone gave little Davy Hutchinson a few pebbles.
> Tessie Hutchinson was in the center of a cleared space by now, and she held her hands out desperately as the villagers moved in on her. "It isn't fair," she said. A stone hit her on the side of the head.
> Old Man Warner was saying, "Come on, come on, everyone." Steve Adams was in the front of the crowd of villagers, with Mrs Graves beside him.
> "It isn't fair, it isn't right," Mrs Hutchinson screamed, and then they were upon her. (Jackson, *Lottery*, 15)

The height of inhumanity is that even little Davy is given "a few pebbles" to throw at his mother.

The story is particularly stirring in that it is told by an absolutely uninvolved, seemingly empathy-less narrator. The details of the inhuman ritual are registered unemotionally in all sobriety:

> There was a great deal of fussing to be done before Mr Summers declared the lottery open. There were the lists to make up – of heads of families, heads of households in each family, members of each household in each family. There was the proper swearing-in of Mr Summers by the postmaster, as the official of the lottery; at one time, some people remembered, there had been a recital of some sort, performed by the official of the lottery, a perfunctory, tuneless chant that had been rattled off duly each year; some people believed that the official of the lottery used to stand just so when he said or sang it, others believed that he was

> supposed to walk among the people, but years and years ago this part of the ritual had been allowed to lapse. [...] Mr Summers was very good at all this; in his clean white shirt and blue jeans, with one hand resting carelessly on the black box, he seemed very proper and important as he talked interminably to Mr Graves and the Martins. (Jackson, *Lottery*, 11)

The narration's sobriety, which is inappropriate to the content, is based on figural coloring, reflecting the mentality of the villagers, who relate to the monstrous as to a self-evident normality.

The denial of the inhumane and the evocation of the normal already characterizes the beginning of the story, which emphatically evokes the mood of the everyday:

> The morning of June 27th was clear and sunny, with the fresh warmth of a full-summer day; the flowers were blossoming profusely and the grass was richly green. The people of the village began to gather in the square, between the post office and the bank, around ten o'clock; in some towns there were so many people that the lottery took two days and had to be started on June 26th, but in this village, where there were only about three hundred people, the whole lottery took less than two hours, so it could begin at ten o'clock in the morning and still be through in time to allow the villagers to get home for noon dinner. (Jackson, *Lottery*, 9–10)

Before the reader learns what the lottery is about, the narrator's reference to the punctual end before noon dinner contributes decisively to the downplaying of what is to happen. This forced trivialization of the horrific is the decisive element in the figural coloring of the narrative report.

4.14 Foreshadowing: William Faulkner, "Elly"

William Faulkner's short story "Elly" (1934) begins with a description of a wooden railing, or more precisely, a description of the actions that the wooden railing seems to take in the gaze of an observer. The selection and evaluation of these actions is clearly figurally colored:

> Bordering the sheer drop of the precipice, the wooden railing looked like a child's toy. It followed the curving road in thread-like embrace, passing the car in a flimsy blur. Then it flicked behind and away like a taut ribbon cut with scissors.

Who is the observer? Whose mindset colors the description? The next sentence names candidates:

> Then they passed the sign, the first sign, Mills City 6 mi and Elly thought, with musing and irrevocable astonishment, "Now we are almost there. It is too late now."

Obviously it is "they" who are the observers we are looking for. The rest of the text then reveals that "they" are the young Ailanthia, known as Elly, and her boyfriend Paul de Montigny, who are going to Mills City to visit her grandmother. It remains unclear why the narrator has chosen the wooden railing as the first motif to be created. The first three sentences of the short story seem to have no particular relation to its further course. Only at the very end of the story is the significance of the railing for the narrative revealed.

The wooden railing appears twice more in the story before the end. Elly tries to convince Paul of her plan to get rid of her strict, hated grandmother, who rejects Paul for racist reasons, in a car accident. He is supposed to drive back with the grandmother and cause an accident at the place with the wooden railing, which would end fatally for the old woman.

> "Listen. You remember that curve with the little white fence, where it is so far down to the bottom? Where if a car went through that little fence..."
> "Yes. What about it?"
> "Listen. You and she will be in the car. She won't know, won't have time to suspect. And that little old fence wouldn't stop anything and they will all say it was an accident. She is old; it wouldn't take much; maybe even the shock and you are young and maybe it won't even... Paul! Paul!"

Paul is outraged and wants to hit Elly. Elly changes her plan when Paul persistently answers negatively to her repeated questions about whether he will marry her. Elly now plans to kill both Paul, who does not want to marry her even though he makes love to her, and the hated grandmother. She decides on a double murder.[21]

On the drive home from Mills City, Elly asks Paul one more time, the last time, why he is not willing to marry her.

> "But why? Why, Paul?" He didn't answer. The car fled on. Now it was the first sign which she had noticed; she thought quietly, 'We must be almost there now. It is the next curve.' She said aloud, speaking across the deafness of the old woman between them: "Why not, Paul? If it's that story about nigger blood, I don't believe it. I don't care."
> 'Yes,' she thought, 'this is the curve.' The road entered the curve, descending.

When Paul also answers this very last question in the negative, his fate is sealed:

---

21 Melvin Bradford (1968) is led by far-fetched socio-philological interpretations of the story that assume the murder of only one person into a detailed argument that amounts to what is clearly stated in the text anyway, namely that Elly intends to kill not only her grandmother but also her lover, who is unwilling to marry her.

"All right," she said. She sat back; at that instant the road seemed to poise and pause before plunging steeply downward beside the precipice; the white fence began to flicker past. As Elly flung the robe aside she saw her grandmother still watching her; as she lunged forward across the old woman's knees they glared eye to eye the haggard and desperate girl and the old woman whose hearing had long since escaped everything and whose sight nothing escaped for a profound instant of despairing ultimatum and implacable refusal. "Then die!" she cried into the old woman's face; "die!" grasping at the wheel as Paul tried to fling her back. But she managed to get her elbow into the wheel spokes with all her weight on it, sprawling across her grandmother's body, holding the wheel hard over as Paul struck her on the mouth with his fist. "Oh," she screamed, "you hit me. You hit me!" When the car struck the railing it flung her free, so that for an instant she lay lightly as an alighting bird upon Paul's chest, her mouth open, her eyes round with shocked surprise. "You hit me!" she wailed. Then she was falling free, alone in a complete and peaceful silence like a vacuum. Paul's face, her grandmother, the car, had disappeared, vanished as though by magic; parallel with her eyes the shattered ends of white railing, the crumbling edge of the precipice where dust whispered and a faint gout of it hung like a toy balloon, rushed mutely skyward.

Of the three occupants of the car, Elly is the only one to survive. Any solidarity with the self-pitying murderer, which dominates in the socio-philological interpretations,[22] becomes absurd when one considers the final situation:

"Something happened," she whimpered. "He hit me. And now they are dead; it's me that's hurt, and nobody will come."

Ella does not kill herself "by implication," as Skei (1979,16) suggests. The text clearly says that she survives, only slightly wounded and full of sniveling self-pity. She has broken glass in her bleeding hand and is whimpering, complaining that the cars are speeding by above the precipice and no one is looking to see if she is hurt.

Notwithstanding any argument with the critical literature on Faulkner's widely underappreciated story, the main question that interests us here is the function of the initial description of the wooden railing in the mode of FCN. Two things are highlighted about the railing: behind it falls a steep precipice, and the railing is fragile like a child's toy.

---

22 The critical attitude of Melvin Bradford (1968) toward the heroine of the story is criticized by Hans Skei (1979). However, Skei's insensitive and inattentive reading of the story becomes clear from the following socio-philological mainstream generalization: "Faulkner has apparently taken a special interest in this kind of extreme juxtaposition of the young, burning desire and the society which cherishes and values virginity and innocence – not the least as a means of gaining and maintaining control over the upcoming generation" (Skei 1979, 15).

The first paragraph of the story, with its description of the wooden railing, can be interpreted as the narrator putting himself into Elly, who is looking for a suitable place for the planned accident and murder on the car ride to Mills City and whose gaze is caught by the wooden railing looking like a child's toy. It is not Elly who is currently perceiving the railing; the narrator is reproducing a vision that Elly has already saved in her revengeful mind. This reproduction of an internalized figural view is foreshadowing on the part of the narrator that the reader cannot understand at this point in the text and will only understand after the final catastrophe.

Elly's thinking, with musing and irrevocable astonishment, on the way to Mills City – "Now we are almost there. It is too late now" – could be interpreted as meaning that she intended to cause a fatal accident for Paul at a dangerous spot she already knew about, and that she now realizes that they have already gone too far for that. The motive for the murder plan is Paul's persistent refusal to marry her. Elly misses the moment for a possible attack on Paul on the drive to Mills City, probably because she wants to give her lover one last chance. When she asks him, on this drive to Mills City, after having passed the fateful spot, whether he will marry her, it is not coincidental that she thinks of how a man was watching them when they came out of the woods, with Paul carrying the motor robe, and got back into the car.

On the drive to Mills City, she remembers the rendezvous in the woods that took place just before "with a certain detachment and inattentiveness." This is because something "dreadful" that she had completely forgotten has come back to mind: the grandmother with her inescapable cold eyes waiting in Mills City. And at that moment she plans to kill the grandmother, too. And the connection of the two murders happens because Paul does not stop rejecting her marriage plans.

In this way, the wooden railing perceived through the heroine's eyes and deeply imprinted in her consciousness receives a convincing motivation. But the reader can only see this in hindsight.

5 Limiting and Uncertain Cases

5.1 Figural Coloring without a Figure

5.1.1 Katherine Mansfield, "At the Bay"

In his *Theory of Narrative* (1979, 225; tr. 1984, 172), Franz Stanzel cites Katherine Mansfield's short story "At the Bay," among others, as a conspicuous example of what he calls "reflectorization of the teller-character." If we look at the work more closely, we find that here we have a special case of FCN: figural coloring without a figure, or – in Stanzel's terms – "reflectorization" without a reflector.

> Very early morning. The sun was not yet risen, and the whole of Crescent Bay was hidden under a white sea-mist. The big bush-covered hills at the back were smothered. *You could not see* where they ended and the paddocks and bungalows began. [...] Drenched were the cold fuchsias, round pearls of dew lay on the flat nasturtium leaves. *It looked as though* the sea had beaten up softly in the darkness, *as though* one immense wave had come rippling, rippling – how far? *Perhaps if you had waked* up in the middle of the night you might have seen a big fish flicking in at the window and gone again. ... [...] *There ahead* was stretched the sandy road with shallow puddles; the same soaking bushes showed on either side and the same shadowy palings. Then *something immense came into view*; an *enormous shock-haired giant* with his arms stretched out. It was the big gum-tree outside Mrs. Stubbs' shop, and as they [the shepherd and his flock] passed by there was *a strong whiff of eucalyptus*. And *now* big spots of light gleamed in the mist. The shepherd stopped whistling; he rubbed his red nose and wet beard on his wet sleeve and, screwing up his eyes, glanced in the direction of the sea. The sun was rising. It was *marvelous* how quickly the mist thinned, sped away, dissolved from the shallow plain, rolled up from the bush and was gone *as if in a hurry to escape*; big twists and curls jostled and shouldered each other as the silvery beams broadened. The far-away sky – a bright, pure blue – was reflected in the puddles, and the drops, swimming along the telegraph poles, flashed into points of light. *Now* the leaping, glittering sea was so bright *it made one's eyes ache to look at it*. The shepherd drew a pipe, the bowl as small as an acorn, out of his breast pocket, fumbled for a chunk of speckled tobacco, pared off a few shavings and stuffed the bowl. *He was a grave, fine-looking old man.* As he lit up and the blue smoke wreathed his head, the dog, watching, looked proud of him. (Mansfield, *Stories*, 165–166; italics mine – W. Sch.)

The text, which begins in an entirely narratorial, objective manner, is increasingly interspersed with signs of a perceiving and evaluating instance (italicized in the quotation). Who is that instance? The only character on stage is the shepherd. But he is not presented as perceiving and evaluating, and is rather an object than a subject of perception. In the text, there is also no recognizable collective to which the signs of subjectivity could be sensibly attributed. We have to imagine a potential reflector that is not represented by the narrator but projected. The

https://doi.org/10.1515/9783110763102-006

narrator represents what this imaginary reflector, with his selection and evaluation of the world by the bay, could perceive.[1]

5.1.2 Virginia Woolf, *The Waves*

Ann Banfield's very abstract "empty deictic center," which she proposed with reference to Virginia Woolf's *The Waves* (Banfield 1987), offers no salvation, no solution to the problem of figural coloring without a figure.

Let us look at the beginning of *The Waves*:

> The sun had not yet risen. The sea was indistinguishable from the sky, except that the sea was slightly creased as if a cloth had wrinkles in it. Gradually as the sky whitened a dark line lay on the horizon dividing the sea from the sky and the grey cloth became barred with thick strokes moving, one after another, beneath the surface, following each other, pursuing each other, perpetually. (Woolf, *The Waves*, 3)

The first thing that catches the eye, or rather the ear, is the non-standard character of this prose. We have here a type of prose that can be called *poetic* or *ornamental prose* (Schmid 2014d). This prose is characterized by, among other features, poetic devices such as rhythmization and sound repetition, i.e., phonic equivalence. Both procedures are well represented in the quotation. This prose text reads like poetry. The layer of poetic procedures is not integrated into the perspective structure of the text but is located on the substrate of the narration as its own layer. As a rule, poetization does not participate in the perspectival treatment of the text and does not exercise the expressive function (in Bühler's sense) that is usual for narrative texts. This means that poetic procedures are usually not indicative of the narrator but go back to the author. In relatively rare cases, the poetic structuring is to be attached to the narrator – if he is depicted as a poet, for example.

In Russia, ornamental prose dominates the narrative literature of modernism (1880–1910) and the avant-garde (1910–1940). In contrast to realist prose, consistently characterized by perspectivization, psychological motivation, and stylistic diversification, Russian ornamental prose unfolds the archaic, mythic-unconscious imagination. In texts of Russian ornamental prose from Andrej Belyj to Evgenij Zamjatin, the relevance of differing points of view is abolished, the psy-

---

1 A similar conclusion has already been drawn by Monika Fludernik (1996, 148–150), who, subjecting this passage to a minute analysis, speaks of "an evocation of story-internal consciousness."

chological motivation is, at best, weakened, and the style is homogenized in a poetic manner.

In German literature, where ornamental prose plays a lesser role, the high point of this type of narrative, characterized in German philology as "lyrical," "poetical," or "rhythmical," coincides with the age of symbolism, a time when the continuum of the genre system was dominated by its poetic pole. An example of German high ornamentalism is Rainer Maria Rilke's *The Lay of Love and Death of Cornet Christopher Rilke* (Die Weise von Liebe und Tod des Cornets Christoph Rilke, 1906):

> Ein Tag durch den Tross. Flüche, Farben, Lachen –: davon blendet das Land. Kommen bunte Buben gelaufen. Raufen und Rufen. Kommen Dirnen mit purpurnen Hüten im fluten-den Haar. Winken. Kommen Knechte, schwarzeisern wie wandernde Nacht. Packen die Dir-nen heiß, dass ihnen die Kleider zerreißen. Drücken sie an den Trommelrand. Und von der wilderen Gegenwehr hastiger Hände werden die Trommeln wach, wie im Traum poltern sie, poltern –.
>
> [...] Rast! Gast sein einmal. Nicht immer selbst seine Wünsche bewirten mit kärglicher Kost. Nicht immer feindlich nach allem fassen; einmal sich alles geschehen lassen und wis-sen: was geschieht, ist gut. (Rilke, *Weise*, 144–47)

The following translation reproduces the ornamental element well:

> A day full of baggage and curses, colors and laughter that drown the whole country. Bois-terous boys come running, brawling and bawling. Wenches come winking with purple hats in their flowing hair. Soldiers come iron-dark as the wandering night, seizing the women with lust and tearing their clothes, pressing them hard against the edge of the drums. And the drums leap to life awakened by violent resistance of passionate hands, and as in a dream they rattle and roll –.
>
> [...] Rest! For once to be a guest. No longer to feed on meager fare. No longer to snatch greedily. For once to let everything come and know: all that happens is good. (Rilke, *Lay*, 43–55)

This text, in "verse-infected prose," as Rilke later called it somewhat contemptu-ously, is an extreme case of the poetic stylization of a narrative text, with its dense instrumentation of sounds in which rhythmization, alliteration, assonance, and paronomasia play a large part. In the Rilke text, we can observe the aperspectiv-ism of ornamental prose and the weakening of the expressive function. The as-cription of text segments to narratorial or figural perspective is barely discernible. This is because the opposition between the narrator's text and the characters' text is, if present at all, only weakly marked, since overdetermining ornamentaliza-tion largely eliminates the ideological and linguistic expressive function of nar-rating and speaking subjects. The narrative text directs the reader's attention toward the authorial poetic principle, which is not the expression of realistic, objective thinking, but rather evokes a poetic, mythical mode of thought.

In anglophone literature, a high-water mark for the poetization of narrative prose is Woolf's *The Waves*. We have already drawn attention to the phonic poetization of the beginning. Although the six people who appear as characters each have their own nature and worldview, perspectivity is limited in that the characters' ways of speaking are not individualized but fit into the highly stylized language of ornamental prose. The linguistic perspective of the characters' discourse is not developed.

In *The Waves*, we find the mythical thinking that was mentioned as a hallmark of ornamental prose. In the next section of the text, the children's game of hide and seek turns into a metamorphosis, the basic form of mythical thinking. Louis turns into a flower stalk:

> "Now they have all gone," said Louis. "I am alone. They have gone into the house for breakfast, and I am left standing by the wall among the flowers. It is very early, before lessons. Flower after flower is specked on the depths of green. The petals are harlequins. Stalks rise from the black hollows beneath. The flowers swim like fish made of light upon the dark, green waters. I hold a stalk in my hand. I am the stalk. My roots go down to the depths of the world, through earth dry with brick, and damp earth, through veins of lead and silver. I am all fibre. All tremors shake me, and the weight of the earth is pressed to my ribs. Up here my eyes are green leaves, unseeing. I am a boy in grey flannels with a belt fastened by a brass snake up here. Down there my eyes are the lidless eyes of a stone figure in a desert by the Nile. I see women passing with red pitchers to the river; I see camels swaying and men in turbans. I hear tramplings, tremblings, stirrings round me.
>
> "Up here Bernard, Neville, Jinny and Susan (but not Rhoda) skim the flower-beds with their nets. They skim the butterflies from the nodding tops of the flowers. They brush the surface of the world. Their nets are full of fluttering wings. "Louis! Louis! Louis!" they shout. But they cannot see me. I am on the other side of the hedge. There are only little eyeholes among the leaves. O Lord, let them pass. Lord, let them lay their butterflies on a pocket-handkerchief on the gravel. Let them count out their tortoise-shells, their red admirals and cabbage whites. But let me be unseen. I am green as a yew tree in the shade of the hedge. My hair is made of leaves. I am rooted to the middle of the earth. My body is a stalk. I press the stalk. A drop oozes from the hole at the mouth and slowly, thickly, grows larger and larger. Now something pink passes the eyehole. Now an eye-beam is slid through the chink. Its beam strikes me. I am a boy in a grey flannel suit. She has found me. I am struck on the nape of the neck. She has kissed me. All is shattered." (Woolf, *Waves*, 6–7)

Returning to the beginning of *The Waves*, it cannot be overlooked that in the second paragraph, a group of persons is mentioned: "As they neared the shore." And it is now obvious that the unmistakable signs of subjective perception, which the beginning contains, are to be traced back to these perceivers. As in the case of

Čexov's "Rothschild's Violin," which we discussed above (section 1.2), a perception is shaped before a possible perceiving entity enters the stage of the story.

If the protagonists do not qualify as the sought-after carriers of perception, the perspective has to be determined as that of a reflector projected by the narrator, similar to the case of Katherine Mansfield's "At the Bay."

5.1.3 Guzel' Jaxina, *My Children*

A not infrequent limiting case of FCN is the description of a landscape to open a novel. Such descriptions, which set the scene for the novel's action, are very often narratorial in form. This is the case, for example, in Theodor Fontane's novel *Der Stechlin* (1898), where the landscape of the county of Ruppin is presented in an almost geographical description. But it is also not uncommon for the exposition of the place of the action to take place with a sprinkling of figural selection and evaluation. We have such a case in the novel *My Children* (Deti moi, 2019) by the Russian-Tatar author Guzel' Jaxina.[2]

> Волга разделяла мир надвое. Левый берег был низкий и желтый, стелился плохо, переходил в степь, из-за которой каждое утро вставало солнце. Земля здесь была горька на вкус и изрыта сусликами, травы — густы и высоки, а деревья — приземисты и редки. Убегали за горизонт поля и бахчи, пестрые, как башкирское одеяло. Вдоль кромки воды лепились деревни. Из степи веяло горячим и пряным — туркменской пустыней и соленым Каспием.
>
> Какова была земля другого берега, не знал никто. Правая сторона громоздилась над рекой могучими горами и падала в воду отвесно, как срезанная ножом. По срезу, меж камней, струился песок, но горы не оседали, а с каждым годом становились круче и крепче: летом — иссиня — зеленые от покрывающего их леса, зимой — белые. За эти горы садилось солнце. Где-то там, за горами, лежали еще леса, прохладные остролистые и дремучие хвойные, и большие русские города с белокаменными кремлями, и болота, и прозрачно-голубые озера ледяной воды. С правого берега вечно тянуло холодом - из-за гор дышало далекое Северное море. Кое-кто называл его по старой памяти Великим Немецким. (Jaxina, *Deti*, 13)

---

2 Guzel' Jaxina was born in Kazan' in 1977. She spoke Tatar at home and learned Russian only after she started going to daycare. In 1999, she moved to Moscow. In 2015, she graduated from the Moscow School of Film with a degree in screenwriting. Her first novel, *Zuleikha* (Zulejxa otkryvaet glaza, 2015; English translation 2019; literal translation of the original title: *Zulejxa Opens Her Eyes*), which is set against the background of Stalin's dekulakization and was initially rejected by several publishers, has received numerous literary awards and has been translated into more than thirty languages.

*The Volga divided the world in two. The left bank was low and yellow, spread out unevenly and passing into the steppe, from behind which the sun rose every morning. The land here was bitter to the taste and riddled with gophers, the grass was dense and tall, and the trees were stumpy and sparse. Fields and gourds, as colorful as a Bashkir blanket, ran beyond the horizon. There were villages along the edge of the water. There was a smell of hot and spicy Turkmen desert and salty Caspian Sea from the steppe.

Nobody knew what the land on the other shore was like. The right side of the river loomed over the river like a mighty mountain and fell steeply into the water, like a knife cut off. But the mountains did not sink, they grew steeper and stronger with every year: blue-green in summer from the forest that covered them, and white in winter. The sun was setting behind these mountains. Somewhere over there, beyond the mountains, lay still forests, cool, sharp-leaved, and dense conifers, and large Russian cities with white-stone kremlins, and swamps, and clear-blue lakes of icy water. On the right bank there was a perpetual chill: the faraway North Sea was breathing from behind the mountains. Some people called it, in old memory, the Great German Sea.

The landscape is clearly described from the point of view of its inhabitants. The division of the world into the left and right banks of the river, the view of the fields ("as colorful as a Bashkir blanket"), and the specific aromas ("a smell of hot and spicy Turkmen desert and salty Caspian Sea from the steppe") give the description local specificity. When the distant North Sea seems to breathe down from the mountains, it is perceived from an axiological point of view, with the nostalgia of the Volga German population. The collective of Germans settled on the Volga emerges as reflector of the description. They will be the hero of *My Children*, whose title refers to Catherine the Great's designation of the Volga Germans

5.2 Character or Narrator?

In the case of the works by Mansfield and Woolf that we have considered, the most plausible explanation of the perspective is that the narrator projects a reflector that is not represented in the narrated world. Stanzel may have had this possibility in mind when he spoke – not entirely clearly – of "reflectorization of the teller-character." In neither Mansfield nor Woolf can the narrator be seen without further ado as the subject of perception, for the text contains too many signs of the perception of an instance that we find ourselves locating on the level of the narrated characters.

The momentum of a character's subjective perception becomes clear in Mansfield's "At the Bay":

> Very early morning. The sun was *not yet* risen, and the *whole* of Crescent Bay *was hidden* under a white sea-mist. The big bush-covered hills at the back were smothered. *You could not see* where they ended and the paddocks and bungalows began.

The Waves begins very similarly, in a mode whose subjectivity is related to a reflector:

> The sun had *not yet* risen. The sea was *indistinguishable* from the sky, except that the sea was slightly creased *as if a cloth had wrinkles in it.*

The solution advocated here – a reflector imagined by the narrator – is admittedly not the only one. We could also see the narrator himself in the role of the reflector – a subjectively selecting narrator who expresses himself through his choices.

In the following section, we will consider a narrative beginning in which determining the subject of perception (narrator or character) is difficult.

5.2.1 Johann Wolfgang Goethe, *Novella*

Let us have a look at the novella that Goethe produced in 1828 as a prose reworking of the originally planned verse epic *The Hunt* (Die Jagd) and titled with the genre designation *Novella* (Novelle):

> Ein dichter Herbstnebel verhüllte noch in der Frühe die weiten Räume des fürstlichen Schlosshofes, als man schon mehr oder weniger durch den sich lichtenden Schleier die ganze Jägerei zu Pferde und zu Fuß durcheinander bewegt sah.
>
> Die eiligen Beschäftigungen der Nächsten ließen sich erkennen: man verlängerte, man verkürzte die Steigbügel, man reichte sich Büchse und Patrontäschchen, man schob die Dachsranzen zurecht, indes die Hunde ungeduldig am Riemen den Zurückhaltenden mit fortzuschleppen drohten.
>
> Auch hie und da gebärdete ein Pferd sich mutiger, von feuriger Natur getrieben oder von dem Sporn des Reiters angeregt, der selbst hier in der Halbhelle eine gewisse Eitelkeit, sich zu zeigen, nicht verleugnen konnte.
>
> Alle jedoch warteten auf den Fürsten, der, von seiner jungen Gemahlin Abschied nehmend, allzulange zauderte. (Goethe, *Novelle*, 141)

> The thick fog of an early autumnal morning obscured the extensive courts which surrounded the prince's castle; but through the mists, which gradually dispersed, a stranger might observe a cavalcade of horse and foot, already engaged in their early preparations for the field. The active employments of the domestics were already discernible. These latter were engaged in lengthening and shortening stirrup-leathers, preparing the rifles and ammunition, and arranging the game-bags whilst the dogs, impatient of restraint, threatened to break away from the slips by which they were held. Then the horses became restive, from their own high mettle, or excited by the spur of the rider, who could not resist the tempta-

tion to make a vain display of his prowess, even in the obscurity by which he was surrounded. The cavalcade awaited the arrival of the prince, who was delayed too long while
taking leave of his young wife. (Goethe, *Novella*)

That the narrator is the reflector is suggested by the narrative style, the literary
character of the lexis and syntax. That a character is the reflector is suggested by
the trace in the last sentence of the presence and evaluation of the situation by a
figural participant: "the prince, who was delayed *too long* while taking leave of
his young wife."

However, the "too long" can again be interpreted in two ways: first, as a
transposition of the narrator, who until now has been narrating from his own
point of view, into a participating observer; or, second, as a signal that the preceding description is to be regarded as a rendition of a figure's observations.

But can the inconspicuous "too long" change the perception of the entire
paragraph before it? We have to leave this question open or – better – leave the
answer to the reader.

Whatever we decide in such cases – for or against the narrator as subject of
perception – the decision is always going to be accompanied by doubts. Such
uncertainty, however, is the norm when making judgments about who is speaking, thinking, and perceiving in FCN.

5.2.2 Otto Ludwig, *Between Sky and Earth*

The question of the subject of the figural coloring also arises in this novel by Otto
Ludwig. Let us first consider the beginning of the novel:

Das Gärtchen liegt zwischen dem Wohnhause und dem Schieferschuppen; wer von dem
einen zum andern geht, muss daran vorbei. Vom Wohnhaus zum Schuppen gehend hat
man's zur linken Seite; zur rechten sieht man dann ein Stück Hofraum mit Holzremise und
Stallung, vom Nachbarhause durch einen Lattenzaun getrennt. Das Wohnhaus öffnet jeden
Morgen zweimal sechs grün angestrichene Fensterladen nach einer der lebhaftesten Stra-
ßen der Stadt, der Schuppen ein großes graues Tor nach einer Nebengasse; die Rosen an
den baumartig hochgezogenen Büschen des Gärtchens können in das Gässchen hinaus-
schauen, das den Vermittler macht zwischen den beiden größern Schwestern. Jenseits des
Gässchens steht ein hohes Haus, das in vornehmer Abgeschlossenheit das enge keines Bli-
ckes würdigt. Es hat nur für das Treiben der Hauptstraße offene Augen und sieht man die
geschlossenen nach dem Gässchen zu genauer an, so findet man bald die Ursache ihres
ewigen Schlafes; sie sind nur Scheinwerk, nur auf die äußere Wand gemalt. (Ludwig, *Romane*, 331)

*The garden lies between the dwelling house and the slate shed; you have to go past it if
you cross from one to the other. Going from the dwelling house to the shed, it is on your left;

to the right, you can see a piece of courtyard with a wooden shed and stables, separated from the neighboring house by a picket fence. Every morning, the house opens twice six green-painted shutters onto one of the liveliest streets in the town, the shed a large gray gate onto a side street; the roses on the tree-like bushes of the garden look out into the alley that acts as an intermediary between its two bigger sisters. On the other side of the alley there stands a tall house, which in noble seclusion does not dignify the narrow one with a glance. It has eyes open only for the hustle and bustle of the main street, and if you look more closely at the ones closed to the alley, you will soon find the cause of their eternal sleep; they are only sham work, painted only on the outer wall.

The mention of the previously unintroduced garden as the first object of the narrative, almost the first agent of the narrative, and the drawing of the describing agent into the situation by means of deictic indications of place ("on your left," "to the right"), point to a reflector familiar with the overall situation. But there is not a single character in the whole novel who could play this role. Therefore, the narrator is the only instance left that can take on this position and be familiar with the habits of the inhabitants. Consider in this context the remark "Every morning, the house opens twice six green-painted shutters onto one of the liveliest streets in the town." This observation, and the corresponding remark, would hardly have been made by one of the acting characters.

The first paragraph of the novel is full of anthropomorphizing metamorphoses: "the house *opens* ... shutters," "the roses ... *look* out into the alley that acts as an intermediary between its two bigger sisters," "a tall house ... that does not *dignify* the narrow one with a *glance* ... has *eyes open* only for the hustle and bustle of the main street," one "will soon find the cause of ... eternal *sleep*" of the *closed eyes*. Who else but the narrator should be responsible for these metaphors?

There is also another decision to be made. The metaphors may also have a symbolic meaning: the anthropomorphically described houses may express the mentality of their inhabitants, as when the pedantically laid out, "anxiously circled" garden later becomes recognizable as an image of Apollonius's way of thinking (cf. Schmid 2017, 213–232). The origin of the symbolic intentions may be none other than the narrator (and behind him the author).

This example allows us to conclude that in certain cases a coloration that seems figural cannot be linked back to any other entity than the narrator. There is no need for the postulate of an "empty deictic center." However, the point of view effective in Ludwig's novel is clearly also axiologically concretized.

5.3 FCN Subsumed by FID: Thomas Mann, "A Weary Hour"

In the example of Wellershoff's narrative "The Normal Life," we saw how FCN can be embedded in FID. In that case, the alternation between the narrator and the character as the instance responsible for the propositional content of the statements was relatively clear. In many other cases, the fluctuation between the two instances is so imperceptible that entire passages of FCN can seem like FID and are indeed taken by many critics to be exactly that.

The fluctuation between FCN and FID can be observed well in Thomas Mann's short narrative "A Weary Hour" (Schwere Stunde, 1905). This novelistic study of Friedrich Schiller's creative struggle in his work on *Wallenstein* presents an extended interior monologue in the mode of FID. At some points, the character's interior monologue is interrupted by the narrator's discourse, which is infected by or reproduces expressions and evaluations from the character's text. But these narratorial parts are so densely embedded in the interior monologue that they are, as it were, subsumed by it and do not appear as forms of presentation in their own right. In the following examples, what I consider FCN is underlined, and what appears to be FID is italicized.

> Das war ein besonderer und unheimlicher Schnupfen, der ihn fast nie völlig verließ. Seine Augenlieder waren entflammt und die Ränder seiner Nasenlöcher ganz wund davon, und in Kopf und Gliedern lag dieser Schnupfen ihm wie eine schwere, schmerzliche Trunkenheit. *Oder war an all der Schlaffheit und Schwere das leidige Zimmergewahrsam schuld, das der Arzt nun schon wieder seit Wochen über ihn verhängt hielt?* (Mann, VIII, 371)

> It was a particular, a sinister cold, which scarcely ever quite disappeared. It inflamed his eyelids and made the flanges of his nose all raw; in his head and limbs it lay like a heavy, sombre intoxication. *Or was this cursed confinement to his room, to which the doctor had weeks ago condemned him, to blame for all his languor and flabbiness?* (Mann, *Stories*, 290)[3]

> Er stand am Ofen und blickte mit einsam raschem und schmerzlich angestrengtem Blinzeln hinüber zu dem Werk, von dem er geflohen war, dieser Last, diesem Druck, dieser Gewissensqual, diesem Meer, das auszutrinken, dieser furchtbaren Aufgabe, die sein Stolz und sein Elend, sein Himmel und seine Verdammnis war. *Es schleppte sich, es stockte, es stand – schon wieder, schon wieder! Das Wetter war schuld und sein Katarrh und seine Müdigkeit. Oder das Werk? Die Arbeit selbst? Die eine unglückselige und der Verzweiflung geweihte Empfängnis war?* (Mann, VIII, 372)

---

3 Lowe-Porter's translations of Thomas Mann, which were crucial for the whole reception of Mann in the anglophone world, are characterized by such a great distance from the original that the subtle difference between FCN and FID might not come to light at all.

He stood by the stove and blinked repeatedly, straining his eyes across at the work <u>from which he had just fled; that load, that load, that weight, that gnawing conscience, that sea which to drink up, that frightful task which to perform, was all his pride and all his misery, at once his heaven and his hell.</u> *It dragged, it stuck, it would not budge – and now again ...! It must be the weather, or his catarrh, or his fatigue. Or was it the work? Was the thing itself an unfortunate conception, doomed from its beginning to despair?* (Mann, *Stories*, 290–291)

I am aware of the fact that the attributions can be made differently from how I have indicated. But either way, the impression remains that the narration, which partially takes the shape of FCN, is, as it were, subsumed by the hero's interior monologue. The narrator's part in this seemingly purely figural stream is often overlooked.

5.4 Diegetic Narrators: Fëdor Dostoevskij, *The Adolescent*

FCN, like FID, does not seem to be possible with diegetic narrators (i.e., so-called first-person narrators), for narrator and character seem to coincide in a single instance.[4] Structurally and functionally, however, they are two entities, which in narratology are called the narrating and narrated self.[5] The two instances can be endowed with different mental traits. This is the more the case, the greater the temporal distance between the two states of the same person.

Wayne C. Booth (1961, 150) considers the distinction between first- and third person narrators overestimated: "[...] we can hardly expect to find useful criteria in a distinction that throws all fiction into two, or at most three, heaps." This is, however, contradicted by the practice of literary production. Stanzel (1979, 114–116) provides examples in which authors change a novel that has already been begun from one form to the other on the basis of artistic considerations, from the non-diegetic to the diegetic (Gottfried Keller's *Green Henry*) and the reverse, from the diegetic to the non-diegetic (Franz Kafka's *The Castle*).[6]

Dostoevskij's notebooks for *The Adolescent* (Podrostok, 1875) are enlightening in this context. After a long vacillation between the two forms, as is documented in the extensively preserved notebooks (Dostoevskij, *PSS*, XVI), Dostoevskij decided on a diegetic narrator. The decisive factor was that the "first-person"

---

4 For counter-examples cf. Cohn 1969.
5 On the dichotomy of diegetic and non-diegetic narrators, see Schmid 2010, 68–74.
6 The latter case has already been analyzed by Cohn 1978, 169–172.

narration of a twenty-year-old narrator was "more original" and demanded "more love, more artistry" than a "third-person" novel.[7]

The events narrated in *The Adolescent* unfold in the tension between the nineteen-year-old Arkadij Dolgorukij and his biological father Andrej Versilov. Arkadij, born out of wedlock, grew up without parents in the care of strangers. In the Moscow boarding house where he was educated, teachers and students made him painfully aware of his illegitimate origins. He responded to this by retreating into dreams that revolved primarily around his unknown father, and he developed the "idea" of becoming a Rothschild. When Arkadij meets his father, whom he has only seen once before, when he was ten years old, he is swept up in a "whirlwind" of events that give the youthful hero a picaresque character (Gerigk 1965).

Under the pen of the twenty-year-old Arkadij, the chronicle of turbulent events takes the form of confessions. In this context, it is not without significance that the novel, like other late works of Dostoevskij, was born from the germ of the concept for a *Vita of a Great Sinner* (Žitie velikogo grešnika), a plan that was ultimately not realized in *The Adolescent* or in other works.[8] Arkadij is not guilty of any real offenses, but in the exegetic time he finds his thoughts and some of the behaviors of the diegetic time, which was only a few months ago, extremely embarrassing. As narrating self he is particularly unpleasantly touched by his former naivety. Extremely critical of himself, he relentlessly exposes the real and supposed embarrassments of his past, but at the same time, in order to stand up to himself and his reader, he emphasizes his distance from his former self.

The large time gap between a young narrated self and a mature narrating self, which is characteristic of the confessional novel, is here reduced to a short period of no more than eight months. In May of an unnamed year, Arkadij reports on the adventures he experienced between September 19 and mid-December in the previous year.

Arkadij Dolgorukij is the most strongly profiled narrator in all of Dostoevskij's work (cf. Hansen-Löve 1986; 1996). Apart from the explicit self-representation, the image of the narrator is also strongly conveyed by indices, through the thematic, axiological, and stylistic symptoms that his narration contains. In the complexes relevant for adolescent consciousness, the following characteristics are most notable: insecurity, vulnerability, shame, desire for recognition. Arkadij

---

7 For this chapter I refer to my article Schmid 2015.

8 In the drafts, under August 12, 1874, we still find the sentence with which the novel was evidently intended to begin: *"I am nineteen years old and am already a great sinner" («Мне девятнадцать лет, а я уже великий грешник»; *PSS*, XVI, 47).

is an amiable, unspoiled, somewhat naive adolescent who desires nothing more than to be recognized by the adult world, and especially by his father. Stylistically, the adolescent narrator, who is quite educated and has a wide range of expressive possibilities, makes himself known through specifically adolescent expressions, especially at the beginning of his narration. When Arkadij thematizes his narrative or reports on things that concern his tense relationship with his surroundings, the overall dominant representational function of language is often displaced by the functions of expression and appeal (in the sense of Bühler 1934). The lexis is then interspersed with colloquial elements that are characteristic for an adolescent: defiantly showy hyperbole, carelessly boyish expressions, and stereotypical terms from adolescent vocabulary.

The adolescent narrator has a tense relationship with his addressee, whom he imagines as a critical adult who sneers at his naivety. Wherever Arkadij presents his thoughts and actions, impression comes to the fore as a function of the narrative. The selection of what is narrated, the euphemistic self-assessments at certain points, as well as the weighty rhetorical gestures all indicate that Arkadij wants to impress his addressee, to convince him of himself and his dignity.

The narrative is dominated by the figural perspective. In this respect, the novel can be seen as having an FCN macrostructure. Arkadij tries to put himself completely in the place of his former self, and describes the central twelve days in which the events are concentrated almost entirely from the temporal position of the narrated self. It is his declared effort to describe "in strict order" (Dostoevskij, *Adolescent*, 295; «в строгом порядке», *PSS*, XIII, 241) the events that have come upon him with such speed that now he still wonders how he has withstood them. In doing so, he generally refrains from explaining contexts that only became known to him later. For large sections of the text, Arkadij communicates to his reader only what he, as the narrated self, knew, thought, perceived, felt, and spoke at the narrated moment in question. The external world is described only insofar as it was perceived by the narrated self as received reality.

Adolescence is a phase of violent axiological change. At the age of nineteen for the narrated self and twenty for the narrating self, Dostoevskij has chosen ages in which one's view of the world is in a constant state of flux. The novel foregrounds the development of the young man in three time phases.

In the action, Arkadij experiences more and more new sides of reality, obtains information about the people close to him and their past histories, and evaluates his environment on the basis of growing insight and with constantly changing accents. The clearest sign of Arkadij's maturation is that in his first days in St. Petersburg after September 19, the "idea" of becoming a Rothschild, which had been his life's purpose in Moscow a month before, what he lived for in the world, is gradually forgotten and finally dropped altogether or decisively redefined.

What is quite obvious is the maturation that Arkadij experiences during writing and through narration. At the end of his notes, he can only look at the narrative self of the first sentences, which has become alien to him, with a distance:

> Кончив же записки и дописав последнюю строчку, я вдруг почувствовал, что перевоспитал себя самого, именно процессом припоминания и записывания. От много отрекаюсь, что написал, особенно от тона некоторых фраз и страниц, но не вычеркну и не поправлю ни единого слова. (PSS, *XIII*, 447)

> On finishing my notes and writing the last line, I suddenly felt that I had re-educated myself precisely through the process of recalling and writing down. I disavow much that I've written, especially the tone of certain phrases and pages, but I won't cross out or correct a single word. (*Adolescent*, 554)

Arkadij intends to present the events of the diegesis "in a way characteristic of [him] then" (*Adolescent*, 30; «с тогдашнею характерностью», *PSS*, XIII, 25) in order to "restore the impression" (*Adolescent*, 120; «чтобы ... восстановить впечатление», *PSS*, XIII, 100). This explains why he conceals important facts that became known to him only later. In retrospect, some evaluations given from the temporal position of the present of the action prove to be misleading. In this respect, we could call the narrative self "unreliable," were it not for the fact that every narrator is unreliable in some sense. Toward the end of the novel, the narrator reveals his perspective and corrects the evaluation of "aunt" Tat'jana Pavlovna Prutkova, which has so far been given in figural perspective:

> Одно добавлю: мне страшно грустно, что, в течение этих записок, я часто позволял себе относиться об этом человеке непочтительно и свысока. Но я писал, слишком воображая себя таким именно, каким был в каждую из тех минут, которые описывал. (*PSS*, XIII, 447)

> I'll add one thing: I'm awfully sorry that in the course of these notes I have frequently allowed myself to refer to this person disrespectfully and haughtily. But as I wrote I imagined myself exactly as I was at each of the moments I was describing. (*Adolescent*, 554)

The Adolescent provides a wealth of examples of FCN. We can say that FCN forms the basic structure in the relationship between the voices of narrator (narrating self) and figure (narrated self). Two circumstances support the occurrence of FCN in this diegetic novel, and specifically two-voiced FCN. One is the figural perspective, i.e., the perception and evaluation from the point of view of the narrated self; the other is the actual or claimed distance between the narrated and the narrating self.

Let us look at an example. The situation is as follows: Arkadij, despite his firm intentions, let himself get carried away when speaking of his idea of becoming a Rothschild before the socialists gathered at Dergačëv's, revealing his immature views on the world and women, and attacking the revolutionaries. The assembled people responded with a "loud and most unceremonious burst of laughter" (*Adolescent*, 58; «Громкий и самый бесцеремонный залп хохота», *PSS*, XIII, 51). This is, of course, an indelible disgrace for the nineteen-year-old. Nevertheless, he closes the chapter with the words "I wasn't ashamed of anything" (*Adolescent*, 58; «Я ничего не стыдился», *PSS*, XIII, 51). The following chapter then begins with the words "Of course, between me as I am now and me as I was then there is an infinite difference. Continuing to be 'not ashamed of anything,' I caught up with Vasin while still on the stairs" (*Adolescent*, 59; «Конечно, между мной теперешним и мной тогдашним — бесконечная разница. Продолжая „ничего не стыдиться", я еще на лесенке нагнал Васина», *PSS*, XIII, 51).

At first, Arkadij as narrated self defiantly denies the obvious embarrassment of the situation. "I wasn't ashamed of anything" reflects the position of the narrated self. Then, in the next chapter, the narrating self asserts a profound change that has allegedly taken place in him in the intervening months, finally denying the defiant denial of embarrassment in ironic self-quotation. The irony of the self-quotation is reinforced by the fact that the assertion of not being ashamed of anything is made linguistically dependent on the participle "continuing," which gives the sentence a comic touch. The irony toward his own words is obviously caused by the imagined frown of the imagined skeptical reader.

In other points, Arkadij unapologetically admits the shame of his former self, but in these instances a certain exaggeration of contrition is noticeable:

> Позор! Читатель, я начинаю теперь историю моего стыда и позора, и ничто в жизни не может для меня быть постыднее этих воспоминаний! (*PSS*, XIII, 163)

> Disgrace! Reader, I am now beginning the history of my shame and disgrace, and nothing in life can be more shameful for me than these memories! (*Adolescent*, 199–200)

> Но стыдился я сам и себя самого! Я сам был судьею себе, и — о боже, что было в душе моей! (PSS, XIII, 420)

> But I was also ashamed of myself! I was my own judge and – God, what there was in my soul! (*Adolescent*, 521)

On the other hand, Arkadij can at certain points refrain from claiming an "infinite difference" from his earlier self and can, on the contrary, affirm an allegedly unchanged position of meaning. But in such cases defiance is at play. In a conversation with the old Prince Sokol'skij, he has explained vehemently why he does not like women, to Sokol'skij's not inconsiderable annoyance. He naturally senses that his "tirade" must seem immature, and seeks to offset the feared ridiculous impression by defiantly asserting that he still clings to his earlier ideas:

> Хоть я и выписываю этот разговор несколько в юморе и с тогдашнею характерностью, но мысли эти и теперь мои. (*PSS*, XIII, 25)

> Though I'm writing down this conversation somewhat humorously here, and in a way characteristic of me then, the thinking is still mine. (*Adolescent*, 30)

The embarrassments of the past occasionally overwhelm the narrator to such an extent that he relapses into the defiant misanthropy of the past year in the present. After presenting his embarrassing role in the meeting at Dergačëv's, he notes:

> Воспоминание скверное! Нет, мне нельзя жить с людьми; я и теперь это думаю; на сорок лет вперед говорю. Моя идея — угол. (PSS, XIII, 48)

> A nasty recollection! No, it's impossible for me to live with people; I think so even now; I say it for forty years to come. My idea is – my corner. (*Adolescent*, 55)

The monophonic variant of FID is often encountered in *The Adolescent*. In the following two examples, which illustrate this single-voiced FID, the disappointment of the narrated self in his natural father is expressed; this is triggered by reports about Versilov's problematic behavior in Bad Ems:

> Итак, вот человек, по котором столько лет билось мое сердце! (PSS, XIII, 61)

> So this was the man after whom my heart had been throbbing for so many years! (*Adolescent*, 72)

> Но ведь оказывается, что этот человек — лишь мечта моя, мечта с детских лет. Это я сам его таким выдумал, а на деле оказался другой, упавший столь ниже моей фантазии. Я приехал к человеку чистому, а не к этому. И к чему я влюбился в него, раз навсегда, в ту маленькую минутку, как увидел его когда-то, бывши ребенком? Это «навсегда» должно исчезнуть. (*PSS*, XIII, 62)

> But it turned out that this man was only my dream, my dream since childhood. I had thought him up that way, but in fact he turned out to be a different man, who fell far below my fantasy. I had come to a pure man, not to this one. And why had I fallen in love with him, once and for all, in that little moment when I saw him while still a child? This "for all" had to go. (*Adolescent*, 73)

Although Arkadij, as the narrator, has already developed a different relationship to his father at this point, he does not yet show any distancing from his earlier evaluation. And at this point, the reader knows nothing of the son's later, more conciliatory view.

Double-voiced text interference presupposes a signaling of evaluative distance. On the one hand, Arkadij puts himself in the present of the action and his earlier self, using an expression symptomatic of that time, and on the other hand, he distances himself from that expression and the evaluative position embodied in it. The most frequent signal of distance are quotation marks, which assign an expression to the narrated self. This is the type of text interference that I call *direct figural designation*.

In *The Adolescent*, direct figural designation is a frequently employed device for reducing the words of third persons to their characteristic designations and thematic core, while at the same time overlaying them with additional narrative valuation:

[Макар] «жил почтительно», — по собственному удивительному его выражению [...]. (*PSS*, XIII, 9)

[Makar] "lived deferentially," – in his own amazing expression. (*Adolescent*, 9)

Где бы Версиловы ни были [...] Макар Иванович непременно уведомлял о себе «семейство». (*PSS*, XIII, 13)

Wherever the Versilovs were [...] Makar Ivanovič never failed to inform "the family" of himself. (*Adolescent*, 15)

Это была целая орава «мыслей» князя, которые он готовился подать в комитет акционеров. (*PSS*, XIII, 22)

It was a whole crowd of the prince's "thoughts," which he had prepared to submit to the shareholders' committee. (*Adolescent*, 26)

With the help of direct figural designation, Arkadij also distances himself from his own earlier thoughts. Thus, the idea of becoming a Rothschild, which the narrated self conceived in Moscow and still pursues in his first days in St. Petersburg, usually appears in the text of the narrating self in quotation marks. Other key terms that reveal the narrator's ironic distancing from his former self mostly concern this idea and its implementation:

В это девятнадцатое число я сделал еще один «шаг». (*PSS*, XIII, 36)

On this nineteenth day of the month, I took one more "step." (*Adolescent*, 43)

[...] и хоть теперешний "шаг" мой был только *примерный*, но и к этому шагу я положил прибегнуть лишь тогда, когда кончу с гимназией, когда порву со всеми, когда забьюсь в скорлупу и стану совершенно свободен. Правда, я далеко был не в «скор-лупе» [...]. (*PSS*, XIII, 36; italics in the original)

[...] though my present "step" was only *tentative*, even this step I had resolved to resort to only when I had finished school gymnasium, when I had broken with everyone, when I had shrunk myself into my shell and become completely free. True, I was still far from being in the "shell" [...]. (*Adolescent*, 43; italics in the original)

We have previously called FCN the macrostructure of the whole novel. The hidden contagion of the narrative discourse by the evaluations of the narrated I, which is not signaled by quotation marks, characterizes the whole work.

Thus, it is noticeable that Arkadij wants to place the journey from Moscow to his family in St. Petersburg under a new omen each time he mentions it. While at one point he claims to have traveled only to take stock of his father, the center of his thinking, at another time he plays the role of Versilov's savior. On a third occasion the "document," the compromising letter of Katerina Axmakova in which she declares her father to be insane, is put forward as the reason for the journey, while Arkadij reveals at still another point that it is the longed-for encounter with this woman whom he secretly loves that has induced him to make the trip. Behind all these disguises, the real reason shines through: the longing of the lonely young man for happiness in his family. The truth in the insincerity is based on the fact that the opposing reasons are not simply inventions of the narrating self but correspond to the changing motivations of the narrated self, whose relationship to the narrating self corresponds to the relationship of the character to the narrator in non-diegetic narration. In this respect, FCN is the basic structure of *The Adolescent*.

6. Summary and Conclusions

6.1 Definition

Figurally colored narration is a fifth way of representing characters' minds besides the narratorial consciousness report, direct discourse, indirect discourse, and free indirect discourse. The term *mind* here means the inner world of a character, including consciousness, emotion, and what Mixail Baxtin refers to with his term *smyslovaja pozicija*, which can be translated as *mindset*.

In FCN, we can only speak with reservations of representation of a figure's consciousness. Since FCN, unlike FID, does not reflect the figure's current consciousness, it is only a fragmentary representation of the figure's mind, and less of his or her current consciousness than of his or her general mindset.

Among the devices of speech and mind representation, FCN is closest to FID. As in FID, in FCN the character's text is broken by the narrator's text. But unlike FID, FCN does not refer to a character's current mental acts but to typical, characteristic segments of the character's text in which the character's way of thinking is expressed.

FCN is often difficult to distinguish from FID. This may be one reason why, unlike FID, with which the scholarly community is enamored, FCN is poorly understood. Many scholars simply equate it with FID.

FCN is also found in works with a diegetic narrator (traditionally called a first-person narrator). Here the narrator–figure relationship is replaced by the narrating self–narrated self relationship. Since both instances (narrating and narrated self) converge in a single person in different temporal situations, the identification of FCN is more difficult with diegetic than with non-diegetic narrators. But, as shown by Dostoevskij's *Adolescent*, the narrating self can be very distant from the narrated self, like a critical third-person narrator relative to a character.

Despite the categorial difference between FCN and FID, both patterns have common origins in everyday speech. Any reporter will usually incorporate expressions and evaluations of the person he is telling about into his report. It is on this tendency of everyday narrative that the naturalness of FCN is based.

In both patterns, in FCN as in FID, empathetic and critical intentions can be distinguished. A reporter can more or less consciously adopt the expressions and evaluations of his object person either with a consonant tendency or in order to distance himself from that person. In this latter case, the reporter's criticism may refer more to the content of the character's text or to its form of expression.

https://doi.org/10.1515/9783110763102-007

Criticism of expression can imply criticism of the way of thinking revealed in that expression.

In oral performance, the distancing is effected by certain intonations. In the fixed form of the written text, the indexical role of intonation is taken over by contextualization.

6.2 Approaches

FCN has been described, albeit not known by that name, since the 1920s. One of the first scholars to treat FCN was Leo Spitzer, who calls the device "a kind of 'contagion' [*Ansteckung*] of the author's language by the character's language," thus choosing a term that was subsequently taken up by many scholars in English (*contagion*) and Russian (*zaraženie*).

Inspired by Spitzer, Mixail Baxtin offers the first Russian approach to FCN in a book published in 1929 under the name of Valentin Vološinov with the misleading title *Marxism and the Philosophy of Language*. Using the example of Dostoevskij's story "A Nasty Anecdote," Baxtin/Vološinov demonstrates and analyzes the device he calls "anticipated and disseminated someone else's speech."

In his book *Discourse in the Novel*, Baxtin (1934/35) treats FCN as a manifestation of the phenomenon of *heteroglossia*. For him, the examples he cites from Dickens's *Little Dorrit* illustrate a "double-accented, double-styled hybrid construction" in which "two utterances, two languages" intermingle.

The most fundamental contribution to FCN in Russian Literary Studies was made by Natal'ja Koževnikova in her works from the 1970s. She calls the device *improperly authorial narration*. Although it is often not possible to clearly demarcate *improperly authorial narration* (FCN) from *free indirect discourse* (FID), especially since the former often initiates or includes the latter, it is important to distinguish between the two devices. FID serves to reproduce characters' speech or thoughts, whereas FCN is a mode of description or narration by the narrator. Koževnikova uses examples from Russian literature of the 1920s to discuss in detail various perspectival and stylistic nuances of the figuralization of narration. Her observations are very careful, but suffer from an overly simple concept of point of view, which excludes axiological and stylistic facets.

The approach presented here differs from Koževnikova's concept in two further respects. First, Koževnikova does not make a distinction between marked and covert forms of figural designation; the criterion of markedness does not play a role for her. Second, in her examples, Koževnikova focuses mainly on the reproduction of a character's discourse and narrative, i.e., on forms of external speech. Naturally, she is especially interested in dialectisms and folk language.

The present book is not about the narrative repetition or imitation of specific characters' expressions but about the adoption of axiological and stylistic features of the genotypical characters' text, the mental subject sphere of a figure or a collective.

Elena Padučeva, addressing FCN under the heading *quotation*, pays similarly little attention to the problem of markedness to Koževnikova. Her comparison of FCN and FID is problematic. In "quotation" (i.e., FCN) there are two voices "singing together" (Baxtin's *double voicedness, bivocality*), whereas FID "tends towards the monological interpretation" (i.e., univocality). It seems questionable whether there is such a rigid, static, and simple opposition between "quotation" (FCN) and FID.

The German Slavist Johannes Holthusen coined the term *uneigentliches Erzählen* (*improper narration*) and documented the device in his studies of Russian narrative prose of the 1960s.

In my book *The Text Structure in Dostoevskij's Stories* (Schmid 1973), I referred to the frequent occurrence in Russian prose of the phenomenon whereby "a narratorial report is interspersed with individual words or parts of sentences that in their thematic, evaluative, lexical, syntactic, and/or language-functional characteristics betray that they do not actually belong to the narrative text, but rather come from the horizon of consciousness and the linguistic repertoire of the portrayed characters." For the still-unnamed device, I distinguished two types: *Ansteckung* (*contagion*) and *Reproduktion* (*reproduction*).

In my *Elemente der Narratologie* (Schmid 2013), I took up Holthusen's term *uneigentliches Erzählen* and illustrated the procedure with examples from Dostoevskij, Čexov, and Solženicyn. In the English translation of the book, *Narratology* (Schmid 2010), I suggested the term *figurally colored narration*.

In the anglophone world, the term "Uncle Charles Principle," introduced by Hugh Kenner (1978) on the basis of a quotation from Joyce's *Portrait of the Artist as a Young Man*, has become established for the device of FCN. The "Uncle Charles Principle" says that "the narrative idiom need not be the narrator's."

Kenner's point that the "Uncle Charles Principle" in Joyce not only affects lexis but can also encompass syntax is picked up by Susan Swartzlander in a study of Ernest Hemingway's early narrative "Up in Michigan." She shows that for Hemingway, as for Joyce, the syntax and rhythm of characters' speech can also infect narrative discourse.

Following in Kenner's footsteps, the American writer Lucy Ferriss and her students find the "Uncle Charles Principle" in a number of American short stories. However, Ferriss seems to have a different understanding of the "Uncle Charles Principle" than the FCN on which this book is based. FCN in our sense is rarely to be found in the texts she studied. In them, a figural coloring is dominant only in passages in which the consciousness of the corresponding figure is presented, which thus correspond to FID. Our stipulation that FCN does not present a character's current acts of consciousness is not met in Ferriss's findings.

In German Literary Studies, the discussion of perspective and mind representation since the 1950s has been dominated by the work of Franz Stanzel. In his comprehensive book *Theory of Narrative*, Stanzel – a little awkwardly – calls FCN *reflectorization of the teller-character* or *assimilation of a teller-character to a reflector-character*. The term *assimilation*, which implies a certain solidarity, in many cases does not express what the reader actually encounters. In the example from Katherine Mansfield's story "The Garden Party," the narrator seems to distance himself from the characters' expressions.

Unfortunately, Stanzel did not take note of Russian theories in his *Theory of Narrative* (1979; tr. 1984), although at least Vološinov's book had been available in English since 1973.

Stanzel's student Monika Fludernik took up the concept of *reflectorization*, defining it as "the narrator's taking on the personality (linguistic and ideological) of a character or [...] a group of characters whose views are presented as if 'through their minds'" (1996, 135). In creating the construct of a "reflectorized teller character," Fludernik obviously succumbs to Stanzel's problematic formula of the "adaptation of a narrator figure to a reflector figure." It would be more appropriate to speak of the adoption of the figural perspective (in all its facets) by the one and only narrator, who does not directly express his (and the author's) distance from the characters' evaluations but lets it be deduced.

Fludernik (1996) splits Stanzel's category of reflectorization into two concepts: 1. her own concept of *reflectorization*, for which she uses Stanzel's name, 2. an alternative mode that she calls *figuralization*. The main differences between these concepts are as follows. 1. Reflectorization presupposes a character present in the story whose way of thinking and speech is reproduced in the narrative text outside of direct or free indirect discourse. Reflectorization is double-voiced and serves as an ironic distancing. The narratorial presentation clashes with the figural point of view. 2. Figuralization cannot be attributed to a figure or a narrator. Figuralization is monophonic and serves empathic immersion. In figuralization, the story is perspectivized in ways that have no relation to a focalizer.

FCN is a special case of what Mieke Bal (1977a) calls "focalisation transposeé" and Irene de Jong (1987, 2001) "embedded focalization."

6.3 FCN as Text Interference

FCN is a form of text interference, the overlapping of the rendered character's text by the rendering narrator's text. The interference results from the way that, in one and the same segment of the narrative text, certain thematic, semantic, stylistic, and grammatical features point to the narrator's text and others, in contrast, to the character's text. As a result of the distribution of features from both texts and the expressive function (in Bühler's sense) pointing in two directions, these texts are simultaneously realized in one and the same segment of the narrative text.

The way the character's text and the narrator's text are represented in text interference can be illustrated by profiling their features: 1. thematic features, 2. evaluative or ideological features, 3. grammatical features – person, 4. grammatical features – tense, 5. grammatical features – orientation system, 6. features of language function, 7. stylistic features – lexis, and 8. stylistic features – syntax.

We can distinguish two main modes for the adoption of evaluations and designations from the character's text in FCN: *contagion* and *reproduction*.

In the first mode, *contagion*, the figural elements of the narrative text reflect evaluations and designations of the character, without these being part of a current act of his or her consciousness. The difference from FID is that in the latter the character's current acts of consciousness are presented, whereas in FCN the content of the narrative statements belongs entirely to the narrator. Following Leo Spitzer (1923a) we call this adoption of individual figural evaluations and designations *contagion* or *infection* of the narrative discourse by the character's text.

In the second mode, *reproduction*, the figurally colored elements of the narrative discourse reflect evaluations and terms typical of the character's text.

The question, which has been controversial since the discovery of FID, of whether text interference serves more to express empathy or irony, divides scholars into two parties: univocalists (Bally, E. Lerch, Lorck, Banfield, Padučeva) and bivocalists (Spitzer, Baxtin, Pascal). This question can only be answered by considering what position the narrator, whose text reproduces and overlays the character's text, generally takes regarding the character's evaluations. Ascertaining that is a matter of interpretation, and thus a problem of hermeneutics. The structurally conditioned bitextuality of FCN (and indeed text interference in general) does not necessarily take on a two-voiced, double-accented character as postulated by Baxtin/Vološinov, who was fixated on agonal relations.

Thus, a line can be drawn under the old controversy about how many voices FCN and the other devices of text interference imply by taking the relationship between narrator and character into account. How many voices are assumed depends on how the reader perceives that relationship. We must be prepared for a double dynamic here. On the one hand, the relationship between the two instances in a given work can change, for example when the hero or the narrator change their views and values. On the other hand, an interpretation of the relationship between narrator and character can change in the course of the reading history of even one and the same reader.

6.4 Functions and Areas of Application

We mainly find FCN in passages where the normal functions of a narrator are fulfilled: introducing or concluding a story, describing a landscape, characterizing a figure or a collective with more or less critical accents, describing a figure empathetically or satirically, telling a life story. Very often, FCN is used to give an overview of a longer period of time, to present flashbacks, or to describe a situation. FCN is widely used to incorporate expressions from the simple vernacular of the people into narrative discourse; this is especially common in Russian literature. Special functions emerge in the narrator's play with ontological levels, e.g., creating an illusory reality or presenting dreams as reality.

In chapter 4 these functions were demonstrated using examples from English, Russian, and German literature.

Typically, FCN is rarely used in children's literature, unlike FID, which is applied widely. This can be explained by the fact that FCN always causes a degree of confusion about who is responsible for the coloring of the narration. Children do not like such confusion and do not understand irony. When FID is used in children's literature, it is always clear who sees and thinks. FCN withholds from children the security, the familiarity, that they need in stories.

One curious thing stood out in the countless stories and novels that I considered when preparing this book. Little FCN is to be found among authors for whom FID plays a special role. This is true of Jane Austen, to whom the rise of FID is dated, of Goethe's *Elective Affinities*, where we find a lot of FID, and of Arthur Schnitzler, for instance, a grandmaster of text interference in German modernism. Only with difficulty can FCN be found in the works of these three authors.

Not by chance, authors who use FCN widely are considered difficult writers. And they are authors who operate intensely with perspective and voices. Among them, Dostoevskij, James Joyce, and Virginia Woolf deserve special mention.

A remarkable number of examples in this book were taken from works by Dostoevskij. This does not simply spring from my predilections as a Slavist. There is hardly any author in the European literatures who works so sensitively and subtly with the axiology of voice and ways of thinking as Dostoevskij. The view of him as an author who was mainly interested in soul, philosophy, and tension fails to recognize his stylistic mastery, especially in conducting a concert of multiple voices. It is no coincidence that Baxtin used Dostoevskij's work to develop his philosophy of many-voicedness and polyphony.

Dostoevskij did not write in a wild furor, little concerned about questions of aesthetics, as legend has it. In reality, Dostoevskij gave thorough attention to formal and, in particular, narrative aspects, as is documented, for example, in the surviving notebooks for the novel *The Adolescent*, in which Dostoevskij comments on the advantages and disadvantages of the first- and third-person form. Thus, *The Adolescent*, which begins with the words "Unable to restrain myself, I have sat down to record this history of my first steps on life's career, though I could have done as well without it" (Dostoevskij, *Adolescent*, 5), becomes a kind of meta-novel on the theme of how to describe one's own life.

6.5 Limiting Cases

The Adolescent was treated as the last work under the heading "Limiting Cases." The novel is a special case because it is told by a diegetic (first-person) narrator. This narrator, as a twenty-year-old narrating self, has a tense relationship with his nineteen-year-old narrated self. The entire novel can be seen as having FCN as its macrostructure. The narrating self tries to put himself completely in the place of his former self, and describes the events almost entirely from the temporal and hence axiological position of the narrated self. It is his declared effort to describe "in strict order." Without describing the events in free indirect perception or FID, the narrating self uses the character's (i.e., his former self's) evaluations and expressions.

Three works fall into the borderline case of figural coloring without a figure.

Katherine Mansfield's narrative "At the Bay" begins in an entirely narratorial, objective manner but is increasingly interspersed with signs of a perceiving and evaluating instance. But there is no reflector to be found. We have to imagine instead a potential reflector who is not represented by the narrator, but projected. The narrator represents what this imaginary reflector could or should perceive, with his selection and evaluation of the world at the bay.

Virginia Woolf's *The Waves* is a similar case. If the protagonists do not qualify as the subjects of perception for which we are looking, the perspective will have to be determined as that of a reflector projected by the narrator.

The description of a landscape at the opening of a novel is not an uncommon limiting case of FCN. We have such a case in the novel *My Children* (2019) by the Russian-Tatar author Guzel' Jaxina. The landscape on both sides of the Volga is clearly described from the point of view of its inhabitants. The collective of Germans settled on the Volga emerges as a reflector of the description.

In some works, the narrator himself functions not only as the subject of the narrative text but also as the subject of perception. We have encountered two works where it is hard to deny that the narrator is the source of perspective and the subject of perception. They are Goethe's *Novella* and Otto Ludwig's novel *Between Sky and Earth*. In the former, the initial description points to the narrator as reflector. In the latter, the description of the garden that opens the work can only be traced back sensibly to the narrator as observer. These two examples allow us to conclude that in certain cases a coloration that seems figural cannot be traced back to any other entity than the narrator.

In some works, the fluctuation between narrator and figure is so imperceptible that entire passages of FCN can seem like FID, and are indeed taken by many critics as exactly that. An example of this is Thomas Mann's short narrative "A Weary Hour," a novelistic study of Friedrich Schiller's creative struggle in his work on *Wallenstein*. The narrative presents an extended interior monologue in the mode of FID. At some points, however, the character's interior monologue is interrupted by the narrator's discourse, which is infected by or reproduces expressions and evaluations from the character's text. But these narratorial parts are so deeply embedded in the interior monologue that they are, as it were, subsumed by it.

⋆

One might well ask which of the three literatures touched upon in this FCN and FID are narrative siblings, sometimes even twins. They have common traits, are based on the same principle, and are occasionally mistaken for each other or mixed up. But they each have their own identity. Both have their basis in interference between narrator's text and character's text, but it is also here that a crucial difference emerges. FCN is essentially narratorial; FID expresses figural content. Even though in both cases the narratorial text functions as the governing regimen, the quoting text, in FID the figural propositional content is granted a certain independence. Nevertheless, FCN should not be underestimated because of its stronger narratoriality. Narration is ultimately based on the intentional, selective, and accentuating activity of the narrator.

⋆

One might well ask which of the three literatures touched upon in this book is most prominently marked by FCN. To this I can only give a highly subjective answer. In my extensive search for works in the three literatures where FCN might be present, my richest findings were in Russian literature. This may, of course, be related to the fact that I am a Slavist and am familiar with more Russian than German or English texts. But it could also be that the phenomenon of perspective, which occurs in the narrative traditions of all three literatures, is in Russian literature most strongly manifested in the treatment of voice. It is perhaps no coincidence that the theory of narrative voice was developed, in the Russian 1920s, on the basis of Russian realism (Dostoevskij), postrealism (Čexov), and the experimental, voice-loving avant-garde of the 1920s.

7. Works Cited

7.1 Literary Sources

Austen, *Emma* = Jane Austen: *Emma*. 200th-Anniversary Annotated Edition. Edited with an Introduction by Juliette Wells. New York: Penguin Books, 2015.

Bellow, *Mr Green* = Saul Bellow: Looking for Mr Green. *American Short Stories Since 1945*. Edited by John G. Parks. New York and Oxford: Oxford UP, 2002. 260–274.

Broch, *Schlafwandler* = Hermann Broch: *Die Schlafwandler. Eine Trilogie*. Frankfurt a. M.: Suhrkamp, 1994.

Broch, *Sleepwalkers* = Hermann Broch: *The Sleepwalkers. A Trilogy*. Translated from the German by Willa and Edwin Muir. Vintage 1996.

Čexov, *PSS* = Anton P. Čexov: *Polnoe sobranie sočinenij i pisem v 30 t. Sočinenija v 18 t.* Moscow: Nauka, 1974–1982.

Čexov, *S* = *Anton Chekhov's Selected Stories*. Texts of the stories, comparison of translations, life letters, criticism. Selected and edited by Cathy Popkins. New York: Norton, 2014.

Čexov, *ShSt* = *Anton Chekhov's Short Stories*. Texts of the stories, backgrounds, criticism. Selected and edited by Ralph E. Matlaw. New York: Norton, 1979.

Dickens, *Dorrit* = Charles Dickens: Little Dorrit. https://www.gutenberg.org/cache/epub/963/pg963-images.html (accessed November 9, 2021)

Dostoevskij, *PSS* = Fëdor Dostoevskij: *Polnoe sobranie sočinenij*. 30 Vols. Leningrad: Nauka, 1972–1990.

Dostoevskij, *Adolescent* = Fyodor Dostoevsky: *The Adolescent*. Translated from the Russian by Richard Pevear and Larissa Volokhonsky. With an Introduction by Richard Pevear. Vintage Classics, 2003.

Dostoevskij, *BK* = Fjodor Dostojewski: *Die Brüder Karamasoff*. Aus dem Russischen von E. K. Rahsin (= Elisabeth Kaerrick). Munich: Piper, 1920.

Dostoevskij, *Double* = Fyodor Dostoevsky: *The Double and The Gambler*. Translated from the Russian by Richard Pevear and Larissa Volokhonsky. With an Introduction by Richard Pevear. Vintage Classics, 2005.

Dostoevskij, *CaP* = Fyodor Dostoevsky: Crime and Punishment. A Novel in Six Parts with Epilogue. Translated and Annotated by Richard Pevear and Larissa Volokhonsky. Vintage Classics, 2007.

Dostoevskij, *Eternal Husband* = Fyodor Dostoevsky: *The Eternal Husband and Other Stories*. Translated by Richard Pevear and Larissa Volokhonsky. New York: Modern Library, 1997. 65–230.

Dostoevskij, *Letters* = *Letters of Fyodor Michailovitch Dostoevsky to His Family and Friends*. Translated by Ethel Golburn Mayne. London: Chatto & Windus, 1917.

Dostoevskij, *Nasty Anecdote* = Fyodor Dostoevsky: *The Eternal Husband and Other Stories*. Translated by Richard Pevear and Larissa Volokhonsky. New York: Modern Library, 1997. 3–64.

Goethe, *Novella* = Johann Wolfgang Goethe: *Novella*. Translation by Thomas Carlyle and R.D. Boylan. https://germanstories.vcu.edu/goethe/novelle_e.html (accessed April 4, 2021)

https://doi.org/10.1515/9783110763102-008

Goethe, *Novelle* = Johann Wolfgang Goethe: DTV-Gesamtausgabe. Vol. 20. Munich: dtv, 1962. 141–161.

Gogol', *Sobr. soč* = Nikolaj Gogol': *Sobranie sočinenij*. 7 Vols. Moscow: Xudožestvennaja literatura, 1966.

Gogol', *O* = Nikolai Gogol: *The Overcoat*. Translated by Constance Garnett. http://www.fountainheadpress.com/expandingthearc/assets/gogolovercoat.pdf (accessed June 6,2020)

Hemingway, *Michigan* = Ernest Hemingway: "Up in Michigan." In *The Snows of Kilimanjaro and Other Stories*. London: Penguin Books, 1973. 34–39.

Homer, Odyssey = Homer: *The Odyssey*. Translated by A. T. Murray and G. E. Dimock. 2 Vols. Cambridge, MA, and London: Harvard University Press, 1995.

Jackson, *Lottery* = Shirley Jackson: The Lottery. *American Short Stories Since 1945*. Edited by John G. Parks. New York and Oxford: Oxford UP, 2002. 9–15.

Jaxina, *Deti* = Guzel' Jaxina: *Deti moi. Roman*. Moscow: Izdatel'stvo AST, 2019.

Joyce, *Ul* = James Joyce: *Ulysses*. London: Penguin Books, 1974.

Leskov, *Sobr. soč.* = Nikolaj Leskov: Sobranie sočinenij v 6 tomax. Moscow: Izdatel'stvo Pravda, 1973.

Ludwig, *Romane* = Otto Ludwig: *Romane und Romanstudien*. Herausgegeben von William J. Lillyman. Munich: Hanser, 1977.

Mann = Thomas Mann: *Gesammelte Werke in 13 Bänden*. Frankfurt a. M.: Fischer, 1990.

Mann, *Death in Venice* = Thomas Mann: *Death in Venice and Other Stories*. Translated and with an introduction by David Luke. New York: Vintage, 1998.

Mann, *Magic Mountain* = Thomas Mann: *The Magic Mountain*. New York: Fred A. Knopf, 1949.

Mann, *Stories* = Thomas Mann: *Stories of Three Decades*. Translated from the German by Helen T. Lowe-Porter. London: Secker & Warburg, 1936.

Mansfield, *Stories* = *The Collected Stories of Katherine Mansfield*. With an Introduction by Stephen Arkin. Ware, Hertfordshire: Wordsworth Classics, 2006.

Puškin, *PSS* = Aleksandr Puškin: *Polnoe sobranie sočinenij*. 17 vols. Moscow and Leningrad: Izd. Akademii Nauk SSSR, 1937–1959.

Puškin, *Prose* = Alexander Pushkin: *Complete Prose Fiction*. Translated, with an Introduction and Notes by Paul Debreczeny. Stanford: Stanford UP, 1983.

Rilke, *Weise* = Rainer Maria Rilke: *Die Weise von Liebe und Tod*. Frankfurt a. M.: Suhrkamp, 1974.

Rilke, *Lay* = Rainer Maria Rilke: *The Lay of the Love and Death of Cornet Christopher Rilke*. Tr. by Leslie Phillips and Stefan Schimanski. London: L. Drummond, 1948.

Solženicyn, *MSS* = Aleksandr Solženicyn, *Maloe sobranie sočinenij*. Moscow: Inkom NV, 1991.

Solženicyn, *OD* = Alexander Solzhenitsyn: *One Day in the Life of Ivan Denisovich*. Translated by Ralph Parker. New York: Dutton, 1963.

Tolstoj, *Povesti* = Lev Tolstoj: *Povesti i rasskazy*. V dvux tomax. Moscow: Xudožestvennaja literatura, 1966.

Trifonov, *Sobr. soč,* = Jurij Trifonov: *Sobranie sočinenij v četyrex tomax*. Moscow: Xudožestvennaja literatura, 1986.

Trifonov, *LG* = Yury Trifonov: *The Long Goodbye. Three Novellas*. Translated by Helen P. Burlingame and Ellendea Proffer. New York: Harper & Row, 1978.

Weldon, Weekend = Fay Weldon: Weekend, https://www.teachingenglish.org.uk/sites/teacheng/files/weekend_text_0.pdf; (accessed March 28, 2021)

Wellershoff, *NL* = Dieter Wellershoff. Das normale Leben. In: D. W., *Im Dickicht des Lebens.*
Ausgewählte Erzählungen. Cologne: Kiepenheuer & Witsch, 2015. 129–203.
Woolf, *Waves* = Virginia Woolf: *The Waves.* London: Vintage, 2000.

7.2 Criticism

Bal, Mieke (1977a). Narratologie. Essais sur las signification narrative dans quatre romans
modernes. Phil. Diss. Rijksuniversiteit te Utrecht. Paris: Klincksieck.
Bal, Mieke (1977b). "Narration et focalisation. Pour une théorie des instances du récit." *Poétique*
29. 107–127.
Bal, Mieke (1978). *De theorie van vertellen en verhalen. Inleiding in de narratologie.* 5th edition.
Coutinho 1990
Bal, Mieke (1981). "Notes on Narrative Embedding." *Poetics Today* 2. 41–59.
Bal, Mieke (1983). "The Narrating and the Focalizing: A Theory of the Agents in Narrative." *Style*
17. 234–269
Bal, Mieke (1985). *Narratology: Introduction to the Theory of Narrative.* 4th illustrated edition.
Toronto: Toronto UP, 2017.
Banfield, Ann (1982). *Unspeakable Sentences: Narration and Representation in the Language of
Fiction.* Boston: Routledge.
Banfield, Ann (1987). "Describing the Unobserved: Events Grouped Around an Empty Center." In
The Linguistics of Writing. Arguments between Language and Literature. Edited by Nigel
Fabb, Derek Attridge, Alan Durant, and Colin MacCabe. New York: Methuen. 265–285.
Baxtin, Mixail (1929). *Problemy tvorčestva Dostoevskogo.* Leningrad: Priboj, 1929. In M. M. B.
Sobranie sočinenij. Vol. 2. Moscow: Russkie slovari, 2000. 5–175.
Baxtin, Mixail ([1934/35] 2012). "Slovo v romane." In M. Baxtin. *Sobranie sočinenij.* T. 3.
Moscow: Jazyki slavjanskix kul'tur, 2012. 9–179. Tr. Baxtin 1981.
Baxtin, Mixail [Bakhtin, Mikhail] (1981). "Discourse in the Novel." In *The Dialogic Imagination.
Four Essays by M. M. Bakhtin.* Edited by Michael Holquist. Translated by Caryl Emerson and
Michael Holquist. Austin, TX: University of Texas Press. 259–422
Belov, Sergej (1979). *Roman F. M. Dostoevskogo Prestuplenie i nakazanie.* Pod red. D. S. Lixačë-
va. Leningrad: Prosveščenie.
Bočarov, Sergej (1993). "Ob odnom razgovore i vokrug nego." *Novoe literaturnoe obozrenie* 2.
70–89.
Booth, Wayne C. (1961). *The Rhetoric of Fiction.* Chicago: Penguin.
Bradford, Melvin E. (1968). "Faulkner's *Elly*: An Exposé." *The Mississippi Quarterly* 21. 179–187.
Brinton, Laurel (1980). "'Represented Perception': A Study in Narrative Style." *Poetics* 9. 363–
381.
Bühler, Karl (1918/20). "Kritische Musterung der neueren Theorien des Satzes." *Indogerma-
nisches Jahrbuch* 4. 1–20.
Bühler, Karl (1934). *Sprachtheorie. Die Darstellungsfunktion der Sprache.* Frankfurt a. M.:
Gustav Fischer, 1978. Engl.: Bühler 1990.
Bühler, Karl (1990). *Theory of Language. The Representational Function of Language.* Translated
by Donald Fraser Goodwin. Amsterdam: Benjamins.
Bühler, Willi (1937). *Die "Erlebte Rede" im englischen Roman. Ihre Vorstufen und ihre
Ausbildung im Werke Jane Austens.* Zürich and Leipzig: Niehans.

Chatman, Seymour (1975). "The Structure of Narrative Transmission." In: *Style and Structure in Literature. Essays in the New Stylistics*. Edited by Roger Fowler. Ithaca, NY: Cornell UP. 213–257.

Cohn, Dorrit (1966). *The Sleepwalkers: Elucidations of Hermann Broch's Trilogy*. 's-Gravenhage: Mouton.

Cohn, Dorrit (1969). "Erlebte Rede im Ich-Roman." *Germanisch-romanische Monatsschrift*. Neue Folge 19, 305–13.

Cohn, Dorrit (1978). *Transparent Minds: Narrative Modes for Presenting Consciousness in Fiction*. Princeton: Princeton UP.

Doležel, Lubomír (1958). "Polopřímá řeč v moderní české próze." *Slovo a slovesnost* 19. 20–46.

Doležel, Lubomír (1960). *O stylu moderní české prózy. Výstavba textu*. Prague: Nakladatelství Československé akademie věd.

Doležel, Lubomír (1965). "Nejtralizacija protivopostavlenij v jazykovo-stilističeskoj strukture epičeskoj prozy." In *Problemy sovremennoj filologii. Sbornik statej k semidesjatiletiju V. V. Vinogradova*. Moscow: Nauka. 116–123.

Doležel, Lubomír (1967). "The Typology of the Narrator: Point of View in Fiction." In *To Honor Roman Jakobson. Essays on the Occasion of his 70. Birthday*. Vol. 1. The Hague and Paris: Mouton. 541–552.

Doležel, Lubomír (1973). *Narrative Modes in Czech Literature*. Toronto: University of Toronto Press.

Doležel, Lubomír (1993). *Narativní způsoby v české literatuře*. Prague: Český spisovatel.

Emerson, Caryl (1984). "The Tolstoy Connection in Bakhtin." Reprinted in *Rethinking Bakhtin. Extensions and Challenges*. Edited by Gary Saul Morson and Caryl Emerson. Evanston, IL: Northwestern University Press, 1989. 149–170, 282–286.

Fehr, Bernhard (1938). "Substitutionary Narration and Description: A Chapter in Stylistics." *English Studies* 20. 97–107.

Ferriss, Lucy (2008). "Uncle Charles Repairs to the A&P: Changes in Voice in the Recent American Short Story." *Narrative* 16. 178–192.

Fludernik, Monika (1993). *The Fictions of Language and the Language of Fiction. The Linguistic Representation of Speech and Consciousness*. London and New York: Routledge.

Fludernik, Monika (1996). *Towards a "Natural" Narratology*. London and New York: Routledge.

Frank, Joseph (1995). *Dostoevsky: The Miraculous Years, 1865–1871*. Princeton: Princeton UP.

Genette, Gérard (1972). "Discours du récit". In G. G., *Figures III*. Paris: Seuil. 67–282. Engl.: Genette 1980.

Genette, Gérard (1980). *Narrative Discourse*. Translated by Jane E. Lewin. Ithaca, NY: Cornell UP.

Gerigk, Horst-Jürgen (1965). *Versuch über Dostoevskijs "Jüngling". Ein Beitrag zur Theorie des Romans*. Munich: Fink.

Gerigk, Horst-Jürgen ([2006] 2013). *Lesen und Interpretieren*. 3rd edition. Heidelberg: Mattes.

Gerigk, Horst-Jürgen (2013). *Dostojewskijs Entwicklung als Schriftsteller. Vom "Toten Haus" zu den "Brüdern Karamazov."* Frankfurt a. M.: Fischer. Russian translation: *Literaturnoe masterstvo Dostoevskogo v razvitii. Ot „Zapisok" iz Mertvogo doma" do "Brat"ev Karamazovyx."* Translated by K. Ju. Lappo-Danilevskij. Sankt-Peterburg: Izdatel'stvo Puškinskogo Doma; Nestor-Istorija, 2016.

Grund, Simon (forthcoming). "Eventfulness in Classical Greek and Latin Literature." In *Handbook of Diachronic Narratology*. Edited by Peter Hühn, John Pier, Wolf Schmid. Berlin and Boston: De Gruyter.

Günther, Werner (1928). *Probleme der Rededarstellung: Untersuchungen zur direkten, indirekten und „erlebten" Rede im Deutschen, Französischen und Italienischen*. Marburg: Elwert, Braun.

Hamburger, Käte (1957). *Die Logik der Dichtung*, Stuttgart: Klett.

Hamburger, Käte (1968). *Die Logik der Dichtung*, 2., wesentlich veränderte Auflage. Stuttgart: Klett.

Hansen-Löve, Aage A. (1986). Nachwort. In: F. M. Dostoevskij, *Der Jüngling*. Piper-Verlag: Munich. 874–917.

Hansen-Löve, Aage A. (1996). "Diskursivnye processy v romane Dostoevskogo *Podrostok*." In *Avtor i tekst*. Edited by Vladimir M. Markovič and Wolf Schmid. St. Petersburg: Izdatel'stvo S.-Peterburgskogo universiteta, 1996, S. 229–267.

Herdin, Elis (1905). *Studien über Bericht und indirekte Rede im modernen Deutsch*. Uppsala: Almquist & Wikksels.

Holthusen, Johannes (1968). "Stilistik des 'uneigentlichen' Erzählens in der sowjetischen Gegenwartsliteratur." *Die Welt der Slaven* 13, 225–245.

Hough, Graham (1970). "Narrative and Dialogue in Jane Austen." *Critical Quarterly* 12. 201–229.

Hough, Graham (1978). *Selected Essays*. Cambridge: Cambridge UP.

Jakobson, Roman (1957). *Shifters, Verbal Categories and the Russian Verb*. Cambridge, MA: Harvard UP.

Jensen, Peter Alberg (1979). *Nature as Code. The Achievement of Boris Pilnjak. 1915–1924*. Copenhagen: Rosenkilde and Bagger.

Jong, Irene de (1987). *Narrators and Focalizers. The Presentation of the Story in the Iliad*. Amsterdam: Grüner.

Jong, Irene de (2014). *Narratology and Classics. A practical Guide*. Oxford: Oxford UP.

Kenner, Hugh (1978). *Joyce's Voices*. Berkeley and Los Angeles: University of California Press.

Koževnikova, Natal'ja (1971). "O tipax povestvovanija v sovetskoj proze." In *Voprosy jazyka sovremennoj russkoj literatury*, Moscow: Nauka. 97–163.

Koževnikova, Natal'ja (1977). "O sootnošenii reči avtora i personaža." In *Jazykovye processy sovremennoj russkoj xudožestvennoj literatury. Proza*, Moscow: Nauka. 7–98.

Koževnikova, Natal'ja (1994). *Tipy povestvovanija v russkoj literature XIX–XX vv.* Moscow: Institut russkogo jazyka Rossijskoj Akademii Nauk.

LaCapra, Dominick (1982). *Madame Bovary on Trial*. Ithaca: Cornell UP.

Lachmann, Renate (1971). "Die Zerstörung der 'schönen Rede'. Ein Aspekt der Realismus-Evolution der russischen Prosa des 19. Jahrhunderts." *Poetica* 4. 462–477.

Leech, Geoffrey N.; Michael Short (1981). *Style in Fiction: A Linguistic Introduction to English Fictional Prose*. London and New York. 2nd edition. Harlow: Pearson, 2007

Lerch, Eugen (1928). "Ursprung und Bedeutung der sog. 'Erlebten Rede' ('Rede als Tatsache')." *Germanisch-romanische Monatsschrift* 16, 459–478.

Levitan, Lija (1976). "Sjužet i kompozicija rasskaza A. P. Čexova 'Skripka Rotšil'da'." *Voprosy sjužetosloženija* 4. Riga: Zvajgzne. 33–46.

Lorck, Etienne (1921). *Die "Erlebte Rede." Eine sprachliche Untersuchung*. Heidelberg: Winter.

Marnette, Sophie (forthcoming). "Free Indirect Discourse in Medieval and Modern French Literature." In *Handbook of Diachronic Narratology*. Edited by Peter Hühn, John Pier, Wolf Schmid. Berlin and Boston: De Gruyter.

McHale, Brian (1978). "Free Indirect Discourse: A Survey of Recent Accounts." *PTL. A Journal for Descriptive Poetics and Theory of Literature* 3. 249–287.

McHale, Brian (2014). "Speech Representation." In *Handbook of Narratology*. Edited by Peter Hühn, Jan Christoph Meister, John Pier, Wolf Schmid. 2nd edition, fully revised and expanded. Berlin and Boston: De Gruyter. 812–824. Online-Version in *The Living Handbook of Narratology*. URL = http://www.lhn.uni-hamburg.de/article/speech-representation (accessed April 6, 2014).

Padučeva, Elena (1996). "Semantika narrativa." In E. V. P., *Semantičeskie issledovanija*. Moscow: Jazyki russkoj kul'tury. 193–418.

Padučeva (Paducheva), Elena (2011). *The Linguistics of Narrative. The Case of Russian*. Saarbrücken: LAP Lambert Academic Publishing, 2011

Palmer, Alan (2002). "The Construction of Fictional Minds." *Narrative 10.1. 29–46.*

Palmer, Alan (2004). *Fictional Minds*. Lincoln and London: University of Nebraska Press.

Pascal, Roy (1977). *The Dual Voice: Free Indirect Speech and Its Functioning in the Nineteenth-Century European Novel*. Manchester: Manchester UP.

Perry, Menakhem (2007). "Counter-Stories in the Bible: Rebekah and her Bridegroom, Abraham's Servant." *Prooftexts* 27. 275–323

Schmid, Wolf (1968). "Zur Erzähltechnik und Bewusstseinsdarstellung in Dostoevskijs 'Večnyj muž'." *Die Welt der Slaven* 13. 294–306.

Schmid, Wolf (1973). *Der Textaufbau in den Erzählungen Dostoevskijs*. Munich: Fink. 2nd ed. (with an afterword: "Eine Antwort an die Kritiker"). Amsterdam: Grüner, 1986.

Schmid, Wolf (1979). "Thesen zur innovatorischen Poetik der russischen Gegenwartsprosa." *Wiener Slawistischer Almanach* 4. 55–93.

Schmid, Wolf (1989). "Vklad Baxtina/Vološinova v teoriju tekstovoj interferencii." *Russian Literature* 26. 219–236.

Schmid, Wolf (1997). "Modi des Erkennens in Čechovs narrativer Welt." In *Anton P. Čechov – philosophische und religiöse Dimensionen im Leben und im Werk*. Edited by Vladimir B. Kataev, Rolf-Dieter Kluge, Regine Nohejl. Munich: Kubon & Sagner. 529–536.

Schmid, Wolf (1998). "Mnimoe prozrenie Ivana Velikopol'skogo (*Student*)." In Vol'f Šmid, *Proza kak poėzija. Puškin – Dostoevskij – Čexov – avangard*. Izd. vtoroe, ispravlennoe, rasširennoe. Sankt-Peterburg: Inapress. 278–294.

Schmid, Wolf (2005). "Defamiliarisation." In *The Routledge Encyclopedia of Narrative Theory*. Edited by David Herman, Manfred Jahn, Marie-Laure Ryan. London: Routledge. 98.

Schmid, Wolf ([2003] 2008). *Narratologija*. Vtoroe, ispravlennoe I dopolnennoe izdanie. Moscow: Jazyki slavjanskoj kul'tury.

Schmid, Wolf (2010). *Narratology. An Introduction*. Berlin and New York: De Gruyter.

Schmid, Wolf ([1996] 2013). *Proza Puškina v poėtičeskom pročtenii. "Povesti Belkina" i "Pikovaja dama"*. Izd. 2-oe, ispravlennoe i dopolnennoe. Sankt-Peterburg: Izdatel'stvo S-Peterburgskogo universiteta.

Schmid, Wolf (2014a). *Elemente der Narratologie*. 3rd ed. Berlin and Boston: De Gruyter. (1st ed. 2005; originally Russian: *Narratologija*. Moscow: Jazyki slavjanskoj kul'tury, 2003; 2nd ed. 2008)

Schmid, Wolf (2014b). "Implied author." In *Handbook of Narratology*. Edited by Peter Hühn, Jan Christoph Meister, John Pier, Wolf Schmid. 2nd edition, fully revised and expanded. Berlin and Boston: De Gruyter. 288–300. Online-Version in *The Living Handbook of Narratology*. URL = www.lhn.uni-hamburg.de/article/implied-author-revised-version-uploaded-26-january-2013 (accessed April 25, 2020).

Schmid, Wolf (2014c). "A Vicious Circle: Equivalence and Repetition in 'The Student'." In *Anton Chekhov's Selected Stories. Texts of the Stories, Comparison of Translations, Life and*

Letters, Criticism. Selected and ed. by Cathy Popkin. New York and London: Norton. 646–649.

Schmid, Wolf (2014d). "Poetic or Ornamental Prose." In *Handbook of Narratology*. Edited by Peter Hühn, Jan Christoph Meister, John Pier, Wolf Schmid. 2nd edition, fully revised and expanded. Berlin and Boston: De Gruyter. 720–725. Online-Version in *The Living Handbook of Narratology*. URL = https://www.lhn.uni-hamburg.de/node/62.html (accessed September 10, 2020)

Schmid, Wolf (2014e). "Skaz." In *Handbook of Narratology*. Edited by Peter Hühn, Jan Christoph Meister, John Pier, Wolf Schmid. 2nd edition, fully revised and expanded. Berlin and Boston: De Gruyter. 787–795. Online-Version in *The Living Handbook of Narratology*. URL = http://www.lhn.uni-hamburg.de/article/skaz (September 10, 2020)

Schmid, Wolf (2015). "Zeit und Erzählperspektive. Am Beispiel von F. M. Dostoevskijs Roman *Der Jüngling*." In *Zeiten erzählen. Ansätze – Aspekte – Analysen*. Herausgegeben von Antonius Weixler und Lukas Werner (= Narratologia 48). Berlin und Boston: De Gruyter. 343–368.

Schmid, Wolf (2017). *Mentale Ereignisse. Bewusstseinsveränderungen in europäischen Erzählwerken vom Mittelalter bis zur Moderne* (= Narratologia 69). Berlin and Boston: De Gruyter. Tr.: Schmid 2021.

Schmid, Wolf (2018b). "Anton Čechov: 'Skripka Rotšil'da' ('Rothschilds Geige')." In *Die russische Erzählung*. Edited by Bodo Zelinsky. Cologne: Böhlau. 370–384, 723–727.

Schmid, Wolf (2020). *Narrative Motivierung. Von der romanischen Renaissance bis zur russischen Postmoderne*. Berlin and Boston: De Gruyter.

Schmid, Wolf (2021). *Mental Events. Changes of Mind in European Narratives from the Middle Ages to Postrealism*. Hamburg: Hamburg University Press.

Schmid, Wolf (2023). "Free Indirect Discourse in German and Russian Literature." In *Handbook of Diachronic Narratology*. Edited by Peter Hühn, John Pier, Wolf Schmid. Berlin and Boston: De Gruyter.

Semino, Elena; Michael Short (2004). *Corpus Stylistics: Speech, Writing and Thought Representation in a Corpus of English Writing*. London and New York: Routledge.

Siever, Holger (2001). *Kommunikation und Verstehen. Der Fall Jenninger als Beispiel einer semiotischen Kommunikationsanalyse*. Frankfurt: Verlag Peter Lang, 2001

Skei, Hans H. (1979). "The Trapped Female Breaking Loose: William Faulkner's *Elly* (1934)." *American Studies in Scandinavia* 11. 15–24.

Sokolova, Ljudmila (1968). *Nesobstvenno-avtorskaja (nesobstvenno-prjamaja) reč' kak stilisti-českaja kategorija*. Tomsk: Izdatel'stvo Tomskogo universiteta.

Spitzer, Leo (1923a). "Sprachmischung als Stilmittel und als Ausdruck der Klangphantasie." *Germanisch-romanische Monatsschrift*. 11. 193–216. Under the title „Sprachmengung als Stilmittel und als Ausdruck der Klangphantasie" in: L. Spitzer, *Stilstudien II*, München: Max Hueber, 1928. 2nd ed. 1961, 84–124.

Spitzer, Leo (1923b). "Pseudoobjektive Motivierung bei Charles Louis Philippe." In L. Spitzer, *Stilstudien II*, München: Max Hueber, 1928. 2nd ed. 1961, 166–207.

Spitzer, Leo (1928). "Zur Entstehung der sogenannten erlebten Rede." *Germanisch-romanische Monatsschrift* 16. 327–332.

Stanzel, Franz K. (1975). "Die Personalisierung des Erzählaktes im *Ulysses*." In *James Joyces "Ulysses": Neuere deutsche Aufsätze*. Herausgegeben von Therese Fischer-Seidel. Frankfurt a. M.: Suhrkamp.

Stanzel, Franz K. (1979). *Theorie des Erzählens*. Göttingen: Vandenhoeck & Ruprecht. Tr.: Stanzel 1984.

Stanzel, Franz K. (1984). *Theory of Narrative*. Translated by Charlotte Goedsche. Cambridge: Cambridge UP.

Stanzel, Franz K. (1991). "Zur Problemgeschichte der 'erlebten Rede.' Eine Vorbemerkung zu Yasushi Suzukis Beitrag 'Erlebte Rede und der Fall Jenninger'." *Germanisch-romanische Monatsschrift* 41. 1–4.

Steinberg, Günter (1971). *Erlebte Rede: Ihre Eigenart und ihre Formen in neuerer deutscher, französischer und englischer Erzählliteratur*. Göppingen: Alfred Kümmerle.

Suzuki, Yasushi (1991). "Erlebte Rede und der Fall Jenninger." *Germanisch-romanische Monatsschrift* 41. 5–12.

Swartzlander, Susan (1989). "Uncle Charles in Michigan." In *Hemingway's Neglected Short Fiction. New Perspectives*. Edited by Susan F. Beegel. Luscaloosa and London: University of Alabama Press, 1992. 31–41.

Tjupa, Valerij (2014). "Heteroglossia". In *Handbook of Narratology*. Edited by Peter Hühn, Jan Christoph Meister, John Pier, Wolf Schmid. 2nd edition, fully revised and expanded. Berlin and Boston: De Gruyter. 219–226. Online-Version in *The Living Handbook of Narratology*. URL = http://www.lhn.uni-hamburg.de/article/heteroglossia (accessed March 9, 2021).

Toolan, Michael (2006). "Speech and Thought: Representation of." In *Encyclopedia of Language and Linguistics*. Edited by Keith Brown. 2nd ed. Amsterdam: Elsevier, 2006 [1st ed. 1993, ed. Ron Asher]. Vol. 12, 698–710.

Tunimanov, V. A. (1971). "Nekotorye osobennosti povestvovanii v Gospodine Proxarčine." In *Poètika i stilistika russkoj literatury. Pamjati akademika V. V. Vinogradova*. Leningrad: Nauka. 203–212.

Uspenskij, Boris (1970). *Poètika kompozicii. Struktura chudožestvennogo teksta i tipologija kompozicionnoj formy*. Moscow: Iskusstvo. Tr: Uspenskij 1973.

Uspenskij, Boris (1973). *A Poetics of Composition. The Structure of the Artistic Text and Typology of a Compositional Form*. Translated by Valentina Zavarin and Susan Wittig. Berkeley, Los Angeles and London: University of California Press.

Vinogradov, Viktor (1922). "Stil' peterburgskoj poèmy *Dvojnik*." In *Dostoevskij. Stat'i i materialy*. Sb. 1. Pod red. A. S. Dolinina. Peterburg 1922. 211–256.

Vinogradov, Viktor (1939) "O jazyke Tolstogo (50–60-e gody)." In *L. N. Tolstoj I* (= Literaturnoe nasledstvo 36–36). Otv. red. P. I. Lebedev-Poljanskij. Moscow: Izdatel'stvo Akademii Nauk SSSR. 117–220.

Vološinov, Valentin (1927). *Frejdizm. Kritičeskij očerk*. Moscow and Leningrad: Gosudarstvennoe izdatel'stvo.

Vološinov, Valentin (1929). *Marksizm i filosofija jazyka: Osnovnye problemy sociologičeskogo metoda v nauke o jazyke*. Moscow 1993. Tr.: Vološinov 1973.

Vološinov, Valentin (1973). *Marxism and the Philosophy of Language*. Translated by Ladislav Matejka and I. R. Titunik. Cambridge, MA and London: Harvard UP.

Wächter, Thomas (1992). *Die künstlerische Welt in späten Erzählungen Čechovs*. Frankfurt a. M.: Peter Lang.

Wierzbicka, Anna (1970). "Descriptions or Quotations?" In *Sign, Language, Culture*. Vol. I. The Hague and Paris: Mouton. 627–644.

8. Index of Authors and Works

Pages listed under an author's work do not appear under his or her name. In Russian names and titles of works, emphasis is indicated by accents.

https://doi.org/10.1515/9783110763102-009

www.ingramcontent.com/pod-product-compliance
Lightning Source LLC
Chambersburg PA
CBHW030832090426
42737CB00009B/975